WALKING THE FRENCH GORGES

A view of the Verdon Grand Canyon from the Brèche Imbert. (Day 8)

WALKING THE FRENCH GORGES

A trail through Provence and the Ardèche

by
ALAN CASTLE

Illustrated by the author

CICERONE PRESS
MILNTHORPE, CUMBRIA

© Alan Castle 1993
ISBN 1 85284 114 1

British Library Cataloguing-in-Publication Data. A catalogue record for this book is available from the British Library.

ACKNOWLEDGEMENTS

Thanks go, as always, to my wife, Beryl Castle, for all her encouragement during the planning and writing of this guidebook and for accompanying me on many of my walks through France. Her expert tuition on the use of word processors and computers resulted in a considerable saving of time and effort in the production of the manuscript for this book. My French mother-in-law, Andrée Cain, was also a great help in unravelling the complexities of the French language.

Dedicated to the memory of Kurt Wehner
a fellow traveller in Provence

Advice to Readers

Readers are advised that whilst every effort is taken by the author to ensure the accuracy of this guidebook, changes can occur which may affect the contents. It is advisable to check locally on transport, accommodation, shops etc but even rights-of-way can be altered and, more especially overseas, paths can be eradicated by landslip, forest fires or changes of ownership.

The publisher would welcome notes of any such changes

Other Cicerone titles by Alan Castle

The Corsican High Level Route - Walking the GR 20
The Tour of the Queyras: GR 58
The Pyrenean Trail: GR 10
The Robert Louis Stevenson Trail
Walks in Volcano Country

CONTENTS

INTRODUCTION

Roam on! the light we sought is shining still.
Our tree yet crowns the hill,
Our scholar travels yet the loved hillside

Matthew Arnold

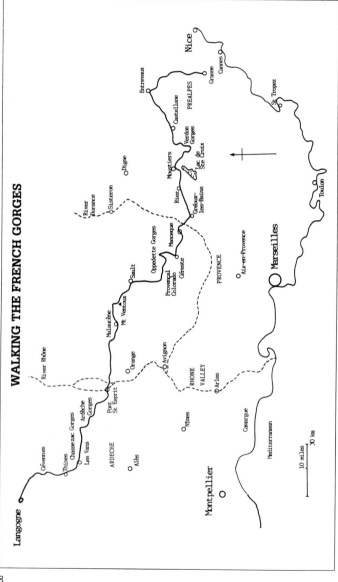

WALKING THE FRENCH GORGES

Nice

Entrevaux

Grasse

Cannes

PREALPES

Castellane

St Tropez

Verdon
Gorges

Moustiers

Digne

Lac de
Ste Croix

Riez

Sisteron

Gréoux-
les-Bains

River
Durance

Toulon

Manosque

Oppedette Gorges

Marseilles

Gréoux

Provençal
Colorado

Sault

PROVENCE

Aix-en-Provence

Malaucène

Mt Ventoux

Avignon

Orange

RHONE
VALLEY

Arles

River Rhône

Cévennes

Thueyts

Chassezac Gorges

Ardèche
Gorges

Les Vans

Pont
St Esprit

ARDECHE

Nîmes

Camargue

Alès

Mediterranean

Langogne

Montpellier

10 miles

30 km

INTRODUCTION

GRANDES RANDONNEE
France has a very extensive network of long distance paths called Grandes Randonnées (literally "Big Walks"), commonly abbreviated to "GR". Each GR route has been designated a number, eg. GR 5, GR 20, etc. The principal long distance trails usually carry a low number, eg. GR 4, GR 6, whereas shorter, circular routes, variations or links have two or three digit numbers. Trails in a particular area, or in the vicinity of a "single digit" GR route, all carry the same first number. For example along with the GR 4 there are the GR 41, GR 412, GR 44, GR 441, etc., the GR 6 has the associated GR 60 and GR 65, and so on. The system has analogies with the road numbering system in Britain: M6, M62, etc. Some GR trails are known by a name as well as a number, eg. the Tour of the Queyras in the French Alps, otherwise known as the GR 58. Note that GR routes that are circular are generally referred to as *Tours*. There are at present some 25,000 miles (40,250km) of GR trails throughout France and the network is still expanding. Further details of the several *Grandes Randonnées* encountered on the walk described in this book are given in Appendix 2.

A WALK FROM THE COTE D'AZUR TO THE MASSIF CENTRAL.
THE GR 4, GR 6 AND GR 9
The trail described in this book follows, for the most part, a section of the ultra-long distance path known as the GR 4. This is one of the great footpaths of France stretching from east to west across the southern half of the country, through Provence and the Massif Central and on through Aubusson, Limoges and Saintes to finish at the Atlantic coast at Royan (for more details see Appendix 2). Various detours are taken from the standard path of the GR 4 in order to take in a more interesting route, visit a place of interest, include a good viewpoint or cover more spectacular country. In particular, in the Lubéron the GR 4 is abandoned altogether for two to three days in order to take a more interesting route through this attractive mountainous area. For this section the route follows part of the GR 6 and later the GR 9. The former is another ultra-long distance east to west route across southern France, running from the southern Alps to a point south-east of Bordeaux. The GR 9 is a long distance route running north to south across the eastern part of France linking the Jura with the Côte d'Azur (for more details of both the GR 6 and the GR 9 see Appendix 2).

The walk described in this book (henceforth to be referred to as the Trail) explores some of the best countryside to be found in southern France; the splendour and variety of the natural scenery is interspersed with numerous man-made places of interest which echo with the rich history and culture of this ancient land. Much of the Trail passes through limestone country, sometimes traversing mountains and ridges or high exposed limestone plateaux, at other times rambling through ancient woodland, alongside river banks or across fields of lavender and orchards of cherry, apricot, apple and pear. In many places mountain torrents have, through the long geological ages, worn great gashes through the limestone creating immense gorges with huge vertical and overhanging walls, and labyrinthine underground cavern systems. The walk can, in one sense, be thought of as a long distance walking trail linking several of the finest and most impressive gorges in the south-east of France. The Trail includes a day-long walk along the *Sentier Martel*, which threads its way through the Grand Canyon of the Verdon Gorges, one of the most spectacularly beautiful landscapes in all Europe. Further west the rim of the mighty Oppedette Gorge is followed, whilst once across the Rhône both the Ardèche and the Chassazac Gorges are on the itinerary.

The Trail is for the most part a mountain walk. Several mountain ranges are traversed, the principal being the Préalpes, north of Grasse, the hills between Entrevaux, Castellane and Moustiers, the Lubéron ranges and the Vaucluse hills, the Mont Ventoux massif and, finally, the mountains of the Cévennes in the south-eastern sector of the Massif Central. Each of these ranges has its own special character, some dry, rocky and rugged, others sylvan, gentle and tranquil. The mountain highlight of the walk must surely be the ascent of Mont Ventoux, at 6268ft (1912m), the highest peak in mainland France, outside the Alps and Pyrenees. The view from this summit on a clear day includes an extensive panorama of virtually all of the French Alps.

The real joy of this walk is its variety; indeed it is the diversity and beauty of the landscape, together with the many different places of interest visited en route, which combine to make this a very special trail, one of the finest to be found anywhere in Europe. Apart from the high mountains and deep gorges the walker passes picturesque medieval villages perched precariously on hillsides, as though straight out of an artist's portfolio, crosses fields of cultivated lavender, and hillsides and meadows rich with the smell of a myriad wild and scented herbs. The Trail includes a crossing of the world-famous vineyards of the Rhône Valley and visits many historical remains, particularly those from the Roman period, before finally climbing up into the wooded hills of the Cévennes.

The GR 4 and this Trail both commence their long journey across France from Grasse, a town, famed for its perfume industry, situated above the Côte d'Azur, a little way inland from Cannes. For the first few days the Trail heads northwards across a region sometimes known as the Préalpes, or foothills of the principal Alpine ranges further north. This is limestone country par excellence. After the picturesque medieval walled town of Entrevaux in the valley of the Var, the route swings to the west to cross the high Col de Vauplane to descend to Castellane, the tourist gateway to the famous Verdon Gorges, beloved of the modern rock gymnast. After a memorable day through the Grand Canyon, the

Trail continues through more spectacular mountain country to Moustiers-Sainte-Marie, famous for its pottery. From here the nature of the walk changes for a few days from high mountains and rocky gorges, to fields of lavender, woodland glades and a series of towns and villages, including the spa town of Gréoux-les-Bains, which lead to the large town of Manosque in the valley of the Durance. Here there is an opportunity to take a day off from the walk by taking a train to nearby Aix-en-Provence.

For those wishing to divide the walk into two or more shorter holidays, Manosque is a good place from which to leave for home. But those who continue now climb into the Lubéron, a lush region of wooded hills, sparsely populated and designated a Regional Nature Park. It is here that the GR 4 is left in preference to the GR 6 which is followed to explore the Oppedette Gorges and later to visit the Provençal Colorado, an area of bizarre ochre rock formations resembling those of Colorado in the United States. The Trail parts company with the GR 6 at the town of Saint Saturnin d'Apt to take a section of a *Petite Randonnée* path (q.v.) and the GR 9, climbing high over the Lubéron mountains to rejoin the GR 4 for a mountain ridge walk to Sault. From the terraces of this ancient town the huge massif of Mont Ventoux is in full view. A traverse of this mighty peak will occupy the walker for the next two days. There is also an opportunity to make a detour to the nearby Nesque Gorges. After Malaucène, to the west of Mont Ventoux, the Trail passes in sight of the serrated Dentelles de Montmirail to the charming ancient village of Séguret, home of a colony of artists. From here the landscape changes once again to provide a couple of day's walking through vineyards to Pont-Saint-Esprit and the Rhône Valley.

The final section of the walk is across the Ardèche, to the west of the Rhône. Part of the Trail in this area follows the ultra-long distance European Footpath No. 4 (the E 4). Firstly the Trail traverses the Bas-Vivarais, visiting the spectacular gorges of the Ardèche and Chassazac, no less impressive than their cousins further east. The upland area of the Massif Central is approached for several days until eventually a long climb begins into the mountains of the Cévennes. The gem of this section is the tiny mountain village of Thines, with its dramatic lonely situation and beautiful ancient church. The Trail leads over these delightful wooded hills to reach its final destination, Langogne, in the valley of the River Allier.

Although the Trail described in this book terminates here, the GR 4 itself continues ever onwards towards the west. Those who wish to sample more of this ultra-long distance footpath can follow it through the Massif Central along the "Traverse of the High Auvergne" described in a companion Cicerone guidebook, *Walks in Volcano Country* (see Bibliography). Those who continue will have the satisfaction of having walked across southern France from the Côte d'Azur to the Auvergne - quite an achievement.

The Trail encompasses three Régions of France, Provence-Côte d'Azur,

Languedoc-Roussillon and Rhône-Alpes, and five départements. From Grasse to just before Castellane (Day 6) the walk traverses the département of Alpes-Maritimes, followed by the Alpes-de-Haute-Provence to a little before Viens (Day 14). Here the route enters the département of Vaucluse, where it remains until it crosses the Rhône to enter, briefly, the département of Gard at Pont Saint Esprit (Day 21). The rest of the walk is across the département of the Ardèche, the ancient Vivarais, to Langogne, on the border with the Lozère département.

The Trail is principally a mountain walk, although for the most part it is not particularly strenuous and demands no specialist mountain skills (unless the high sections are walked in winter), nor a head for heights. Those British walkers who have spent time in the mountains of the Lake District, Wales or Scotland should have no difficulties on these mountains. Walkers who have no experience of mountain country would be well advised to restrict themselves to the lower sections of the Trail (ie. the stages for which no topographical profiles have been included in this guide) or else first get advice and practice hill walking in Britain before attempting the mountain sections. The walk should particularly appeal to those who enjoy mountain walking and who would like to try a walking holiday on the continent, but are somewhat daunted by the very long, steep and sometimes unnerving climbs that can be encountered in the Alps and Pyrenees.

Those who walk regularly in the hills of Britain should experience no great problems on this walk. However, if exercise has not been taken for some time, then obviously some programme of training in the months preceding the trip would be beneficial. An unfit person would find parts of the Trail a great strain and therefore would lose much of the enjoyment of the walk, both for him/herself and for his/her companions. Before travelling to France it would be advisable to take a few short walks with a pack, in order to become accustomed to carrying a load. Even those making exclusive use of gîtes d'étape and hôtels will probably have to carry at least 14lbs of equipment and personal effects. Backpackers will have to carry significantly more.

The trek along the Grand Canyon of the Verdon Gorges and the ascent of Mont Ventoux are undoubtedly the highlights of the Trail, but there is a great deal more to delight the adventurous walker on this outstanding walk across southern France. Peakbaggers will be able to increase their score of summits attained by making some of the optional ascents of neighbouring peaks passed en route. There is much to interest the amateur geologist, botanist, ornithologist, historian, archeologist and photographer and all those fascinated by the traditional life, culture, crafts and practices of a unique part of Europe.

PROVENCE

The ancient province of Provence occupies the south-eastern segment of the country, between the Rhône Valley and the border with Italy. Today, as the Région Provence-Côte d'Azur, it comprises the départements of Alpes-Maritime, Alpes-de-Haute-Provence, Var, Vaucluse and the Bouches-du-Rhône. The region, which has varied in size throughout the ages, has a long and complex history, being occupied both by the Greeks and, more importantly, by the Romans (it was a Roman Provincia, hence its name). The Romans built many towns and roads in the area, and Provence today preserves the best Roman monuments of any region in France. Several Roman roads, bridges and important monuments are passed on the Trail described in this book (eg. in Riez on Day 10 and at Céreste on Day 13), whilst several of the most significant Roman ruins in France (eg. at Orange and at Vaison-la-Romain) can be visited by short detours from the route. For a brief period in the ninth century Provence was a kingdom, whilst during the Middle Ages it was held by Alphonso, King of Aragon, Charles of Anjou, King of Naples, and others. In the fourteenth century, Provence, part of the Holy Roman Empire, was home to the Avignon Popes, who built several palaces (eg. at Groseau, near Malaucène, Day 18) in the region. Finally, in 1481 it was ceded to Louis XI of France and since that time has remained a part of France.

Provence encompasses a variety of landscapes from alpine summits and foothills in the Alpes-de-Haute-Provence and Alpes-Maritime, to Mediterranean scrub and forested hills that drop steeply down to the sea's edge, much of which is devoted to sun worshipers and millionaires. In central Provence the high, sparse plateaux are cut by numerous limestones gorges, including the deepest cleft in the surface of Europe, the Grand Canyon of the Verdon Gorges. Some of the wildest and most rugged alpine country in the southern Alps is found in the Mercantour National Park in the Alpes-Maritime, whilst the extensive ranges that comprise the foothills of the true Alpine summits (known to the French as the Préalpes) cover much of Haute (High) Provence. The broad vistas of the limestone Préalpes offer a landscape quite different from any found in Britain. The mountains to the north of the Côte d'Azur, the Préalpes de Grasse, are traversed during the first few days of the walk to the ancient fortified town of Entrevaux on the River Var, on the frontier with Savoy to the north.

Much of Provence is rural and remote, the populace living either in small villages perched high up on the hillsides, or in remote farmhouses. The *village perchés* were originally built for reasons of defence, but their old quarters *(vieilles villes)* with narrow winding streets and passageways have an air of timeless tranquillity. The Provençal stone-built house in the country is known as a "mas" and generally has easily recognised characteristics, such as a shallow sloping roof of terracotta tiles with a decorative frieze under the eaves. Several of these isolated old buildings are passed en route, and several of the stages are between the many medieval hill-top towns and villages. Provence is noted for the clarity of its Mediterranean light and for its clear deep blue skies and wide vistas. The land certainly has, as Robert Louis Stevenson wrote "an indescribable air of the South". The walker should experience this to the full.

THE LUBÉRON

The Lubéron is a large mountainous region situated between Manosque and Cavaillon, bounded between the valley of the Durance to the south and the Vaucluse Plateau in the north. The hills for the large part are wooded, but there are numerous rocky outcrops and many old, picturesque villages perched on the hillsides. It is a region of great charm, criss-crossed with ancient paths and *drailles,* ideal for walking.

The range consists basically of a gigantic fold of limestone, running in an east-west direction. It is divided into two unequal halves by the Combe de Lourmarin, south of Bonnieux, along which there is a motorable road. To the west lies the Grand Lubéron, which contains the range's highest point, the Sommet du Mourre Nègre (3688ft; 1125m), whilst to the east the Petit Lubéron, which only occasionally rises above 2250ft (686m), stretches almost to the outskirts of Cavaillon. The north and south-facing slopes of the 35-mile (56km) long chain show considerable differences, the northern side being cooler, damper, covered in oak woods and deeply ravined, whereas the sunny southern slopes carry a more typical Mediterranean vegetation and are more cultivated.

The area has been inhabited by man since prehistoric times. Many villages were built high up on the hillsides during the medieval period, particularly on the more fertile southern slopes. The land supported a considerable community, the region forming a remote, and therefore safe, refuge for those persecuted during the Wars of Religion in the seventeenth and eighteenth centuries. The main livelihoods involved sheep, olives, vines, lavender and silkworms. Low drystone walls were erected to form fields and whilst working away from home the men lived in drystone huts or *bories*. All these features, as well as the ruins of several hillside villages abandoned with the demographic changes of the twentieth century (eg the ruins of Travignon on Day 16), will be seen whilst on the Trail through the Lubéron.

The Parc Naturel Régional du Lubéron (Luberon Regional Nature Park), created in 1977, covers an area of 463 square miles, including a region well to the north of the main Lubéron chain of mountains. However, many sectors around several towns and villages within this area are excluded from the Park, although the land of over fifty communes is represented. The boundaries of the Park overlap the départements of Vaucluse and the Alpes-de-Haute-Provence. The laudable aims of the Park include both protecting the environment from unsuitable development and exploitation, and encouraging the revival of traditional skills and occupations thereby curbing the depopulation of the region. The Headquarters of the Park is at Apt (the Maison du Parc), where there is a Park Information Centre and exhibition. There are strict rules forbidding the taking of geological samples or the removal of wild plants from within the Park. The Trail enters the Lubéron Park after leaving Manosque (Day 13) and leaves it after the long climb north from Saint-Saturnin-d'Apt on Day 16.

VAUCLUSE
The département of the Vaucluse contains a rich diversity of landscapes from high mountains and *garrigues* to fast flowing rivers and valleys carpeted with orchards and vineyards. To the north of the département lies the enormous Ventoux massif, the summit of which, at 6268ft (1912m), is the highest peak in mainland France outside the Alps and Pyrenees. Mont Ventoux is also the highest point reached on the entire Trail between Grasse and Langogne. The high Vaucluse Plateau, between the Lubéron hills to the south and Mont Ventoux and the Lure mountains to the north, is a vast arid area of limestone gorges and complex underground caverns. The Nesque Gorges near Sault can be reached by a detour from the Trail near Sault (Day 16) whilst those of Oppedette are examined in detail during Day 14. Also found in the Vaucluse are the multicoloured ochre mines of Rustrel and Roussillon, the rock striations resembling those of the Colorado in the western United States. The Provençal Colorado is the subject of the walk on Day 15. Before the mountains peter out to the vine-growing areas of the Ouvèze and Rhône valleys, the Dentelles de Montmirail present a rocky defile that belies their modest altitude. The main urban centres in the Vaucluse are the market towns of Apt, Carpentras and Cavaillon, none of which are visited on this walk.

THE ARDECHE, CEVENNES AND THE MASSIF CENTRAL
Once across the Rhône Valley the Trail soon enters the Ardèche, a modern département of France, which under the Ancien Régime was known as the Vivarais, a term still frequently used to describe this largely rural, depopulated and often wild landscape. The area takes its name from the river, a major tributary of the Rhône, which penetrates its heart. The Ardèche shares several of the characteristics of Provence to its east, and indeed many guidebooks to Provence include the area within their pages. The Lower or "Bas-Vivarais" is the scene of the first few days through the Ardèche, a part of the "Midi" noted in particular for its dramatic gorges of the rivers Ardèche and Chassezac, prehistoric ruins and dolmens, spectacular cave systems and for the "limestone forest" of the Bois de Païolive. All these features are passed en route.

On leaving Les Vans the GR 4 begins its long climb up into the Massif Central, into the mountains of the Cévennes. The Massif Central is the term given to the high mountainous plateau of southern central France, a largely remote area of some 36,000 square miles (93,000 square km), a major source of hydroelectric power. The only major city in the region is Clermont-Ferrand, industrial in nature, situated to the north-west of the area covered in this guidebook. Much of the land in the Massif Central is above (3278ft) 1000m in altitude, the highest point being the Puy de Sancy at 1885m above Le Mont-Dore in the Auvergne (see *Walks in Volcano Country*, Bibliography). The mistral wind, which plagues much of the area covered in the present book, originates in the cold air above the Massif Central.

The Cévennes is a rugged, mountainous region which forms the south-eastern edge of the Massif Central. The highest point in the Cévennes is the Pic de Finiels (5570ft; 1699m), part of the high tableland of the Lozère massif, to the west of the area traversed in the walk described herein. It is a land of wooded hillsides and rushing streams; there are many tributaries of the River Gardon forming deep, steep-sided valleys and the River Tarn, famous for its spectacular Gorges, rises in these mountains. The principal town is Alès. Many of the inhabitants are Protestants, descendants of the Huguenots, who in the seventeenth and eighteenth centuries were persecuted terribly by the Catholic rulers of France. The Cévennes was witness to many atrocities during the Camisard's Revolt in the Wars of Religion in the eighteenth century, the violence of which was also experienced in Provence and other parts of southern France. The region is known to the British today largely on account of the book *Travels with a Donkey in the Cévennes,* written by Robert Louis Stevenson after a journey through this country in 1878 (see *The Robert Louis Stevenson Trail,* Bibliography).

The landscape and traditional way of life of the Cévennes is safeguarded by a number of organisations, the oldest (founded in 1894) and most active of which is the Club Cévenol. This organisation has supported various forms of "green tourism" in the Cévennes, including walking, in order to provide work for locals and halt depopulation in the area. A Scots woman, Pat Valette, married to the Editor of the Club's Journal, has done much to encourage walking in the Cévennes, particularly along the Robert Louis Stevenson Trail (see Appendix 3 and Bibliography).

The Parc National des Cévennes (Cévennes National Park), the second largest of the six National Parks in France, covers an area of 91,416 hectares (225,889 acres). The Park was created in 1970 to protect the landscape and curb the commercial exploitation of the region. The Trail does not pass through the main section of the Park, but the area around Malarce and Thines is regarded as an "outer protected zone" (zone périphérique) where most of the rules of the National Park apply.

CLIMATE - WHEN TO GO

The climate of much of the region covered by the Trail is typically Mediterranean. Summers tend to be hot and dry. During July and August the heat can be intense, particularly in the lower lying areas. Some British walkers would find the summer heat too unpleasant for walking; great care must be taken during such periods to avoid sunstroke and dehydration. Furthermore, the period from mid-July to mid-August is the time when the majority of the French go on holiday and consequently finding accommodation during this period can be more of a problem than in early or late season.

Both late spring and early autumn are ideal times to embark on this walk. The general freshness and the flowers of spring make this time of year a delight in Provence and the Ardèche. Late spring/early summer is also the time to see the lavender fields of Provence at their best. However, snow usually lies on the higher mountains until June and this should be considered when making plans for a trip early in the season. Several parts of the Trail pass through ancient deciduous woodland which is seen at its best during the autumn, when the reds, browns and golden yellows of the turning leaves present a riot of colour. Autumn is also the time to witness the annual harvesting of grapes for the wine industry, particularly in the regions around the Durance and Rhône valleys.

Apart from the high temperatures of summer, there are also other adverse weather characteristics of the region which should be borne in mind. Firstly, surprising as it may seem, Marseille has a greater annual rainfall than Paris. However, much of the rainfall in Provence and the Ardèche occurs between October and April, and then mainly during torrential bursts of great violence. The summer months are generally dry, with day after consecutive day of clear blue skies. Thunderstorms can however occur at any time, developing often without warning, particularly after the heat of an oppressive afternoon, and their fury and danger should not be underestimated. Although there are far fewer rainy days than in Britain, rain when it does come can fall with almost unbelievable ferocity. These warnings are given from personal experiences!

The region is plagued between October and April by the mistral, the notorious wind which originates in the cold air above the Massif Central and travels at great speed towards the south-east. It is an icily cold wind which persists for many days without abatement. The mistral is particularly pronounced in the Rhône Valley. If encountered it is advisable to keep to the valleys or lower hills: it would be very difficult even to stand upright on the high tops. Hence it would be dangerous to attempt much of this route under these conditions, particularly as woodland is traversed along several parts of the Trail, where trees can be uprooted and branches broken by this wind.

The lower sections of the route described herein could be walked during the wintertime of most years without encountering any significant difficulties. However, considerable falls of snow occur on the mountains every winter, and consequently the high level sections should be attempted only by those with the necessary winter hillwalking skills and the appropriate equipment. Much of the route included in Profiles 1 to 5 would be in this category. In particular it would be necessary to take an ice-axe and crampons and have the ability to use them. Movement in deep snow can be laborious - skis would be useful. The dangers of strong, bitterly cold winds at altitude, whiteout during heavy snowfall, the drifting of snow and the risk of avalanche, should all be considered.

TRAVELLING TO THE REGION

There are four possible modes of travel to the south of France from Britain: air, train, coach and private transport. Note that any timetable information is liable to change. When consulting timetables remember that France is one hour ahead of Britain for most of the year.

Air

There are three destinations worthy of consideration. British Airways and Air France are the main carriers.

Nice

This is probably the best destination to fly to for this walk. This major Mediterranean holiday destination is served by several flights from the major British airports (flight time is about 1³/₄ hours from London). It is possible to get reduced APEX air fares on scheduled services and Nice is also the destination of several charter flights. Falcon holidays include Nice in their "flight only" holiday listings (see Appendix 3). Further and up-to-date details of all the flights available to Nice can be obtained from any reputable travel agent. Nice airport is situated on the edge of the Mediterranean and is a spectacular place to land. A frequent bus service operates to the city centre (only about 10 minutes' journey).

The start of the walk at Grasse is easily reached from Nice by a relatively short bus journey (or train to Cannes and bus from there to Grasse). If the full walk to Langogne is achieved then a train is easily taken from there back to Nice via Nîmes and Marseille. Similarly, fast and convenient train services to Nice operate from the Durance and Rhône valleys for those contemplating only part of the walk.

Lyon

There is a direct daily service from London, Heathrow to Lyon (flight time approximately 1¹/₂ hours) with connecting flights from other major British airports to Heathrow. A bus service operates between the airport and Lyon city centre (bus departs approximately every 20 to 30 minutes all day Monday to Friday). From Lyon frequent express trains operate down the Rhône Valley to the Côte d'Azur. Alight at Cannes and take the bus to Grasse (see the "Facilities" section of "Day 1" for details) for the start of the walk. Good train services back to Lyon for the flight home can be picked up at either Manosque in the Durance valley, Day 12 (train from here to Marseille, where change for a connection to Lyon) or from the Rhône Valley (Day 21). Those continuing to Langogne (Day 26) can reach Lyon most easily by taking a bus to Le Puy (see "Facilities" for Day 26 for details) and from there a train to Lyon via Saint Etienne (total journey time from Langogne about 3¹/₂ hours).

Paris

Several flights a day operate between London (Heathrow and Gatwick) and Paris (Charles de Gaulle). Flying time is approximately one hour. Scheduled services also operate from Birmingham, Glasgow and Manchester. Charles de Gaulle International Airport is approximately 15 miles from Paris city centre (journey time approximately 45 minutes). There are three possible modes of transport between airport and city: Air France bus, Roissy Rail Train and taxi. Once in Paris an express train can be taken to Cannes for the start of the walk (see "Train" below). Fast and frequent train services operate back to Paris from all the major terminating places of the walk, viz. from Manosque, the Rhône Valley and from Langogne.

The major disadvantage of the airplane for those who do not wish to be tied down to a specific date of return, is that the flight home usually has to be booked in advance. Travel by train allows far greater flexibility.

Train

French Railways or SNCF (Société Nationale de Chemins de Fer) offer a first-rate service throughout the country. Trains are generally fast, punctual, clean, comfortable and not overly priced. The journey to the south of France from Britain is via Paris, and so there are opportunities to spend a day or more in the capital either at the beginning or end of the holiday, before continuing the journey.

There are two principal ways in which the train can be used to travel to and from the south of France.

A. Train and cross-Channel ferry (or via the Channel Tunnel) to Paris, followed by train to Cannes. Return from Langogne (or from Manosque or the Rhône Valley) via Paris.

It is possible to reach the south of France from London in about 16 to 19 hours using train and cross Channel ferry. This journey time will be considerably decreased once the Channel Tunnel is opened in the late autumn of 1993. The journey can be considered in three stages:

a) London to Paris

There are several trains between London and Paris operating daily during the day and night. There are two principal routes:

1. London (Victoria) - - Dover or Folkestone - - Calais or Boulogne - - Amiens - - Paris (Gare du Nord). Journey time is approximately 7 hours. The fast service using the Channel Tunnel will use essentially this route.
2. London (Victoria) - - Newhaven - - Dieppe - - Rouen - - Paris (Gare Saint Lazare). Journey time is approximately 9 hours.

Route 2 involves a longer Channel crossing (about $3^3/4$ hours) than Route 1 (about $1^3/4$ hours). There is also a nightly service from London, Waterloo, to Paris via Portsmouth and Le Havre (journey time approximately 10 hours). Note that cut-price fares sometimes operate between London and Paris, particularly on night crossings. More discounted fares may possibly come available as the ferry companies begin to compete with the much faster Channel Tunnel route. If travelling from Newhaven on a night ferry, check first whether a cheaper fare is available from London. If making independent travel arrangements to the

Channel ports, it is sometimes cheaper to purchase a London to Paris ticket but discard the first part of the ticket to the English port. The same (in reverse) applies for a journey from Paris to Newhaven, ie. a ticket from Paris to London, particularly on a night sailing, can be cheaper than a ticket from Paris to Newhaven! However, things often change, so check first before buying a ticket.

b) Across Paris

Trains from Britain arrive in Paris at either Gare Saint Lazare or Gard du Nord. It will be necessary to cross Paris to the Gare de Lyon for trains to the south of France. The easiest way of travelling across the capital (other than by taxi) is to make use of the Metro (Underground) system. Simply ask for one ticket. There is no need to state the station to which one is travelling as there is a fixed price whatever the destination. Note that if spending some time in Paris it is more economical to buy a *carnet* of ten Metro tickets (a carnet cost 36.50FF in 1992). Crossing Paris can be somewhat of a hassle, particularly if unsure of the system, and so it is a good idea to write down the following brief instructions on a small piece of paper or card which can be kept in the pocket and discarded later. Armed with this it will be unnecessary to consult Metro maps at stations.

1. From Gare du Nord to Gare de Lyon. Line 5 (Direction Place d'Italie) to Bastille (7 stops). Change to Line 1 (Direction Château de Vicennes) to Gare de Lyon (1 stop).
2. From Gare Saint Lazare to Gare de Lyon. Line 12 (Direction Mairie d'Issy) to Concorde (2 stops). Change to Line 1 (Direction Château de Vincennes) to Gare de Lyon (8 stops).

On the return journey:

1. From Gare de Lyon to Gare du Nord. Line 1 (Direction Pont de Neuilly and la Defense) to Bastille (1 stop). Change to Line 5 (Direction Bobigny-Pablo-Picasso) to Gare du Nord (7 stops).
2. From Gare de Lyon to Gare Saint Lazare. Line 1 (Direction Pont de Neuillyand la Defense) to Concorde (8 stops). Change to Line 12 (Direction Porte de la Chapelle) to Gare Saint Lazare (2 stops).

The journey time is approximately half an hour, although it is wise to allow at least an hour (preferably two) between mainline trains arriving from London and departing for the south of France. Small maps of the Metro system (and also the bus and RER services) can be obtained free of charge at metro stations. Ask for a *Petit Plan de Paris* or a *Plan de Poche*. Note that a few mainline trains (SNCF) operate between Gare du Nord and the Gare de Lyon. These are not often convenient.

c) Paris to Cannes and return to Paris from Langogne, the Rhône Valley or Manosque.

Several express trains operate daily between Paris - Gare de Lyon and Nice. The principal stations en route are Dijon, Lyon, Valence, Orange, Avignon, Arles,

Marseille, Cannes, Antibes and Nice. The journey time between Paris and Cannes is approximately 6½ to 7 hours (this will be significantly reduced when TGV services all the way to the Côte d'Azur come into operation). Small blue timetables ("horaires") can be obtained at mainline stations (eg. Paris - Gare de Lyon) which provide information on the current trains operating between Paris and Nice. Timetables No. 551A and 551B are the relevant sheets. The first part of the journey to Lyon can already be taken by TGV if desired. The journey time from Paris to Lyon by TGV is an incredible 1 hour and 59 minutes! An overnight train from Paris to Cannes is very convenient, leaving Paris in the late evening and arriving in Cannes at about 7.20am. If a couchette is taken on this service the walker would be fresh on arrival either to start the walk, or to spend a day sightseeing in Grasse before setting out on the Trail.

Walkers terminating the walk at Manosque can take a train south via Aix-en-Provence to Marseille (St Charles station) from where there are several express trains to Paris (journey time from Marseille to Paris is approximately 5½ hours).

Those finishing the walk in the Rhône Valley will have few problems with a return journey to Paris as the valley is the principal transport artery in the south of France.

The Trail finishes at Langogne which is on the mainline between Paris and Nîmes. The relevant small blue timetable is sheet No. 510. There are two daytime trains from Langogne to Paris (approximately 7 hours' journey time) and an overnight sleeper. The latter is convenient, leaving Langogne at approximately 10.30 in the evening, arriving in Paris just before 7am.

B. Airplane to Paris and train from Paris to Cannes. Return to Paris by train and airplane back to Britain.
This is possibly the best combination of air and train travel. The somewhat lengthy and unpleasant Channel crossing by boat is avoided and the trains from and back to Paris are fast and convenient. The use of airplane to Paris will have less advantages once the Channel Tunnel is open however. Details of the two stages of the journey have been given in the relevant sections above. Air France and SNCF sometimes offer combined air and rail tickets at very reasonable prices, ie. air to Paris and train from there to one's destination.

General Information about rail travel in France

a) Booking
Travel centres in major British Rail stations in most large cities in the UK supply timetable and price information and can also book tickets and make seat and couchette reservations. A seat/couchette reservation is advisable if travelling during the peak holiday season (particularly at weekends), but note however that SNCF reservations will only be accepted within two months of travel date. Note that it is not absolutely necessary to book tickets in Britain for the whole

journey, eg. if staying for a short while in Paris before travelling to the south of France, more flexibility will be available if a ticket to Cannes is purchased at the Gare de Lyon prior to departure. The same is true for the return journey. Buying a ticket at a railway station in France is no more difficult than in Britain. However, there are two problems with this option, viz. all the seats may already have been booked (this is a particular problem in main season at weekends), and if one's French is poor then the wrong ticket may be bought! A ticket purchased in Britain is valid from two months from the date of outward travel. A ticket bought at a railway station in France is valid for two months from the date of purchase. Tickets can be used on any trains, although on certain services (see below) a supplement may be payable. Seat and couchette reservations are extra (second class couchette was 80FF in 1992).

b) Types of Trains

The French are justly proud of their train system, boasting that some 1400 express trains operate every day throughout the country. The high speed network is expanding at a considerable pace. By the year 2010 SNCF plans to have 4,700km (2,919 miles) of line suitable for trains running up to 350km per hour (217mph). All of the rail routes of interest to users of this book are serviced by express trains, and many of these are special trains, such as the air-conditioned Corail Trains. The pride of French Railways is the TGV (Train à Grande Vitesse) which routinely travels up to 270km per hour (168mph). A world record of over 563km per hour (350mph) was set up in the spring of 1990 (not on a passenger train!). The TGV has been so successful that within three years the service between Paris and Lyon had won 56.5% of the market from the air carriers. The rail system along the Rhône Valley is being modernised to take TGV services, thereby linking the capital with the Côte d'Azur by ultra-high speed trains. This is taking place despite strong local protest and opposition from conservation groups. When the Channel Tunnel is open the TGV services in France should compete effectively with air transport from Britain. A small supplement is payable on all TGV services.

All express trains have some form of catering, from a simple "mini-bar" pushed by an attendant passing through the train, to a lavish restaurant car as on TGVs.

Couchettes are equipped with bed linen, pillows and blankets. There are six berths per compartment in second class and four berths per compartment in first class.

c) Types of Ticket

There are several types of "saver" ticket on French railways, which enable savings of up to 50% off the normal fare:

1.   Frances Vacances Pass. This provides unlimited 1st and 2nd class rail travel throughout France on any four days during a period of 15 days or on any 9 days during a period of 1 month.

2. Holiday Return ("Sejour") ticket. 25% reduction on a return or circular journey of a least 1000kms.
3. Rail Europ Family (REF) card. This costs about £5. With it one member of a family group pays full fare whilst all the others qualify for up to a 50% reduction on rail travel and up to 30% on Channel crossings.
4. Rail Europ Senior (RES) card. This is available to those over 60 who are holders of a BR Senior Citizen Railcard. A RES card holder is entitled up to a 50% discount on rail travel and up to a 30% reduction on Channel crossings.
5. For the under 26s Inter-Rail cards and "carte jeune" are available. Note that since May 1991, Inter-Rail tickets have been available for the over 26s, but at a premium of a third over the youth rate. Note also though that in the autumn of 1992 France, together with certain other European countries, declared its intention to withdraw from the Inter-Rail system within the next few years.

Further details can be obtained from major BR Travel Centres and from most railway stations in France. Note also that there is an English language train information service in Paris. This can be dialled on 45.82.08.41.

One cautionary note. Access to railway station platforms is free in France, but tickets must be validated by date stamping before boarding the train. This simple task is performed using the orange coloured machines ("composteurs") which are located on the concourse of nearly all French railway stations. Failure to do so can result in a fine.

Coach

There is not an extensive network of coaches in France comparable to that in the UK. However, Eurolines operate a number of services to France from Victoria Coach Station in London. Long distance coach is probably the cheapest way of travelling to and from the south of France. Coaches leave for Lyon and for other destinations in the Rhône Valley and on the Côte d'Azur. Note also that an inexpensive coach service operates between London and Paris several times a day; this could be used to reach Paris from where a train could then be taken to the south of France. Several stops are made en route except on the London-Paris run which is non-stop. Bookings can be made and further information obtained from principal National Express offices throughout Britain.

Private Transport

There are two disadvantages of driving a car to the south of France to walk this Trail. Firstly, the car will have to be parked somewhere for the duration of the holiday. Sometimes a car can be left in a hôtel car park provided that a night or two is spent in the hôtel at the start and finish of the trip. The second disadvantage is that with a linear route such as this, public transport will have to be used anyway at the end of the walk to get back to the car left at the start.

It is useful to understand the road classification in France. Motorways ("Autoroutes" or "A" roads) are toll roads. Although fast it is fairly expensive to travel across the country by autoroute. The speed limit on Autoroutes is 130km/hr (81mph). "N" or "R.N" roads ("Routes Nationales") are roughly equivalent to British "A" roads. "D" or "Départemental" roads are equivalent to British "B" or "C" roads. The speed limit on dual carriageways is 110km/hr (68mph) and 90km/hr (57mph) on single carriageways. In built-up areas the speed limit is 50km/hr (31mph) unless otherwise indicated. Radar speed traps operate in France and French Police can inflict on-the-spot fines. Seat belts are compulsory on rear as well as on front seats. It is advisable to carry a red warning triangle in case of accident or puncture and to obtain a Green Card level of insurance.

LOCAL TRANSPORT

Public transport in rural France has suffered a similar fate to that in Britain. With a declining rural population and an increasing reliance on the motor car, many bus and local train services have been cut or severely curtailed. However, the public transport network is still reasonably good in many of the areas covered in this guidebook, particularly in the regions favoured by tourists (the Côte d'Azur, Durance and Rhône valleys). Details of the major services that exist are given under the "Facilities" section of each "Day" in the guide section. These public transport listings should not be considered as comprehensive; the situation is continually changing as some services are lost, others change from a regular to an occasional run and a few change routings, omitting some villages whilst including others. There may even be new services created on occasions! It is important to remember that the services outside the main areas of densest population are likely to be infrequent.

Generally winter timetables are inferior to those of the summer. Some bus services only operate during the main summer tourist season (mid-June to mid-September, or sometimes only in July and August) whilst several others run only on certain days of the week (eg. on market days) or during school terms. One important point: reference to a *car* in France refers to a public bus (motor coach) - a private motor car is a *voiture*.

To reach the start of the walk at Grasse it will be necessary to take a bus from Cannes. This service is frequent and inexpensive. Full details are given under "Public Transport" in the "Facilities" section of Day 1.

If the Trail is followed from Grasse to Langogne as described, or terminated at either Manosque or in the Rhône Valley (where there are excellent public transport facilities), no further local public transport will be required, although even the best laid plans sometimes go wrong, when it may be necessary to take a bus journey for a variety of reasons. In addition some walkers may wish to combine part of the walk with general sightseeing in the area and will need at times to make use of local transport to reach some of the main attractions. Even in an area where no bus service operates, a local taxi will usually be found without too much trouble. Taxi fares are generally cheaper than those in Britain. If all else fails try to hitch a lift; the locals are aware of the transport situation and will often oblige by taking the visitor to the nearest bus or train station.

OVERNIGHT ACCOMMODATION

There is a greater variety of accommodation available for walkers to France than in Britain and generally this is less expensive than that at home. Walkers should not be dismayed at the word "hôtel" in France as the 1 and 2-star establishments usually offer rooms and meals at very reasonable prices. The *chambre d'hôte* or French "bed and breakfast" is becoming more and more popular in France, and several of these should be found en route. In addition there is an extensive network of simple, but usually fully equipped hostels or *gîtes d'étape* (q.v.) which cater especially for the needs of walkers. A few farmhouses offer a variety of accommodation, occasionally only in a barn, sometimes in a dortoir, whilst some have provision for a chambre d'hôte. In just a few areas there may be a lack of organised accommodation available, but even in these circumstances, a polite word to the locals may result in a dortoir or simple room being offered for the night, or at the very least it should be possible, with permission, to sleep in a barn *(grange)*. It is not necessary, therefore, to carry tent, stove and cooking utensils whilst walking this Trail.

Those walkers who prefer to backpack, however, will find a number of campsites along the route, as well as several possibilities for wild camping. Some may wish to carry a tent when walking out of season, when the possibilities for overnight accommodation are less numerous. However, remember that most campsites in France close outside the summer season, whereas many of the *gîtes d'étapes* and hôtels remain open during the winter, particularly those in the more mountainous areas where skiing is popular, and in the tourist centres which are frequented all year round. The periods between the summer and winter seasons can sometimes be a problem when the hôtel owners often close down to take their own holidays. Note also that the range of facilities on offer can sometimes vary depending on the time of year that the visit is made. For example, some *gîtes d'étape* are open throughout the year, but have a resident warden who will provide meals, only during the main summer season. In the latter cases there will nearly always be a fully equipped kitchen available in the *gîte*, where food bought in an *épicerie* can be prepared.

This guidebook, it is hoped, gives adequate details of accommodation along the Trail, but further and up-to-date information can be obtained from the various tourist offices and syndicats d'initiative encountered en route. The staff of these establishments (details of which appear in the "Facilities" sections of each "Day") can often book local accommodation by phone (English is occasionally spoken in the larger offices).

There will inevitably always be some degree of uncertainty when walking alone or as an independent couple or group, as to where each night will be spent. Take a positive rather than a negative attitude to this, considering it all part of the experience and challenge of walking in France. It provides a tiny slice of excitement, in a way, never knowing exactly where you will end up each night. Don't become depressed by the uncertainty, as something will always "turn up", even if it means having to spend the night in an old barn! Make polite enquiries and someone will almost certainly provide a room or some sort of shelter for the night. If all else fails a local bar will have a phone which can be used to book accommodation "off-route" and to summon a taxi to travel to the night's accommodation (note that taxis are generally cheaper than in England). If possible try to avoid the period between mid-July and mid-August (Bastille Day to the Feast of the Assumption) when the majority of the French take their holidays and there is consequently a greater risk of finding hôtels and *gîtes d'étapes* full. The areas popular with tourists (eg. Grasse, Moustiers, Gréoux-les-Bains) are likely to be more of a problem at such times, but to compensate these towns have more accommodation on offer than the remote rural areas where hôtels are less likely to fill up. *Gîtes d'étapes* are generally quite crowded at the weekends, but even if bursting at the seams with occupants, the guardian will usually come up with a mattress for the late arrival. Many of the regions featured in this book suffer less from overcrowding than areas such as the Alps or Brittany. Remember that if walking independently you will have the freedom to go when and where you wish, at whatever pace and rate of progress you prefer, and in addition will be saving a considerable sum by not paying for the services of a holiday company, many of whom levy a considerable fee for the security of booked accommodation.

GITES D'ETAPE
There are several thousand of these simple hostels found all over France, particularly along the GR trails. They provide basic and cheap accommodation for the outdoor enthusiast, especially the walker. Many of these establishments are located on or near to the trails described in this book (see Appendix 1). A full list of *gîtes d'étape* throughout the country, and in the neighbouring regions, will be found in the latest edition of *Gîtes d'Etape de Randonnée et Refuges* (see Bibliography). The *gîte d'étape* should not be confused with the *gîte rural* which is the term usually reserved for a rented holiday cottage (in just a few cases *gîtes d'étape* are referred to, rather confusingly, as *gîtes ruraux;* eg the establishment at Villars (Day 7) is termed a "*gîte rural* de France")

   Gîtes d'étape come in all shapes and sizes, from converted barns or stables to large houses, school buildings or even parts of hôtels. Few are purpose built. The wardens are often farming folk who use the *gîte d'étape* as an extra source of income. The typical *gîte d'étape* will accommodate between 10 and 30 people in a unisex dormitory, usually on large mattresses. Blankets are usually, but not always, provided (see Equipment section). It will have a kitchen equipped with stoves and cooking utensils and there will also be a dining area.

There are usually hot showers as well as washbasins and toilets. The warden often does not reside in the *gîte d'étape*, but may live in an adjacent house or farm. Meals are often provided by the guardian and these generally represent good value for money.

A few of the *gîtes d'étape* in the Préalpes belong to an organisation known as the GTA (Grande Traversée des Alpes), whilst many of those in the Ardèche are establishments belonging to a concern called Chamina (Association pour le Développement de la Randonnée Pédestre dans le Massif Central) whose logo is a green walking man equipped with cloak and walking stick. *Gîtes d'étape* which are referred to as *gîtes communal* are hostels provided by the village or commune, and often tend to be more spartan than private *gîtes d'étape*. The latter are often more expensive than the *gîtes communal*, but generally are more comfortable and usually provide meals of restaurant standard. The owners of private *gîtes* want as many customers as possible and so these establishments tend to be well signposted along the trails and in the neighbouring villages and towns. *Gîtes communal* can sometimes be a little tricky to locate! Whatever the nature of the hostel and whoever owns the building, it is not necessary to be a member of any organisation to spend the night at a *gîte d'étape*. No discount is offered to members of any clubs or associations. *Gîtes d'étape* offer inexpensive accommodation: all *gîtes* belonging to a particular organisation usually have a standard overnight fee, fixed at the start of each yearly season (eg. the standard rates for Chamina *gîtes d'étape* was 35FF, about £3.50, in 1992). *Relais d'étape* (see below) are cheaper, whist some private *gîtes* and those belonging to more prestigious organisations often charge somewhat more for an overnight stay (45FF was common in 1992).

Several of the areas through which the Trail passes are popular horse riding centres, with an extensive network of bridleways. Stabling facilities are available at some of the *gîtes d'étape* (eg. at Moustiers, Day 9, and at Malaucène, Day 18) and it is also possible at these gîtes to hire out horses or ponies on an hourly, or daily basis. Guided horse and pony trekking is also widely available and makes a relaxing change from walking the Trail.

Gîtes d'étape are primarily intended as overnight accommodation for walkers hiking the various trails, so one is not normally encouraged to spend more than a few nights at any one gîte. They do, however, make ideal bases to sit out a spell of bad weather in the company of other like-minded people. Sometimes a small fee is payable for use of the *gîte d'étape* during the daytime. *Gîtes d'étape* can on occasions become very crowded, although this is generally less common in many of the areas covered by this book than in the very well known walking and climbing areas of the Alps. The warden will usually seek to accommodate everyone however full the gîte, but sometimes late arrivals may have to go elsewhere. However, if there is no other accommodation available in the vicinity it is most unlikely that entry would be refused however full the gîte, although it may be necessary to sleep on a mattress on the floor. It is possible to book ahead by telephone (telephone numbers of the relevant *gîtes d'étape* are provided in Appendix 1) but good spoken French is required as few guardians speak English. Overcrowded *gîtes d'étape* are most frequently encountered between mid-July and mid-August. Arriving early at a *gîte d'étape* is the best way of reserving a bed for the night. Remember also that dinner, if provided, is usually served between 7 and 8pm at most *gîtes d'étape*, and therefore a late arrival will go hungry if not carrying his or her own food provisions.

Very occasionally the walker will come across a *relais d'étape* (eg. near Rougon, Day 7). This tends to be a very basic establishment, sometimes little more than a rudimentary dormitory, whilst at Rougon the *relais d'étape* consists of a small area of pre-erected tents. In one or two areas an *abri* or rough shelter will be encountered (eg. the Abri du Contrat below the summit of Mont Ventoux, Day 17). These are generally quite small and unsuitable for an overnight stay, but provide welcome shelter during bouts of severe weather. Occasionally the term "refuge" is used for simple shelters or very basic *gîtes d'étape*: do not expect the large, elaborate "refuges" often found in the Alps. The one exception on this route is the large refuge of La Mâline, above the Verdon Gorges (Day 8). This establishment, which belongs to the French Alpine Club (CAF), offers comfortable accommodation and good food for the large number of outdoor enthusiasts who frequent the gorges.

HOTELS

Hôtels in France are star graded on a system very similar to that in use in Britain. The basic hôtel is the one star establishment and this is usually reasonably priced, clean and comfortable. Most of the hôtels in the areas covered by this guidebook carry a one or two star grading, although more luxurious accommodation (three- and even four-star grading) can be found in the centres popular with tourists. Hôtels are generally much cheaper in France than in Britain; expect to pay between 90FF to 180FF (about £9 to £18) per night for a room for two. Payment is for the room, ie. the average room is designed for two people and there is seldom a reduction if only one person occupies the room (although if travelling alone it is always worth asking for a discount). Sometimes the proprietors will provide an extra bed for a third or even fourth person, usually for a small additional charge. Therefore if travelling as a pair, or even as a threesome if there is no objection to sharing, a one- or two-star hôtel can often be little more expensive than a *gîte d'étape*.

It is a good plan to mix accommodation between *gîtes d'étape*, where other like-minded walkers will be encountered, and hôtels, which obviously provide more privacy and comfort. If not carrying a tent it will be necessary, in fact, to use both types of accommodation on this route, as there are several towns and villages where only hôtel accommodation is available, whilst in other areas a *gîte d'étape* is the only place to spend the night. However, those wanting predominantly hôtel accommodation should be able to locate a hôtel on the majority of nights during the walk. Also try the occasional *chambre d'hôte* where available. A list of hôtels can usually be obtained from the local *syndicat d'initiative* or *maison de tourisme*.

Sometimes hôtels or restaurants have associated outbuildings or attics. These *dortoirs* provide basic but cheap accommodation for the night and a meal can be bought here as well. Some villages, whist not boasting a hôtel, may have an *auberge* or similar sort of establishment, often with rooms above a café/restaurant.

CAMPING

It is perfectly possible to backpack along this Trail. Those wishing to camp wild *(camping sauvage)* must do so well away from habitation, roads and agricultural land. Permission will generally be required unless the camp is made high up in the mountains, well away from habitation. On parts of the route this will not be possible, particularly in the lower lying areas close to towns and villages, and in the vine and lavender growing regions. In some areas it is illegal to camp wild during the summer months because of the danger of fires. Particular care should be exercised at all times with matches and stoves, as forest fires are all too common during the hot, dry summers. An uncontaminated water source will have to be located, unless sufficient water is carried from a town or village. Water is not abundant in many of the limestone areas and *garrigues* along the route, and this should be borne in mind if intending to camp wild overnight. The art of the backpacker is to leave no sign of an overnight camp. Leave no litter and take care not to pollute water sources.

There are several campsites in the vicinity of the Trail, although they are considerable distances apart in certain areas, whilst in some places a detour from the route is required. Most campsites are only open during the summer months. It is usually necessary to provide passport details and complete a registration form when staying at a campsite in France. Although camping is extremely popular, tents tend to be of the large frame variety and the French have not taken enthusiastically to backpacking. Therefore a small backpacking tent will often be squeezed in between large family tents. This can sometimes lead to an invitation to a barbecue or picnic, but on the negative side, large family groups often make a lot of late night noise. Simple camping in a farmer's field *(camping à la ferme)* is becoming increasingly popular in France, and several such signs should be seen along the way. Food is sometimes available from the farmer's wife. The facilities at other campsites vary from spartan (merely a water tap) to luxurious, with bars, sports facilities, etc. Most provide hot showers. A star grading system is in operation for official campsites: 1-star is the least pretentious, 4-star has all mod-cons. Note that the overnight fee at some campsites can be as much, or even more, than the cost of a bed in a *gîte d'étape*.

Most people who set out with a tent will almost certainly make use of other forms of accommodation as well, particularly the *gîte d'étape*. Some may wish to carry a lightweight tent for use only on nights when other accommodation cannot be found, although in this case many walkers would find that at the end of the holiday they had carried the extra weight for no reason other than providing an additional feeling of security. Another option is to camp every night,but make use of the many restaurants en route, thereby avoiding the need to carry stove, cooking utensils and extra food.

EATING OUT

France is of course renowned for its cuisine and one of the delights of a walking holiday in Provence and the Ardèche is the opportunity to eat out at several different establishments. Most restaurants have a range of fixed-price menus as well as à la carte. Fixed price menus in most restaurants in southern France range from 50FF to approximately 180FF (about £5 to £18, 1992 prices). The average meal costs around 60FF to 90FF. For this price there is usually a choice of hors d'oeuvre, a main course (usually a meat or fish dish) and sweet, fruit and/or cheese. Wine is generally extra, but is cheaper than in Britain. The 180FF menu would probably be a five or six course affair. It is a good idea to finish the holiday with such a meal as a "celebratory dinner". In summary, eating out in restaurants in France is in general cheaper than in Britain and the choice of establishments is much greater. The smallest village will often have one or more restaurants and even in the most isolated and rural parts of the country one can expect food of high quality at reasonable cost.

There are a few differences between eating out in France compared with Britain that should be appreciated. Firstly, the menus for lunch and dinner are usually the same, ie. lunch is a large meal in France. Most walkers will prefer to eat their large meal of the day in the evening, but occasionally it might be appropriate to walk in the morning and evening and escape the heat of the day in a restaurant over a long, slow lunch. Note that if a snack is required at lunchtime then this can often cost as much as a full meal. Dinner is not normally available until 7 to 7.30pm. Breakfasts are continental, consisting only of coffee or drinking chocolate with bread and jam (average cost 20FF to 25FF in 1992). Lastly, one small point: the same knife and fork are generally used for most courses on the menu; do not expect to get clean cutlery with every course.

Many restaurants in France are hôtel-restaurants, but meals are almost always available to non-residents. Quite often a restaurant will double as a café or bar and will serve drinks and snacks to customers not requiring a meal. Several *gîtes d'étape* on or near the Trail provide meals. Food in *gîtes d'étape* is generally of the same quality and price as in a restaurant.

Vegetarians will find life generally a little more difficult in France than in Britain. However, vegetarian meals are becoming more widespread in France, particularly in the cities and fashionable towns. If there is no vegetarian dish on the menu then give your requirements to the waiter; a vegetarian alternative will nearly always be provided on request.

FOOD

Shops tend to open earlier than their equivalents in Britain (usually around 7.30 to 8.00am) and stay open later (often up to 8.00pm). The disadvantage is that they close for much longer during the lunch "hour". A walker arriving in a village anytime between noon and 4.00pm is likely to find the shops closed (particularly from 12.30 to 3.00pm). A supermarket is a *supermarché*; a grocers' shop is an *épicerie* or *alimentation*; bread is sold in a *boulangerie* or *dépôt de pain*; cakes and pastries are sold in a *pâtisserie*, and cold meats, sausages or pâté in a *charcuterie*.

Half or even full day closing for shops is quite common on Mondays in France particularly in the rural areas in the south of the country, and so it is sensible to acquire adequate provisions on Saturdays to last for two full days. However, a few shops open for part or even the whole of the day on Sundays (Sunday opening is most likely to be found in places popular with tourists, particularly during the main holiday season of July and August). Simple provisions (eg. cheese, bread, cooked meats, honey) can sometimes be purchased from the guardian of a *gîte d'étape* or from a farm passed on route, and these opportunities are particularly useful when there is no shop in the immediate vicinity. Mobile shops (grocers, bakers, butchers) visit many of the communities that are too small to support a permanent shop, and these can on occasions be useful to the passing walker.

Dehydrated meals are difficult to obtain in rural France and therefore, if desired, should be purchased in Britain before leaving for France. However, French packet soups are very good and a wide variety of them is on sale everywhere; when supplemented with pasta and perhaps saucisson sec and cheese, they can provide a tasty, basic meal. Fruit, vegetables and cold meats are excellent and widely available. Milk is usually of the UHT variety and the commonest form of bread is the baguette which, although tasty, will become very stale within a few hours. *Biscottes* or French Toasts are an alternative when bread is not available. *Pain d'épice* (spiced "bread") provides a sweet, anytime snack.

WATER

Lack of water can be a problem in some areas, but only for the walker who is unprepared. There are water fountains in many of the villages and hamlets along the Trail and water bottles should always be filled when the opportunity arises. Temperatures during the daytime can become very high at times, particularly during July and August, and heat exhaustion and dehydration can rapidly develop, particularly when carrying a pack on steep mountainsides. Always ensure that an adequate quantity of liquid is consumed.

Note that the French word *source*, when seen along the the Trail, refers to a spring or other source of water. Most, but not all, of the water sources encountered en route are safe to drink, but if in any doubt water purifying tablets should be used. Water taken from sources labelled *l'eau non potable* is not suitable for drinking.

EQUIPMENT

The most important consideration is to ensure that the pack is as light as possible. Nothing ruins a walking holiday more than having to endure the excessive weight of an overloaded rucksack. Be ruthless to ensure that no unnecessary items are taken. If making sole use of hôtel or *gîte d'étape* accommodation there is no reason why the pack should not be small and relatively light.

A pair of lightweight boots is the recommended footwear, preferably well "worn-in". Heavyweight mountain boots should not be necessary except for winter hillwalking. Some form of lightweight shoe is also desirable for rest days, for relaxing in the evenings and for sightseeing. A pair of good quality trainers is recommended as these can be used as an alternative form of footwear on easy sections of the route. The wearing of boots inside *gîtes d'étape* is not allowed and is discouraged in most hôtels.

During the summer months Provence and the Ardèche experience high temperatures, and therefore for much of the time shorts and a tee-shirt will be the most comfortable attire. Walkers need have little fear of exposing bare arms and legs to bracken (recent research has highlighted the dangers of Lyme Disease, transmitted by ticks whose favourite habitat is bracken) as few specimens of this plant will be encountered on this walk. It can become decidedly chilly at night at times, particularly on the high sections of the walk and early and late in the season, and therefore warm clothing should also be carried to allow for this and for possible deterioration in the weather. Rather than carry the weight of traditional breeches it may be preferred, during the summer, to take a pair of lightweight walking trousers which can be worn on the occasional cool day or to protect sensitive skin against sunburn. Such trousers can also be worn whilst relaxing in the evenings. Obviously more warm clothing will be required if walking in spring or autumn and particularly during the winter months. A waterproof and windproof jacket is essential at anytime of the year, and many people would also wish to carry waterproof trousers.

The glare and heat from the sun can be intense, particularly during July and August and in the *garrigue* areas where much bare limestone is exposed. The use of sun-hat, high factor suncream, lip-salve and sunglasses will all help to avoid over exposure to the sun. To ensure that fluid is readily available during the day, at least one 1-litre bottle should be carried per person. Mineral water is often sold in screw-cap plastic bottles in France and these can provide useful additional water carriers.

On the Plateau de la Malle (Day 1)
On the Trail heading towards Aiglun (Day 2)

The gatehouse leading to the medieval walled town of Entrevaux (Day 4)
The village of Ubraye (Day 5)

The rucksack, the size of which will depend on whether camping equipment is to be carried, is probably the most important item of gear. It is vital to inspect the sac thoroughly for wear before leaving for France. Try to ensure that the carrying mechanism is not likely to break whilst on holiday. A dustbin liner for the rucksack and a supply of plastic bags will keep the contents dry in heavy rain. Equipment is best packed in different coloured stuff sacs to enable easy identification and access to various items. Perishable food is best kept in a disposable plastic bag to prevent the accidental soiling of the inside of the rucksack.

The backpacker will need to carry additional equipment, a small lightweight tent being the main requirement. A closed-cell type of insulating mat is advisable to cut down loss of body heat through the ground. A sleeping bag is essential, although a lightweight bag is probably satisfactory during the summer months. Those walkers intending to make use of several *gîtes d'étape* may also wish to consider taking a lightweight sleeping bag, as blankets are not always provided. A sleeping bag will also be very much appreciated if a night has to be spent in a barn, or similar primitive accommodation.

The camper who also intends to cook his or her own food will need some form of stove. The most convenient type to use in France during the summer months is the camping gaz stove. Spare gaz canisters are readily available in France at campsites and in village shops. Methylated spirits *(acool à brûler)* and lead-free petrol can also be purchased in France. If travelling by air it is important to remember that none of these fuels can be carried on board an aircraft, but will have to be purchased on arrival. A small cooking set and lightweight cutlery will also be required. Don't forget a box of matches or a lighter.

It is essential for those walkers intending to walk the section through the Verdon Gorges (Day 8) to carry a torch, as the first tunnel through the Couloir Samson is long and tortuous, not penetrated by light along all of its length. It is exceedingly dark! A small torch would also be found useful in *gîte d'étape* or tent at night. Remember to include a spare bulb (this is best kept in the first aid kit, to reduce the likelihood of breaking the bulb, and mislaying it amongst all your other gear). Spare batteries to fit British torches can, in most cases, be bought in France, so it is not necessary to carry the weight of an additional battery, unless excessive use is anticipated.

There are several other miscellaneous items to consider. It is wise to include a small first-aid kit to treat any minor cuts and bruises, headaches or stomach upsets. Insect repellent may also be worth considering. The first-aid box is a good place to store a whistle as it can be located easily in an emergency. A mini French/English dictionary or phrasebook may help with communication. A Swiss Army knife or similar is useful for cutting bread or salami, etc. If buying such a knife the most useful attachments to consider are a pair of scissors, a can opener, nail file and corkscrew. A very small sewing kit (the sort sometimes given free in conference hôtels, ie. a needle and a few appropriate threads) can save embarrassment if clothes are accidentally torn.

An ice-axe and preferably crampons will be required in the more mountainous regions during the wintertime. Note that snow and ice does not always leave the upper mountain slopes until well into June and so if planning a trip in the springtime an ice-axe may be advisable, unless keeping only to the lower sections of the Trail.

MAPS

The three options available, in descending order of recommendation, are:

1.   Didier & Richard (D & R) maps "Itinéraires Pédestres" at 1:50 000 scale.
2.   IGN maps "Série Verte" at 1:100 000 scale.
3.   IGN maps "Série Orange" at 1:50 000 scale.

The maps required to cover the Trail in each series are as follows:

1.   D & R Maps

Five sheets cover the majority of the route. From east to west these are as follows (words in quotation marks are the title of the sheet, whilst those in brackets describe the part of the Trail covered by the map):

Sheet No. 26 "Au Pays d'Azur de Fréjus à Menton" (covers the route from Grasse to the Col de Saint Jeannet, west of Bay and Entrevaux; Days 1 - 5).

Sheet No. 19 "En Haute Provence de Digne à Saint Auban - Le Verdon" (from Bay to Gréoux-les-Bains; Days 5 - 11).

Sheet No. 14 "Du Lubéron à la Sainte Victoire - Provence" (from Gréoux-les-Bains to Saint Croix-à-Lauze and Viens; Days 12 - 14; a short section of the Trail around Oppedette is missing from this sheet).

Sheet No. 27 "Massif du Ventoux - Dentelles de Montmirail - Monts de Vaucluse - Provence" (from a little before Oppedette to Les Farjons, west of Sainte Cécile-les-Vignes; Days 14 - 20).

Sheet No. 21 "Ardèche Meridionale du Gerbier de Jonc aux Gorges de l'Ardèche - Vivarais" (from Aiguèze to just after the Col du Pendu, north of Le Bez; Days 22 - 26).

The D & R maps do not cover the sections from Sainte Cécile-les-Vignes to Aiguèze (Days 20 - 21) and from Col du Pendu to Langogne (Day 26).

The routes of all GR trails, GR de Pays and some Petites Randonnées (q.v.) are overlaid on these maps with a prominent blue line. Note that the exact geographical limits of these sheets tend to vary with each edition of the maps.

2.   IGN Série Vert

Three sheets cover the entire Trail:

Sheet No. 61 "Nice, Barcelonnette" (covers the Trail from Grasse to Moustiers-Sainte-Marie; Days 1 - 9).

Sheet No. 60 "Cavaillon, Digne-les-Bains - Parc Naturel Régional du Lubéron [Nord]" (from Moustiers-Sainte-Marie to Sainte-Cécile-les-Vignes; Days 10 - 20).

Sheet No. 59 "Privas, Alès - Parc National des Cévennes [Est]" (from Sainte-Cécile-les-Vignes to Langogne; Days 20 - 26).

Parts of the Trail are also found on two other Série Verte maps, viz: Sheet No 68 "Toulon, Nice" (from Grasse to Cipières, Day 1, part of the Verdon Gorges, Day 8, and from Saint Martin-de-Brômes to Gréoux-les-Bains, Day 11).

Sheet No. 67 "Marseille, Carpentras - Parc Naturel Régional du Lubéron" (from Saint Martin-de-Brômes to Verdolier; Days 11 - 17).

GR trails are marked on these maps with a thin orange line.

3. IGN Série Orange

Twenty sheets in all are required to cover the entire Trail from Grasse to Langogne. From east to west these are as follows:

Sheet 3643 Grasse;	Sheet 3642 Roquesteron;	Sheet 3541 Entrevaux;
Sheet 3542 Castellane;	Sheet 3442 Moustiers-Sainte-Marie;	
Sheet 3443 Salernes;	Sheet 3342 Manosque;	Sheet 3242 Reillanne;
Sheet 3241 Sault;	Sheet 3141 Carpentras;	Sheet 3142 Cavaillon;
Sheet 3240 Séderon;	Sheet 3140 Vaison-la-Romaine;	
Sheet 3040 Orange;	Sheet 2940 Pont-Saint-Esprit;	
Sheet 2939 Bourg-Saint-Andeol;		Sheet 2839 Bessèges;
Sheet 2838 Largentière;	Sheet 2837 Burzet;	Sheet 2737 Langogne.

GR trails are not marked on these IGN maps.

By far the best maps to purchase for this Trail are the D & R maps at a scale of 1:50 000. These show considerable detail, have the route of the Trail clearly marked on them and five sheets cover most of the route. The only disadvantage is that a small percentage of the Trail is not covered by the series. However, the small missing sections are both found on IGN sheet No. 59 at 1:100 000 (Série Verte). The Série Verte maps are very useful for the initial planning of the route, but are generally of insufficient detail for use in the field (although coupled with the route description contained in this book some walkers may find them adequate). The Série Orange IGN maps at a scale 1:50 000 are very good, but they suffer from two major disadvantages, viz., the route of the Trail is not marked on them and many sheets are required to cover the whole route - using these maps is therefore a very costly option. In conclusion the author recommends that those planning to walk the entire route should purchase the five D & R maps together with the IGN map No. 59 (Série Verte).

Note that IGN is the abbreviation for the Institut Géographique National, the French equivalent of the Ordnance Survey. All the above maps can be purchased or ordered from certain specialist map shops in Britain (see Appendix 3).

WAYMARKING AND NAVIGATION

Long distance paths in Europe are generally waymarked more thoroughly than those in Britain. This is particularly true in France. Nearly all of the paths described in this guidebook are part of the GR network and as such are waymarked with a standard system of red and white painted stripes. These occur, usually in a horizontal position with white above red, on rocks, boulders, trees, posts, fences, telegraph poles, etc. In some areas a rather novel system has been adopted: tin cans have been painted one half red, the other white, and these have been attached to fence posts and even some tree branches. The overall standard of waymarking on the Trail described in this book is very good. The walker should not continue too far without seeing another red/white waymark. If one is not encountered for some time it is likely that the wrong path has been taken.

The quality of the waymarking does vary somewhat from area to area along the Trail. There are numerous reasons for these variations in standards. Particular groups of workers are allocated to specific sections of the GR Trail; standards vary between these waymarking parties. There is always more waymarking to be done than there is time and volunteers available to waymark the trails, and therefore priorities have to be made; often priority is given to the more popular sections of a path or to where the waymarking is known to be poor. It is often many years before resources are available to re-waymark a section. Paint fades with time and exposure to a fierce summer sun and freezing and thawing in winter. Paint adheres to some surfaces better than others: it often cracks and peals on expanding tree bark. Things often change in the countryside, eg. fences may be changed and trees felled - if these carried waymarks then it is most unlikely that either farmer or forester will replace them. Sometimes landowners object to trails passing over their land and as a result remove waymarks.

It is well to remember, when searching for the next "rouge et blanc", that the waymarking of GR and other trails is usually performed by teams of volunteers. In this guide particular care has been given to the route description in those areas where some difficulties may be experienced. However, areas that were once difficult to negotiate may not be so after the route has been re-waymarked, and this could happen at anytime. Similarly, the loss of a crucial waymark can convert an easily navigable section into one of considerable difficulty. Pay particular attention in woodland where forestry activities quite frequently result in the loss of waymarks on felled trees. Occasionally, new waymarks may indicate a slightly different line from the one indicated in this guidebook. In any such cases the walker should, with due regard to the map, follow the new waymarking, making absolutely sure that this does not refer to another GR or other trail.

Remember that when there are two alternative routes on a GR trail, the *variante* is usually, but not always, waymarked in the same manner as the standard trail, ie. with red/white waymarks. Remember too that all standard GR trails are waymarked with red and white flashes: in areas where two GR routes meet or where a variant leaves the main path, care should be taken to follow the correct GR trail.

In the GR waymarking system various arrangements of red and white lines are used to signify different instructions. Two sets of red/white marks appearing together indicate that a change in direction is imminent. This instruction is sometimes shown by the use of curved red and white markings which point towards the new direction to be taken. The painted cross, usually of one red and one white line, is an important one to recognise as it signals that the route is not in that direction and the walker must go back to pick up the correct trail.

In woodland areas some of the trees bear paint marks which the walker could at first mistake for GR waymarkings. The most common are: 1) a thick white line having a thin red line through its centre. 2) a thick white line sandwiched between two narrow red ones, 3) single white stripes sometimes bearing a black number. When these occur they generally do so in greater numbers than the red and white lines of the GR. Walkers in France should learn to distinguish these forestry and hunting marks on trees from those of the long distance path.

Certain notices should be understood. "Propriété Privée" or "Défense d'Entrer" means that the area is private and entry forbidden. The signs "Réserve du Chasse" and "Chasse Privée" do not refer to walkers, but indicate that hunting rights are reserved for the owner of the land.

"PR" (Petite Randonnée) routes, local footpaths and nature trails (q.v.) are waymarked in a variety of different ways. The majority of the many PR trails encountered will be waymarked with a single paint stripe: the commonest colours used are yellow, green or blue. Orange waymarks, which sometimes occur in the shape of a "hoof-print", signify a bridleway. Regional routes or "GR de Pays" are waymarked with red and yellow paint stripes, ie. exactly like GR trails except that yellow replaces white. Routes to mountain summits are often waymarked with single paint stripes, commonly in red.

Signposts, as distinct from waymarks, will also frequently be seen at intervals along the Trail. These will often carry the number of the GR route and the time to the next village, *gîte d'étape*, col or other landmark. The time generally required to walk to these destinations by an "average" unladen rambler in good conditions is usually given on the signpost. These signboards have either been erected by representatives of the GR authorities or local rambling groups (often volunteers) or by the local Maison de Tourisme. Note that where the term "AR" is given together with a time to a particular destination (commonly to a mountain summit) this refers to the time taken to reach the location and return to the signpost, ie. the time to walk "there and back" ("**A**ller et **R**etour").

It should be possible for much of the time to remain on the Trail by following waymarks and making use of the route descriptions provided in this book. However, it would be foolish to ignore the use of map and compass. These should always be carried and one's position on the map checked frequently. This is particularly important in the high mountain and plateau areas of the route, especially along the sections covered by the five topographical profiles included in this book. Knowledge of one's position on the map and the ability to use a compass will allow a route to be navigated in safety in mist or other bad weather conditions, or if the waymarks have been lost. It is hoped that the route descriptions in this guide are sufficient for the walker to follow the Trail without problems, but if the correct line is lost, for whatever reason, a map will be essential for finding your way back to the GR route. In addition a map is invaluable for the identification of neighbouring peaks, lakes and villages.

Occasionally slight problems may be experienced in reading the finer details of French maps. The appearance of small "white roads" on these maps usually indicates that they are metalled, but sometimes they will be found to be only unsurfaced dirt tracks. Also a few of the tracks indicated by single black lines on the maps have now been made up to surfaced lanes. The tarmacking of minor roads appears to be occurring more frequently nowadays as more grants for improvement in rural areas are becoming available. Parts of the route which have been described as dirt tracks in this guide, may in later years carry a metalled surface. Therefore some care in interpreting the descriptions will be required.

PETITES RANDONNEES, LOCAL ROUTES AND NATURE TRAILS

There are several thousands of miles of waymarked trails in Provence and the Ardèche. Apart from many other GR routes (see Appendix 2) the walker in France will encounter a large number of *Petites Randonnées* or short waymarked trails (abbreviated to "PR"), as well as a number of "GR de Pays" (sometimes rather confusingly referred to as merely *Sentiers Pédestres* or "SP"). The latter are somewhat analogous with Regional Routes in Britain, whereas the *Grandes Randonnées* of France could be compared with our own much less extensive National Trail network. All of the GR trails and most of the GR de Pays are devised and managed by a national organisation, based in Paris, known as the Fédération Française de la Randonnée Pédestre (FFRP). Most of the PR routes and nature trails are the work of local organisations (see Appendix 3) or groups of local walkers and tourist authorities.

The PR trails in the areas covered in this book are far too numerous to mention in detail here, many new ones being added to the network each year as more routes are waymarked and leaflets and booklets become published. They are a delightful way of getting to know rural France, being particularly suitable for those on a car based holiday who wish to do a little walking as well as general sightseeing in various parts of the region. They are also useful for those taking a "rest day" on a GR trail who wish to go for a short walk without the inconvenience of a carrying a pack. PR trails involve anything from twenty minutes' to several hours' walking and are usually precisely numbered and waymarked. Details can be obtained from the numerous local tourist offices and *Syndicats d'Initiative* in the region, or by sending an international reply coupon to the various local walking organisations or Regional or National Parks (see Appendix 3).

It is important to appreciate the various waymarking systems that have been adopted for the various categories of walking trail (see "Waymarking and Navigation").

GEOLOGY: GORGES, CAVERNS AND GARRIGUES

Limestone is the predominant rock encountered on this walk. It is found in a variety of forms and situations, from the sheer walls of the Verdon and other gorges, to barren limestone pavements, jagged ridges and pinnacles and a whole variety of outcrops of all shapes and dimensions. The different features of this walk, the many gorges, the nature of the mountains and high plateaux and the vegetation itself are a result of the properties of the overlying rock. Rainwater mixed with carbon dioxide from the atmosphere forms a weak solution of carbonic acid which dissolves the calcium carbonate in the limestone. This simple fact of chemistry has led to the formation of the many limestone gorges in the area and an extremely extensive network of subterranean rivers and potholes. Some of the caverns, which often have most elaborate arrays of stalagmites and stalactites, are open to the public, including the Aven d'Orgnac near Labastide-de-Virac (Day 22).

A prominent feature of the Provençal landscape is the *garrigue*, the local name for a high, barren, vast limestone plateau or table-land. The vegetation is generally course and sparse, with stunted trees and aromatic herbs growing between scattered limestone outcrops. Good examples of garrigues are encountered on the first day out of Grasse and also on the climb to Montfuron (Day 13) and between Malaucène and Séguret (Day 19). When the sun is shining brightly, as it often does in Provence, the intense reflection from the exposed rock can be painful to the eyes; sunglasses are advisable.

FLORA AND FAUNA

The type of vegetation found in this area of southern France is predominantly the result of two factors: the preponderance of thin and alkaline soils, a consequence of the overlying limestone rock; and the climate of long, hot and sunny summers, but often cold winters, with heavy snowfalls and long periods when the mistral is blowing. The latter has an effect on the location of trees and shrubs on a hillside and their shape (they are often bowed and distorted by the continual wind).

At lower altitudes the flora is typically Mediterranean, the plants being able to withstand extended periods of drought and long exposure to a fierce sun. Holm oaks, olive trees and aromatic herbs predominate. In the higher mountains there are deciduous woods of oak, beech and chestnut mixed in with various pine trees. Wildflowers are numerous and of a large variety. In some areas the expanses of broom and heather are extensive. Herbs such as thyme, mint and tarragon are abundant. Many varieties of mushroom grow in southern France, and the search for and the gathering of these is a popular pastime for the Frenchman. Take care if you follow suit, as there are several very poisonous species as well as the numerous edible varieties (if in doubt take them to a pharmacy where identification tables will be available, and often an expert on hand to give advice).

Forests fires are unfortunately a fairly common occurrence in southern France, usually the result of carelessness, but occasionally started deliberately. Every care should be taken when handling matches, camping stoves and naked flames. Fires start all too easily under the tinder dry conditions that develop during the summer months.

The remoteness of much of the land favours a rich wildlife. Birds of prey are fairly common; buzzards, kestrels, kites and even eagles ride the thermals above the hills. Deer, hare and rabbit roam the woods and are popular with huntsmen. Hunting (La Chasse), particularly shooting, is popular in France and consequently care should be exercised when the sound of gunshot fire is heard; safety procedures are not all they could be at times. Wild boar can still be found, but is rare.

The warm summer climate favours many insects, some of the biting variety (clegs and mosquitos), but also an abundance of colourful and varied butterflies. Grasshoppers are also common. The stridulation of cicadas can be intense and infuriating on a hot, sunny afternoon. Lizards flit across the hot rocks and there are several species of snake, most, but not all, of which are harmless (see "Snakes").

RURAL ECONOMY

The agricultural activities of southern France are quite different from those found in Britain. They will be in evidence throughout the walk and are of considerable interest to the visitor from northern climes.

Lavender Fields

The scent of lavender will be on the air for much of the walk. Lavender, and its less fragrant hybrid, lavandin, which is grown below 2300ft (702m), is cultivated in many parts of Provence. It is grown in long, straight rows in large fields, the mass of purple flowers making a most attractive sight. The flowers are harvested between July and September, usually mechanically, but sometimes still by hand. Large expanses of cultivated lavender will be encountered between Moustiers-Sainte-Marie and Gréoux-les-Bains (Days 10 and 11) and above Saint-Jean-de-Sault (Day 16).

Vineyards

The sun-drenched hillsides and wide valleys of Provence produce wines that are of world renown. The Trail passes through extensive areas of vineyards from the wine-producing villages of the Dentelles, through the Ouvèze valley and on to the Rhône (Days 19 - 21). Important vineyards are also passed at Pierrevert, near Manosque (Day 13) and on the lower slopes of Mont Ventoux, near Malaucène (Day 18).

Orchards
Fruit growing is an important commercial activity in several parts of Provence. Cherry, apricot, pear and apple trees will be seen in several areas along the way, particularly in the Vaucluse and in the valleys of the Ouvèze and Rhône. Almond trees, imported from Asia in the sixteenth century, are also common. The display of blossom in April is quite spectacular.

Olives
The gnarled and twisted trees of the olive grove will become a familiar sight to the walker. They are particularly common on the southern slopes of the mountains. Olives, which grow well on both limestone and sandy soils, were introduced to Provence by the Greeks over 2500 years ago. They start producing fruit after six to twelve years, reach full yield after twenty-five years, but live on for many centuries.

Herbs
Several varieties are cultivated in Provence, including marjoram, basil, and tarragon. Many others (eg. rosemary and thyme) grow wild, but are gathered from the hillsides for local use and for sale. The scent of herbs will soon rise as the walker crushes them with the passing of his or her boots.

Honey
Bee keeping for the production and sale of honey (in French *miel*) is an important small scale industry in southern France. Many hives will be passed whilst on the walk and there will be several opportunities to sample the products, which are on sale at numerous farmhouses and villages en route. The "Bee or Honey Museum" at Riez (see Day 10) is well worth a visit.

Chestnuts
These used to form a major item of the diet of the southern French peasant, particularly in the impoverished regions of the Cévennes and Ardèche. Chestnuts were ground to a "flour" from which a type of bread was baked, prepared and eaten as a porridge, or boiled to form a chestnut stew. They are still gathered by locals in some areas. The oak and chestnut woods are particularly fine on the climb up to Thines in the Cévennes (Day 24)

Sheep

Sheep have been reared in Provence for centuries. The annual *transhumance*, whereby the animals were driven up to higher pastures for the summer months, has largely disappeared, the stock now being transported by truck. The numerous *drailles* or drove roads in southern France provide evidence of the importance of animal stock rearing in the rural economy in years gone by. Several of these drailles form sections of the Trail. In many of the arid, limestone regions passed en route the vegetation is so sparse that sheep graze over vast areas.

MOUNTAIN SAFETY

The well equipped and well prepared walker who is sufficiently skilled in the use of map and compass, should encounter no particular problems on this walk. However, the usual safety precautions applicable to any mountain area should always be undertaken. Always keep an eye open for weather changes, remembering that not only are violent storms dangerous, but also over exposure to the sun can have very serious consequences. Never hesitate to turn back or head for the nearest shelter if weather conditions deteriorate. Plan ahead, look for possible escape routes to be used in an emergency, never overestimate the physical ability of the party and always carry sufficient reserves of food and water. Never be afraid to ask the guardians of *gîtes d'étape* for a weather forecast or other advice, as they are usually more than willing to oblige. Other walkers, particularly those who are walking the route in the opposite direction, are another good source of information about the state of the path ahead.

Learn the International Distress Signal, viz. six audible (eg. whistle) or visual (eg. torch) signals for one minute followed by a minute's pause. The alarm is then repeated. The answer from a party coming to the rescue is three such signals, followed by a minute's silence. Help can also be summoned by using arm signals: raising both arms in the air means "I require assistance"; one arm raised and the other lowered means "I do not need help". It is only advisable to summon the rescue services if it is absolutely essential, as it is an extremely costly business in France (see "Insurance").

SNAKES

The European viper or adder is found in several of the regions through which the Trail passes, and a bite, although unlikely to be fatal, would be exceedingly unpleasant and could have serious consequences in the more sparsely populated regions where help may not be quickly available. Fortunately they are fairly secretive animals, likely to detect a walker's presence by vibrations along the ground and take avoiding action. Nevertheless, keep a good lookout for vipers in order to avoid accidentally treading on one. It is a good idea to familiarise oneself with the markings of the European viper (dark green/black in colour with characteristic zig-zag stripes on the upper surface) in order to identify a specimen if seen. The chances are that the Trail will be completed without catching sight of even one of these reptiles.

A bite from a viper can result in considerable bruising, discolouration and swelling of the surrounding area. If bitten it is necessary to rest, avoid a panic reaction, get medical help as soon as possible, and in the meantime try to suck out the venom. It is possible to buy an aspiratory device for this purpose in pharmacies in France. This apparatus consists of a syringe with variously sized and shaped attachments, which enable venom to be drawn from a wound. It is also possible to purchase a viper venom antidote (antiserum) without prescription in French pharmacies. The application of this requires a self-injection in muscle tissue near the site of injury, but it should only be used in emergencies when medical help cannot be obtained (see also "Insurance").

DOGS
Guard dogs are occasionally a problem when encountered on some of the isolated properties passed on the Trail. The majority of dogs are more "bark than bite", but they can be unnerving at times. They are often chained, but frequently on a long chain, so be sure to keep more than a chain length away from them. Some walkers advocate the use of a stout stick to fend off an attack, but this may simply anger the animal. Never run or walk quickly past an unfriendly dog, as this may release its chase response. Walk slowly, backwards if necessary, facing the animal, keeping it in sight at all times. However, do not stare at the dog, as staring is a threat and the animal may read it as a challenge and is thus more likely to attack. More advice on how to deal with a potentially dangerous dog will be found in the leaflet *How Should You Cope with an Unfriendly Dog?*, produced and issued free by the RSPCA (send SAE to RSPCA, Causeway, Horsham, West Sussex RH12 1HG).

If a bite is sustained, however slight, it is important to seek medical advice as soon as possible. Ask for an anti-tetanus inoculation unless such a jab has been acquired recently. Note that although rabies is still found in continental Europe, it's occurrence is exceedingly rare in humans (fewer than 30 cases in the whole of Europe in the twelve years since 1980 and not a single human death from it in EC countries during that period). An attack from a fierce dog is unlikely, and the possibility should not deter anyone from walking in rural France. The author has walked over 2500 miles in France but, as yet, has not been attacked by a dog, although he has encountered several barking and potentially threatening animals.

THIEVES
Petty crime is no more evident in France than it is in Britain. Indeed in the rural areas through which most of this Trail passes, the chance of having personal effects stolen is much lower than in the urban areas of either France or Britain.

However, walkers should nevertheless not leave valuable items unattended in *gîtes d'étape* or in hôtel bedrooms. The risk is greatly increased along those parts of the Trail frequented by tourists (eg. in Grasse, the Verdon Gorges, Gréoux-les-Bains, Rhône Valley). The problem is most acute along the Côte d'Azur. If a car is taken to the area, try not to leave gear in an unattended vehicle.

PHOTOGRAPHY

Most walkers will wish to have a photographic record of their journey through southern France. The best type of camera to take is probably the 35mm SLR; a wide angle lens (eg. 28 or 35mm) is particularly suitable, whilst a telephoto lens will be useful for capturing details of more distant features. All this camera equipment is unfortunately very heavy, but a compromise would be to use a medium zoom lens (eg. 28 - 80mm) on a SLR body. This would obviate the need to change lenses continually, but nevertheless zoom lenses are themselves heavier than prime lenses. Weight can be radically reduced by using a good quality 35mm compact camera equipped with a reasonably wide-angled lens, or alternatively a zoom lens. The quality can be almost as good as an SLR camera, but the compact camera is light and small, easily fitting into a pocket.

Both used and unused film should be protected from heat by placing it well inside the rucksack. It is advisable to take all exposed film home rather than posting it back to Britain to be processed. It could be lost in the post or damaged by X-ray equipment in the sorting offices.

LANGUAGE

> Never go to France
> Unless you know the lingo
> If you do, like me,
> You will repent, by jingo.
> *Thomas Hood (1799-1845)*

The French, like the British, are not particularly keen on learning foreign languages. Many of the younger people can speak some English, but in general do not expect the level of fluency found in Holland or Germany. English is more likely to be understood on the Côte d'Azur and in the other areas frequented by tourists, (eg. in Grasse, Moustiers, Verdon Gorges) than in the numerous villages and hamlets passed en route. The rural areas in this sparsely populated region of France have a preponderance of elderly folk, who are able to understand only French. Furthermore, many of them speak with a strong "Midi" accent. It is a good idea to brush up on "rusty" French before the holiday, as even the most elementary grasp of the language will pay dividends by enriching the experience of walking in France. However, no true adventurer will be discouraged by an inability to speak the local tongue, even if it will necessitate the occasional use of sign language. Do not take Thomas Hood's ditty too seriously!

Provence had its own language *(Langue d'Oc)* which developed from vulgar Latin as a separate tongue from that used in the north *(Langue d'Oïl)* The *Langue d'Oc* flourished in the twelfth century as the language of the troubadours, but waned after 1539 when it was decreed that the language of the north was to be used for all administrative purposes. It had a revival amongst intellectuals and writers (particularly Frédéric Mistral) in the nineteenth century, but today it remains only in street names and the like (see Rustrel, Day 15), although an Institute of Occitanian Studies is making efforts to keep the language alive. Many of the works of the famous twentieth-century writers of Provence, such as Jean Giono from Manosque (see Day 12) and Marcel Pagnol, are in French, although the culture and identity of Provence are clearly present in their writings.

MONEY - BANKS AND POST OFFICES

The unit of currency is the French Franc. It is advisable to carry a fairly large supply of moderately low denomination notes (50FF, 100FF and 200FF notes are particularly useful). Besides cash, Eurocheques, travellers' cheques and credit cards are all widely used in France. Eurocheques are particularly convenient, the only problem being that sometimes a minimum quantity will have to be exchanged (1400FF in 1992), which is a nuisance if money is required at the very end of the holiday. Alternatively, travellers' cheques may be carried. French Franc travellers' cheques are the most useful as these can sometimes be used in restaurants, hôtels, etc, as immediate payment. Access and Visa cards are accepted widely in France and are a useful form of payment for restaurant meals and rail tickets. However, do not expect all of the establishments passed on route to accept this form of payment.

Walkers may also wish to consider an alternative method of obtaining local currency in France (and indeed in most European countries). Open a Girobank account in Britain and then request a Postcheque card and a book of Postcheques. These can be encashed easily in most post offices of participating countries (no charge is levied). The Girobank account in Britain is debited after the documents reach Girobank headquarters.

Banks will be found in the major towns en route, details of which will be found in the "Facilities" section of each "Day" stage. The banks in the larger towns (eg. Grasse, Manosque, Pont-Saint-Esprit) operate normal banking hours, which in France are from around 9am until midday and from 2-3pm until 4-5pm, on weekdays. Most banks are closed all day on Saturdays, and note that Monday in France (particularly in southern France) is often a "closed" day, when many banks, post offices and shops do not open, or close for a major part of the day. Some of the banks in the smaller towns and villages are open only one or a few days per week, and then perhaps only for a few hours. The larger post offices (PTT) will encash Eurocheques, but several of those passed en route are the equivalent of British sub-post offices and do not have the facilities for encashing Eurocheques. It is advisable to carry sufficient currency from the outset to avoid a time consuming detour to a bank later in the holiday.

INSURANCE
It is advisable to take out travel and medical insurance for the duration of the holiday as rescue and hospitalisation charges are very expensive in France. Ensure that the policy has an adequate medical sum insured and that the cost of mountain rescue is covered. Several companies issue cover within Europe for hillwalking, rambling, scrambling and camping, ie. activities excluding the use of specialist equipment such as ropes and ice-axes. Such a policy would be suitable for the walk described in this book, provided that it was not undertaken when the mountains are covered in snow and ice (see Appendix 3).

There are certain reciprocal rights available for British subjects in France under the National Health Service arrangements within the EEC. Information concerning eligibility for medical cover under this scheme and the necessary E111 form can be obtained from local DHSS offices or from main post offices. It is not, however, advisable to rely solely on Form E111.

TELEPHONE TO BRITAIN
It is becoming increasingly difficult for the visitor to make a simple phone call in France due to the widespread introduction by French Telecom of the phonecard system. During the late 1980s many of the public phoneboxes in France were converted from payphones to those requiring a phonecard. It is particularly difficult in the larger towns and cities in France. In Paris it is now almost impossible to find a public cash payphone, the one exception being in the foyer of Gare Saint Lazare (there is normally a long queue!). There are more coin-operated payphones available in the villages and small towns of Provence and the Ardèche, but whether most of these will eventually be converted to those requiring a phonecard is a matter for conjecture. Payment with coins or direct to a cashier can sometimes be made at post offices. Phonecards (for 50 units and 120 units) can be purchased from most post offices and certain other advertised outlets (look for the *Telecarte* sticker). The only other alternative is to use a phone in a hôtel, café or restaurant, but a call made in this way will be more expensive than in a public phonebox (note that the bill in such establishments can be, by law, no more than thirty per cent higher than the official rate).

Fortunately public telephones are numerous in rural France and found in most of the villages and even some of the hamlets along the Trail. The procedure for placing a call is very simple. Lift the receiver and insert the appropriate coins or phonecard, after which a dialling tone will be heard. A digital exchange system has been in operation in France for far longer than in Britain. First dial 19 (the code for an international line) and pause until a second dialling tone is heard. Next dial 44 (the code for the UK). Pause again before dialling the STD code of the number required, but minus the initial zero. Lastly, dial the number of the line required. For example, to phone a number in Edinburgh (STD code 031) dial: 19, pause, 44, pause, 31 123 4567. Note that reduced rates operate from 9.30pm to 8.00am, Monday to Friday, from 2.00pm on Saturdays and all day Sunday.

PUBLIC HOLIDAYS AND TIME IN FRANCE

There are more public holidays in France than in Britain. Fortunately between June and October there are only two to consider, viz. Bastille Day on July 14th and the Fête of the Assumption on August 15th. On both of these days the public transport system is considerably affected and many shops are closed, although most cafés and restaurants remain open. It is well to bear these days in mind and to plan accordingly, particularly if it is necessary to travel by public transport on either of these days. In addition do not forget the public holidays in Britain which are different from those in France, if planning to leave or enter the UK on those days. In the spring there are public holidays in France on May 1st (May Day), May 8th (1945 Armistice Day) and on Whit Monday. In the autumn there are bank holidays on November 1st (All Saints Day) and November 11th (1918 Armistice Day).

For most of the year French time is one hour ahead of the time in Britain, ie. French summer time is one hour ahead of B.S.T. and French winter time is one hour ahead of G.M.T. For a few weeks in late September and early October Britain and France are on the same time.

WALKING HOLIDAYS OF VARYING LENGTH AND TYPE

The full walk described in this book would take the average rambler twenty-six days to complete plus extra days for sightseeing, excursions, rest, and for travelling to and from the area. Most people do not have this amount of time available - but no matter. There are no prizes for completing the whole of the walk described herein, but a great deal of enjoyment and satisfaction will be gained by walking just a part of it, however small. There are many ways in which the walk can be used as the basis for a fine holiday in Provence and the Ardèche. Several of these possibilities are listed below; individuals can easily devise their own itineraries to suit their taste and ambitions.

Most walkers are "travellers" in the true sense of the word, not merely interested in putting one foot in front of the other, but have a desire to come to grips with the landscape, culture and history of the area at first hand. Many people like to combine walking with general sightseeing, particularly when in a foreign country. For this reason emphasis is given in this guidebook to items and places of interest both on and off-route, with details of how they may be visited and incorporated into the walking holiday. The information provided should enable many optional excursions to be made on full or part "days-off" from the Trail.

1.   A continuous walk of a month's duration

This would be particularly suitable for the retired, those between jobs, students with long vacations or those blessed with long holidays. A walk to be remembered for the rest of one's life.

2.   Two week walking holidays

The following suggestions make best use of the public transport facilities available:

i)   Grasse to Manosque (Day 1 to Day 12). 12 days' walking. A first-rate holiday which includes a traverse of the Préalpes and the trek along the Grand Canyon of the Verdon Gorges. The last few days offer gentle walking through fields of lavender, visiting several towns and villages of interest. There should be time available on the journey home to spend a day sightseeing in Aix-en-Provence.

ii)   Manosque to Langogne (Day 13 to Day 26). 14 day's walking. A superb walk taking in an ascent of Mont Ventoux, the Oppedette, Ardèche and Chassezac gorges, the Rhône vineyards and the Cévennes mountains. Strong walkers should be able to reduce the number of days walking to about 12. Time could also be saved by omitting the GR 6 and GR 9 sections, remaining instead on the GR 4 between Oppedette and Sault (see Days 14 - 16). Those who want a more leisurely holiday could allow two weeks for walking to the Rhône Valley (Day 13 to Day 21) enjoying a number of rest days and taking a number of excursions, by public transport or on foot, to the many places of interest within easy reach of the route. Details of many of the possibilities for optional excursions are given in the text of this book.

iii)   Castellane to Malaucène (Day 7 to Day 18; 12 day's walking) or to the Rhône Valley (to Day 21; 15 days walking). This fortnight's holiday takes in both of the main highlights of the Trail, viz. the Verdon Gorges and the ascent of Mont Ventoux.

3.   One week walking holidays

There are numerous possibilities to use the Trail for shorter walking holidays of one week or less. The following are some of the better and more practical possibilities. Obviously the distance covered will depend very much on the fitness and desires of the party, and whether the holiday is to include general sightseeing.

i)   Grasse to Entrevaux (Day 1 to Day 4; 4 days' walking). Plenty of time in a week's holiday to relax on the Côte d'Azur, as well as walk in the mountains. Excellent public transport connections at either end.

ii)   Grasse to Castellane (Day 1 to Day 6; 6 days' walking). An excellent week's mountain walk. There are several opportunities for extending the walk by climbing several of the summits in the neighbouring areas. These optional ascents can be made either as detours from the Trail or as separate day walks from centres passed en route. Brief details of the major possibilities are given in the text.

iii) Entrevaux to Moustiers-Sainte-Marie (Day 5 to Day 9; 5 days' walking). A mountain walk combined with a trek through the Grand Canyon of the Verdon Gorges.

iv) Castellane to Manosque (Day 7 to Day 12; 6 days' walking). A combination of mountain and low level walking and including the Verdon Gorges. Good rail connection at Manosque.

v) Moustiers-Sainte-Marie to Manosque (Day 10 to Day 12; 3 days' walking) or to Cereste (to Day 13; 4 days walking). Ideal for those seeking a few days of gentle walking through lavender fields, vineyards and ancient woodland, linking a number of towns and villages of interest.

vi) Manosque to Sault (Day 13 to Day 16; 4 days' walking) or to Malaucène (to Day 18; 6 days' walking). This week long trip takes in some of the finest areas in Provence: the Lubéron Regional Park, Oppedette Gorge, Provençal Colorado and a traverse of Mont Ventoux.

vii) Malaucène to Les Vans (Day 19 to Day 23; 5 days' walking). An easy, low level walk taking in many of the best features of the Trail: the Dentelles de Montmirail, the Rhône vineyards, the Rhône Valley, the Ardèche and Chassezac Gorges and many picturesque villages.

viii) The Rhône Valley to Langogne (Day 21 to Day 26; 6 days' walking). A trek across the Ardèche.

4.   Day Walks

A number of day walks can be taken along the Trail for those taking a car based, sightseeing holiday to the south of France, but wishing to sample some of the superb walking in the area. Sufficient details are given in this guidebook to allow for the planning of several such excursions. The place where car or other transport was left can be regained at the end of the walk by using either public transport or hiring a local taxi (not usually too expensive in France, especially if shared by several people). The "Sentier Martel" through the Verdon Grand Canyon can easily be walked in this way (see Day 8 for details). Mont Ventoux could be climbed in a day from Sault if transport is arranged to pick walkers up from the summit at the end of the day - otherwise it would be a fine two-day expedition over the mountain from Sault to Malaucène (public transport available back to Sault), but before leaving it is best to book overnight accommodation in Mont Serein (see Day 17).

5.   Nature Walks

The area is of considerable interest to naturalists. Ornithologists and amateur botanists would particularly enjoy the sections through the Lubéron Regional Nature Park and over the Préalpes and in the Cévennes.

NOTES ON USING THE GUIDEBOOK
Layout of Guide

The Trail across Provence and the Ardèche has been divided into 26 stages, each of a day's duration. Each day (with one exception, see Day 5) has been designed to terminate at a place where there is some form of permanent overnight accommodation, either an hôtel or a *gîte d'étape* and often both. In general the days are not over long, although there is some variation in the length and severity of each section, necessitated by the need to reach suitable accommodation each night. Other possibilities for accommodation along the route are also given and it must not be assumed that the daily itineraries described have to be adhered to rigidly. There are several possibilities for decreasing the length of the various stages and lingering a while, or walking further each day if desired. Walkers carrying a lightweight tent will have much greater flexibility for varying the itinerary. There should be sufficient information in this guidebook about the various facilities available to allow the daily mileage to be varied if required.

Each "Day" opens with a table providing distances and estimated walking times between the various places en route, as well as altitudes above sea level to give an indication of the amount of ascent and descent involved. The summary table is followed in several cases by a reference section detailing alternative routes available and/or optional excursions, so that the walker can see at a glance the various possibilities for the day. A section on the facilities available en route then follows so that the reader can plan ahead for the next day or two with regard to food, accommodation availability and other services. There are sub-sections on "accommodation", "restaurants/cafés/bars", "shops", "public transport", "water" and "miscellaneous". Next comes a "Summary" section which describes the nature of the stage and details the highlights of the day. Places of interest en route are outlined here together with relevant historical and geographical facts which should add to the enjoyment of the walker. Certain places where there is much to see and do, such as Grasse, Manosque and the Rhône Valley, have been described under separate headings. Various detours from the standard route for sightseeing or other "day-off" activities are included here so that the reader can analyse all the various possibilities for spending a holiday walking the Trail. Finally, there is a full description of the route with special reference to potential navigational problems that may be encountered. Allowance should be made for possible slight differences in the route details provided and the current situation on the ground. Remarks such as "waymarking is poor in this area" relate to the time of the survey; things may have improved (or deteriorated further!) since the last visit by the author.

Distances and Altitudes

Distances are given in miles and feet respectively because most English-speaking walkers are familiar with this system, but also in kilometres and metres as this is how they appear on the maps.

A very approximate but easily remembered conversion is:

1000m is approximately 3,300ft

2000m is approximately 6,600ft

To avoid tedious repetition in the description of the route, metric distances only are given in the text for distances less than 1 mile (1.61km). For example, if an instruction "turn left in 300 metres" is given, no conversion to yards or fraction of a mile is provided. This should present no problems if the description of the route is followed using the metric maps. A metre is approximately 1.1 yards. Do not assume that such distances when given carry a high level of accuracy. They merely give an indication of when the walker should look out for the change of direction: in a few seconds, a few minutes or much longer. They should really always be prefixed with "approximately", but this would make the text very laborious to decipher - the author did not use a tape measure each time(!). Distances of 1 mile and greater are quoted in both miles and kilometres. The mileage was calculated arithmetically from distances in kilometres taken from the maps.

Heights are given in both m and ft, the latter calculated arithmetically from data obtained from the metric maps. To avoid confusion in the text, the use of the word "metre" denotes distance (eg. 400 metres), whereas the abbreviation "m" is used to indicate a height (eg. 600m).

Timings

Times as well as distances are given between the various stages. These times take into consideration the amount of ascent and descent involved, the severity or otherwise of the terrain and the ease or difficulty of route finding. However, no allowance is made for stopping to rest and/or admire the scenery, have lunch, etc. This must be taken into account when estimating the time for the day's activities. The times quoted are those that it is considered that the "average" rambler would maintain, but obviously the actual time taken will vary from group to group and depend on the prevalent conditions, although it is useful to have an indication of the time generally required to walk each section. It is a system widely used in Europe.

Topographical Profiles

Height versus distance profiles have been provided for the mountainous sections only, viz. Days 1 - 9 (Profiles 1, 2 and 3), Days 16 - 18 (Profile 4) and Days 24 - 26 (Profile 5). These have been designed to show, at a glance, the major ascents and descents on each of the mountain sections of the Trail. They do not, of course, show the many minor ups and downs of the route, which also may exert their toll on the tired body at the end of a long day. They are intended for use in conjunction with the the Tables at the front of each "Day" stage and with the relevant maps. The relatively small ascents and descents in the other areas of the Trail do not warrant separate profiles, but data on the total ascent and descent is included at the very beginning of every "Day" stage.

Changes and Recommendations
The countryside is constantly changing, particularly in depopulated areas such as Provence and the Ardèche. Although it is not expected that the facilities outlined in this book will change substantially over the next few years, nevertheless new *gîtes d'étape* and hôtels will no doubt open whilst others close, shops and restaurants will change owners and bus services may be reduced or lost altogether. It is a good idea to keep abreast of the current situation. Information about neighbouring *gîtes d'étape* and other facilities is often found on noticeboards in *gîtes d'étape;* alternatively ask the guardian if there are any changes along the next section of the Trail. Fellow travellers, particularly those walking the same trail in the opposite direction, are another good source of information.

Remember that recommendations (eg. for a *gîte d'étape,* hôtel or restaurant) where given in this book, are personal ones, usually made after an enjoyable stay or a pleasant meal experienced by the author. However, guardians of *gîtes d'étape* change from time to time, as do owners of hôtels and chefs at restaurants. Furthermore, the situation often changes throughout the year: a quiet, pleasant restaurant with attentive, friendly staff in the low season may be sheer bedlam in the height of summer.

GUIDE

SUMMARY TABLE

WALKING THE FRENCH GORGES - PROVENCE AND THE ARDECHE

STAGE	DISTANCE		ASCENT		DESCENT		EST TIME	
	MLS	KM	FT	M	FT	M	HR	M
1. GRASSE TO GREOLIERES	14.9	24.0	4829	1473	3232	986	7.45	
2. GREOLIERES TO AIGLUN	6.1	9.7	2777	847	3419	1043	4.20	
3. AIGLUN TO AMIRAT	8.0	12.9	3895	1188	3049	930	5.00	
4. AMIRAT TO ENTREVAUX	6.6	10.5	2065	630	3390	1034	3.35	
5. ENTREVAUX TO LE TOUYET	9.5	15.3	4252	1297	1787	545	5.15	
6. LE TOUYET TO CASTELLANE	12.1	19.6	1705	520	3377	1030	5.50	
7. CASTELLANE TO POINT SUBLIME	11.4	18.2	2262	690	2042	623	4.55	
8. POINT SUBLIME TO LA MALINE	6.7	10.8	2295	700	1947	594	6.10	
9. LA MALINE TO MOUSTIERS	14.5	23.5	1964	599	2823	861	7.40	
10. MOUSTIERS TO RIEZ	11.2	18.0	1000	305	1338	408	4.40	
11. RIEZ TO GREOUX-LES-BAINS	13.9	22.4	1708	521	2128	649	5.25	
12. GREOUX-LES-BAINS TO MANOSQUE	8.2	13.2	515	157	679	207	3.15	
13. MANOSQUE TO CERESTE	12.8	20.5	1921	586	1705	520	6.00	
14. CERESTE TO VIENS	11.4	18.3	2170	662	1541	470	5.10	
15. VIENS TO ST SATURNIN D'APT	12.5	20.0	426	130	1206	368	5.05	
16. ST SATURNIN D'APT TO SAULT	15.8	25.5	2764	843	1419	433	7.35	
17. SAULT TO MONT SEREIN	12.8	20.6	4072	1242	2072	632	6.05	
18. MONT SEREIN TO MALAUCENE	11.3	18.2	1079	329	4596	1402	4.40	
19. MALAUCENE TO RASTEAU	15.2	24.5	1328	405	1711	522	6.40	
20. RASTEAU TO MONDRAGON	18.3	29.5	295	90	754	230	6.15	
21. MONDRAGON TO AIGUEZE	10.7	17.2	426	130	331	101	4.15	
22. AIGUEZE TO SALAVAS	15.3	24.6	1262	385	915	279	6.15	
23. SALAVAS TO LES VANS	18.8	30.3	1439	439	1492	455	7.35	
24. LES VANS TO THINES	11.7	18.9	2862	873	1646	502	5.25	
25. THINES TO LOUBARESSE	10.8	17.3	2587	789	485	148	4.50	
26. LOUBARESSE TO LANGOGNE	17.3	27.8	2282	696	3186	972	7.10	
TOTALS	**317.8**	**511.3**	**54180**	**16526**	**52270**	**15944**	**146.35**	

PROFILE 1 - GRASSE TO ENTREVAUX (PREALPES): DAYS 1 - 4

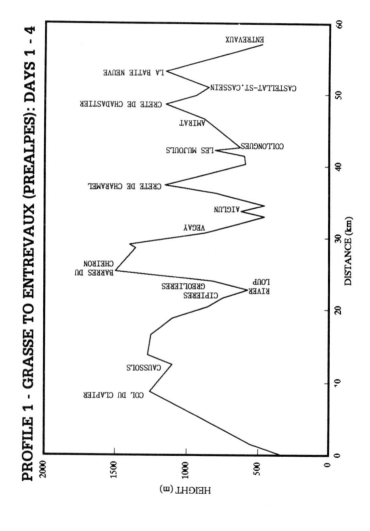

DAY 1
GRASSE TO GREOLIERES

DISTANCE: 14.9 MILES (24km)
TOTAL ASCENT: 4829ft (1473m)
TOTAL DESCENT: 3232ft (986m)
TOTAL ESTIMATED TIME: 7 HOURS 45 MINUTES

| | Height Above Sea Level | | Distance | | | | Est. Time | |
| | Sea Level | | Sect. | | Cum. | | Sect. | Cum. |
	ft	m	mile	km	mile	km	hr m	hr m
GRASSE	1092	333						
START OF GR 4	1836	560	0.9	1.5	0.9	1.5	0.30	0.30
PLATEAU DE LA MALLE	3508	1070	3.3	5.3	4.2	6.8	1.30	2.00
COL DU CLAPIER	4121	1257	1.2	1.9	5.4	8.7	0.35	2.35
CAUSSOLS-SAINT LAMBERT	3606	1100	2.4	3.8	7.8	12.5	1.10	4.45
CIPIERES	2459	750	5.7	9.2	13.5	21.7	2.10	6.55
GREOLIERES	2688	820	1.4	2.3	14.9	24.0	0.50	7.45

ALTERNATIVE START

Purists with plenty of time available who wish to start the walk from the Mediterranean coast could reach Grasse by following the GR 51, which starts a little to the west of Mandelieu, 5 miles (8km) west of Cannes. The route is tortuous and non-direct, as it avoids the sprawling conurbations behind the Côte d'Azur, and so cannot be particularly recommended, although it does pass through some picturesque villages. The route, which is clearly marked on the 1:50 000 Didier & Richard Map No. 26 (Au Pays d'Azur) is via Le Grand Duc, Pégomas, Auribeau-sur-Siagne, Forêt de Pèvgros, Les Bérenguiers, La Martourette, Le Maupas, Le Brusquet, Speracèdes, Cabris and Le Cartinet. The GR 51 meets the start of the GR 4 on the N 85, north of Grasse. The route is about 25 miles (40.2km) long and would require an additional two days of walking.

FACILITIES

Accommodation

Cannes: Accommodation in Cannes, as might be expected, is neither cheap nor easy to obtain, especially during the high summer season. It is therefore advisable to plan to arrive in Cannes during the daytime, allowing plenty of time

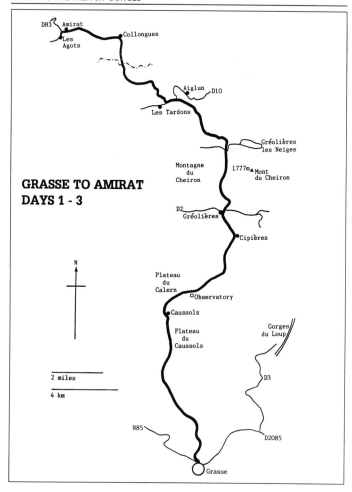

GRASSE TO AMIRAT
DAYS 1 - 3

to travel on to Grasse on the same day (the overnight train from Paris arriving at around 7.45am is particularly convenient). If accommodation is sought in Cannes, help and a free reservation service is available at the railway station (Gare SNCF). There are many hôtels in the city, particularly in the 4- and 5-star categories. It is not usually easy to find a room for less than 200FF. The campsites (eg. Le Ranch Camping, Le Grand Saule, Camping Bellevue) are all

The war memorial at Grasse, starting point of the trail

some way from the city centre and are expensive, and often noisy and overcrowded. The campsites near to the River Siagne at Mandelieu La Napoule, about 5 miles (8km) to the west of Cannes, may perhaps be cheaper and quieter. Flee the Côte d'Azur with all speed!

Grasse: There are several hôtels in the 1- and 2-star categories. The Hôtel-Pension Les Palmiers (17, rue E. Baudoin; tel.93.36.07.24) can be recommended. The Hôtel-Pension St Michel is also in this price category and is near to the centre of town (6, rue du Palais de Justice, tel. 93.36.06.37). The Hôtel Panorama (2, place du Cours, tel. 93.36.80.80), a 3-star establishment, is popular with those wanting more luxury after their tiring journey from Britain and before starting out over the mountains to the north.

Note that although the *gîte d'étape* at the Stade Nautique on the northern outskirts of the town is close to the start of the GR 4, it is an inconvenient base for those wishing to sightsee and/or relax in Grasse before starting the walk. It can be reached from the centre of Grasse by local bus (see below).

There are no conveniently situated campsites in or around Grasse.

Caussols (Saint Lambert): The Auberge de Caussols (tel. 93.09.29.67) has rooms, although it might be foolish to rely on obtaining a bed for the night here without first checking availability, as it is a long way on foot to the next possible place for accommodation.

Note that the former *Relais d'étape* in Cipières is now closed.

Gréolières: La Vieille Auberge (tel. 93.59.95.07) in the place Pierre Merle in the centre of the village, can be recommended. A rate for room and half-board can usually be negotiated, and, unlike in many French hôtels, the lone walker will probably not be asked the full price of a room designed for two guests. If the Vieille Auberge is full, a room in the Gîte de France establishment opposite may possibly be obtained, although these are usually rented out on a longer term basis. The only other alternative is the Hôtel Domaine du Foulon (tel. 93.59.95.02), but this is some 4km (2.5 miles) from the village on the D3 road.

Restaurants/Cafés/Bars
Both Cannes and Grasse have an abundance of good restaurants and cafés to suit most pockets. There are a number of "foreign" restaurants in these two cities (particularly in Cannes) offering a change from French cuisine. Restaurants in Grasse are generally much cheaper than in Cannes. The food at the Hôtel des Palmiers in Grasse is good.

The Auberge de Caussols, passed en route, is a café-restaurant which serves lunch and dinner. Most walkers who set off from Grasse at a reasonably early hour should arrive here at lunchtime, and thus it is conveniently situated for a midday meal.

There is a café-restaurant in the small square in Cipières, and another restaurant in the château in the same village.

Gréolières has at least two restaurants (La Barricade [closed on Mondays] and Le St Hubert) and La Vieille Auberge is a hôtel-restaurant, serving good food.

Shops
There are shops of all types in both Cannes and Grasse. The numerous supermarkets in Grasse are ideal for buying provisions for the first few days in the mountains. Gift shops are also very numerous.

The Auberge de Caussols has a grocer's shop *(épicerie)* on the premises (closed on Wednesdays and Thursdays).

Cipières possesses a bread shop *(boulangerie)* and a simple grocers' shop *(alimentation)*. These are closed on Monday afternoons.

Gréolières has an *épicerie/boulangerie* and a butcher's shop, as well as shops selling local crafts.

Public Transport
Bus from Cannes to Grasse: There is a frequent bus service between Cannes and Grasse (about 20 buses a day, Monday to Friday; 14 buses a day on Sundays and fête days). The bus company is Stavs, tel. 93.39.18.71. The journey time is approximately 45 minutes, and the fare is about 20FF. The bus station (gare

routière) is about 0.5km from the railway station (gare SNCF) in Cannes and is reached from the latter as follows: cross the road outside the railway station and head down any side street to reach the sea front. Here turn right. The bus station will be found at the far end of the old port. Note that some buses stop at Cannes railway station before leaving for Grasse. The gare routière in Grasse is at the east end of the old town at the Notre-Dame des Fleurs (the place de la Foux and the tourist office is a short distance uphill from here).

There is also a local bus from the gare routière in Grasse which is convenient for the start of the GR 4 (see the route description below).

There is a rather infrequent bus service from Gréolières back to Grasse (the bus stop in Gréolières is passed en route).

Water

The Trail passes through limestone country and therefore a scarcity of water can be a problem, particularly during the heat of July and August. The problem is exacerbated by a lack of adequate shade over much of today's route: the walker will probably be exposed to the full strength of the sun for several hours. It is essential for the British rambler, particularly on his or her first day on the Trail, unused to this climate, to carry adequate water (and to take sensible precautions against over exposure to the sun). A spring and well are passed on the descent into Cipières. The water here may well be safe to drink, but it is probably best to carry extra water from Caussols. There is a water fountain in the square in Cipières. Limestone in bright sunlight can be very painful to the eyes, and so sunglasses will not come amiss.

Miscellaneous

Tourist Offices: These will be found in Cannes (Palais des Festivals, Esplanade Georges Pompidou, tel. 93.39.01.01), Grasse (place de la Foux, tel. 93.36.03.56) and Gréolières (in the Mairie, tel. 93.59.95.16).

There are several banks in Grasse, but no others will be encountered until reaching Entrevaux, in 3 or 4 day's time (but see the note on the bank in Entrevaux, under Day 4, Facilities). There is a post office in Grasse and another in Gréolières. Public telephones will be found in Caussols and in Gréolières.

SUMMARY

The first few days of the walk involve a trek to the north over an area known to the French as the Préalpes, or foothills of the principal alpine ranges further north. This is arid, sparsely populated, limestone country, somewhat reminiscent of the area around Malham in Yorkshire, or the area between Shap and Kirkby Stephen in Cumbria, but on a much grander scale and more often bathed in warm sunshine! The area, pockmarked with limestone outcrops of all shapes and sizes, is the land of the "Clues de Haute Provence" - "clues" are the deep limestone gorges gouged into the limestone by torrential rivers. The Gorges du

Loup, formed by the River Loup (crossed between Cipières and Gréolières on the GR 4) are perhaps the most spectacular in this region.

The walk to Entrevaux has been divided into four daily stages in this guidebook. Fit walkers could cover this distance in three days, without too much over exertion, but need to take particular note of the available accommodation in the region. The suggested itinerary for a three day excursion is either Grasse - Gréolières - Amirat - Entrevaux, or Grasse - Gréolières - Aiglun - Entrevaux. The former is recommended, as this allows an early arrival in Entrevaux, for sightseeing and general relaxation, before the start of another hard 2-day stage across the mountains.

The Préalpes de Grasse are more than mere foothills, as the walker will soon realise as the Trail begins with a climb of nearly 3300ft (1007m) from Grasse to the Col de Clapier, where a tremoundous view of limestone peaks and ridges opens out, with distant views of the southern French Alps. After Caussols, the buildings of the Observatoire Gerga, which have been visible for some time, are approached. This astronomical observatory was sited here to make use of the clear southern skies and the lack of artificial light pollution, a feature of so much of modern, urban Europe.

The Trail descends to the picturesque town of Cipières, perched high above the River Loup. On this descent the mountain ranges to be traversed on the morrow are in full view; they appear to be just as daunting as those just crossed. The Château de Cipières is the prominent building that should have been visible during most of the descent. A long descent to the River Loup is followed by an equally steep and arduous climb up to the village of Gréolières, where the walker will, no doubt, be thankful to find a bed for the night.

Grasse

It is a good idea to set aside at least half a day to explore the town of Grasse, before setting off into the neighbouring limestone hills. Those arriving in Cannes on the overnight train from Paris should arrive in Grasse by about 9am; it is advisable to secure a hôtel immediately and spend the rest of the day in relaxation, sightseeing and the stocking of provisions for the journey ahead, which can then be started early the next morning.

Grasse, a large hill-top town overlooking the Côte d'Azur, is the sous-préfecture of the département of the Alpes-Maritime and centre of the French Perfume industry. Up until the sixteenth century the main occupation had been tanning, particularly the manufacture of leather gloves, but, after the introduction of the scent industry by Catherine de Médicis, Henry IV's wife, the town was to develop by the eighteenth century into the perfume capital of the world, a position it still holds today. The town is well situated for this industry having a climate and surrounding landscape which favours the growth of numerous scented herbs (eg. jasmine, thyme, rosemary, lavender and many, many others). These fragrances will almost certainly be smelt on the air as the walker makes his or her way across these mountains in the days to come. There are large herb and flower plantations and lavender fields in the surrounding area which provide the basic materials for the manufacture of perfumes. Despite the presence of tourist shops, Grasse is less ostentatious than the towns and cities of the nearby Côte d'Azur, and still retains much of its old character. It was a favourite resort of Queen Victoria.

There are some thirty perfume factories (parfumeries) in and around Grasse, the most famous being the Parfumerie Fragonard at 20 boulevard Fragonard in the centre of town. Jean-Honoré Fragonard, born in 1732 at 23 rue Tracastel (marked by a plaque), was a minor painter, but regarded as the most important son of Grasse. The daily tours of the factory give a general overview of the processes involved in producing perfume essences, which are then sold to the leading perfume manufacturers who make up their own brand-name perfumes. These tours, which are conducted in English and German as well as in French and include a visit to a small museum concerned with the history of perfume-making, are free, but there is the inevitable visit to the perfume shop at the end of the tour. The perfumes are, however, not overly priced, are light to carry and can be bought in unbreakable containers, and so may therefore be considered as suitable presents to buy even at the start of a walking holiday.

Other places worthy of a visit in Grasse are:

1. Villa-Musée Fragonard. This was the fashionable house, just outside the old town walls, which Fragonard shared with his cousin on returning from Paris after the Revolution. It now houses some of the works of Fragonard. Open 10am to 12pm and 2pm to 5.30pm; closed on Saturdays and in November.
2. Musée d'Art et d'Histoire de Provence. This is housed in the eighteenth-century Hôtel de Cabris at 2 rue Mirabeau: works of art, porcelain, furniture, objets d'art. Same hours as 1. above. Entrance free on Sundays and Wednesdays.
3. The cathedral, which dates from the twelfth-century, contains three paintings by Rubens. A number of concerts are held here every July. The Bishop's Palace is nearby.
4. Musée International de la Perfumerie (opened 1987).
5. Maritime museum.
6. The Place des Aires, the focal point of the old town, is the venue for the daily flower and vegetable market.
7. The old town (Vieux Grasse). There are numerous narrow, winding streets containing interesting sixteenth- to eighteenth-century houses. The most enjoyable pursuit in Grasse, in fact, is strolling round these ancient thoroughfares.

Finally, before leaving Grasse, be sure to gaze out from its several lookout points at the limestone hills to the north: your route lies over these mountains, a march of several days to Entrevaux in the Var valley.

ROUTE

The start of the GR 4 is about a mile to the north of the centre of Grasse and lies 744ft (227m) above it. It is somewhat difficult for the stranger to locate the start of the Trail, but if the instructions given below are followed, no undue problems should arise. The GR 4 can be reached on foot by following the route outlined below, or alternatively a bus can be taken to avoid this initial section of road walking.

By Bus:

Take Bus No. 8-G (Circulaire de la Piscine) from the Gare Routière (Quai 7) in the centre of Grasse. This service runs frequently (approximately every 45 minutes) on weekdays and Saturdays. The journey time is approximately 12 minutes. Alight at the Stade Nautique (altitude 1639ft; 500m). Continue on the road uphill following the route described below.

On Foot:

At the small roundabout above and immediately behind the Tourist Office and in front of the 3-star Hôtel de Parfums in Grasse, take the right exit (no through road sign) named allée Jean Moulin. In 30 metres follow the road to the left, pass to the right of the hôtel and climb the steps (Traverse des Lauriers). At the top of the steps turn right up the boulevard Eugène Charabot, but in about 150 metres, by a bus stop, turn left up a flight of steps (Escalier du Berouard). Turn right at the top of these to reach the N85 at a hairpin bend. Turn right on this main road (an unpleasant busy road, with no roadside footpath - care!) to reach and pass the Stade Nautique (MJC gîte d'étape).

Continue on the road uphill from the Stade Nautique, remaining on the main road in 250 metres as it bends very sharply to the left, to pass above the swimming pool. Soon a series of tennis courts is passed on the right - just before the end of the last court, locate a path on the right signposted as the GR 4 (Entrevaux, 19 hours).

Leave the N85 on this narrow footpath, climbing through scrub and enjoying the good view back to the Mediterranean. After about half-an-hour the path reaches a wider track. Turn right on this to climb gently to the left of a ravine; the track bends right at the top to cross over a small bridge over the ravine (the stream is usually dry). Remain on this track, which now provides level walking for some distance, to reach the wall at the entrance of Saint Christophe, at a hairpin bend. Do not turn left, but continue ahead on the Chemin des Genevriers, the track which now has a metalled surface. There is a superb distant view of the southern Alps and the Mercantour from here.

Climb gently on this lane amidst numerous limestone outcrops and with a most impressive limestone escarpment over to the right. The route is traversing the Plateau de la Malle. Later ignore a turn off to the left on another metalled road, but instead continue ahead on the Chemin de la Malle.

Keep watch for a double red/white sign, indicating a change of direction, which should be found on an electricity pylon just before the road bends to the right. Climb up the bank on the left to follow a footpath through the pine trees. Climb gently on this good path with views out to the Mediterranean and over to the foothills of the Alps. A château (La Malle Château) soon comes into view ahead. This footpath leads back to the minor road, where you turn left. The road bears to the right in front of Les Platanes (no through road sign) and then passes to the left of a solitary house. Soon after this look out for a double red/white sign on a telegraph pole, a few metres after which, take the path on the left. The route soon begins to climb steadily, zig-zagging occasionally, on a well graded footpath up to the Col de Clapier, where an extensive view unfolds of a myriad of limestone peaks, escarpments and ridges, with the Plateau de Caussols, dotted with small trees and scrub, stretching out in front.

Begin a gentle descent on the waymarked path which eventually reaches a track running alongside a line of telegraph poles. The track soon reaches and crosses a metalled road. Continue ahead on a roughly surfaced road through trees (strong smell of pines and of the maquis) passing signs prohibiting the picking of mushrooms and the cutting of wood. Note the observatory on the skyline ahead over to the right. Pass the homestead of La Buissière and descend gradually to the valley on an unsurfaced dirt track, soon reaching a main road (the D12) at Caussols (Saint Lambert). Turn left to enter the village and within 200 metres reach the Auberge de Caussols.

About 80 metres after the auberge, opposite the Mairie and telephone box, turn right to pass over a bridge over a (usually) dried-up stream and begin a climb on the track ahead. Reach the gates of La Cerizaie and take the path with the fence on the left, climbing quite steeply. The path zig-zags before turning to head towards the observatory seen on the crest ahead. The path levels but soon climbs again amongst scrub and scattered, small limestone pinnacles. Meet and cross a grassy track (the latter leads to the observatory) continuing on a thin path amongst limestone, with the observatory buildings over to the right. A neat cairn is reached which marks the boundary between the two communes of Caussols and Cipières. The cairned path heads towards but keeps to the left of the observatory buildings (good waymarking on upright limestone rocks). A series of thin paths and tracks leads to a descending wide track near to a shepherd's hut. The descent to the valley follows more paths and tracks and at one point passes a rather curious arch structure in the rocks, behind which is a spring and well (drinkable[?] water). After passing under high tension electricity cables the descent continues on a good path which leads to a stony dirt track. Descend on this to reach the picturesque village of Cipières.

Take the road just below the Château but soon turn off sharply to the left on a track descending towards the river. At a small building take the right fork steeply down through trees to cross the D603. Descend on a footpath to reach the road again by a bridge. Take the path ahead to the valley bottom to cross

Cipières

over the River Loup by means of an old bridge. The tired walker is then faced with almost 1000ft (305m) of ascent before rest for the night can be obtained at Gréolières. Soon bear left on an asphalt track which leads to a steep and narrow zig-zagging footpath. On reaching a road bear right for 10 metres to take another steep path on the left. This leads to a concrete drive and road. Take the footpath opposite and at a track turn left to continue the climb. Take another path on the left, later crossing a track and continue uphill. This steep, narrow, confined path leads to a flight of steps which gives access to the village of Gréolières.

The village of Rougon perched above the entrance to the Verdon Gorges from Point Sublime (Day 7/8)

At the Baume aux Pigeons, Verdon Gorge (Day 8)

The River Verdon deep within the Grand Canyon (Day 8)

Rock pinnacles and the Lac de Sainte-Croix seen from near the Col de l'Ane (Day 9)

DAY 2
GREOLIERES TO AIGLUN

DISTANCE:	6.1 MILES (9.7km)
TOTAL ASCENT:	2777ft (847m)
TOTAL DESCENT:	3419ft (1043m)
TOTAL ESTIMATED TIME:	4 HOURS 20 MINUTES

	Height Above		Distance				Est. Time	
	Sea	Level	Sect.		Cum.		Sect.	Cum.
	ft	m	mile	km	mile	km	hr m	hr m
GREOLIERES	2688	820						
BARRES DU CHEIRON								
(PAS DE COUTELLADE)	4917	1500	0.9	1.4	0.9	1.4	1.10	1.10
COLLET DU GRAND-PRE (ROAD								
TO GREOLIERES-LES-NEIGES)	4458	1360	2.0	3.2	2.9	4.6	1.10	2.20
VEGAY	2869	875	1.3	2.1	4.2	6.7	0.50	3.10
AIGLUN	2046	624	1.9	3.0	6.1	9.7	1.10	4.20

FACILITIES
Accommodation
The Hôtel Alpina (tel.93.59.70.19) in Gréolières-les-Neiges is open from mid-June to mid-September and from Christmas to Easter. There is also dormitory type accommodation in Gréolières-les-Neiges (see Appendix 1)

There is dormitory style accommodation and a few small rooms in the Auberge le Calendal in Aiglun (tel. 93.05.82.32). This *gîte d'étape* was opened in the late 1980s, replacing the old *gîte communal*.

Wild camping is possible at Haut-Gréolières and on the wide, flat area at Vegay. The latter consists of a few ruined buildings; there is no obvious sign of water, but a stream is crossed 10 minutes further down on the GR 4.

Restaurants/Cafés/Bars
There are two restaurants and a nightclub in Gréolières-les-Neiges (open only during the summer and winter seasons). There are no restaurants in Aiglun, but meals are provided at Le Calendal.

Shops
Stock up with provisions as no shops will be passed today, unless a detour into Gréolières-les-Neiges is planned.

Public Transport
After leaving Gréolières there is no public transport until reaching Entrevaux in 2 to 3 days time.

Water
There is a spring just above the ruins of Haut-Gréolières passed on the ascent to the Barres du Cheiron. Here is a good spot for wild camping. There is a stream at Vegay.

SUMMARY
An overnight stay in Gréolières will have provided sufficient time for the walker to contemplate the sharply rising contours of the Cheiron above the village. Today's walk starts with a long, steep climb of over 2000ft (610m) up the escarpment to cross the massif over the Barres du Cheiron. The Trail traverses the High Cheiron plateau and descends close to the ski resort of Gréolières-les-Neiges (q.v.) and on down to the sad ruins of the hamlet of Vegay (the Vegay waterfall should not be missed here). A slight detour from the GR 4 is required at the end of the day to cross the River Esteron and climb up to the village of Aiglun for overnight accommodation. Aiglun is on the spectacular, switch-backing Route des Crêtes, the D10 road, which clings, somewhat incredulously, to the steep southern slopes of the Montagne de Charamel. There are plenty of good views on today's section, over to the distant high peaks of the Alpes-de-Haute-Provence; a pair of binoculars would be much appreciated.

Strong walkers will be able to combine Days 2 and 3, but, since the closure of the *relais d'étape* at Collongues, it is necessary to continue all the way to the *gîte d'étape* at Amirat. This makes for a very long day's walk.

Gréolières
A picturesque village, situated at the foot of the Cheiron and above the Loup valley, that is at its liveliest during the winter months when the ski station of Gréolières-les-Neiges is operational. The ruins of the original settlement (Haut-Gréolières) are passed en route to the Cheiron. The ornate church is worth a visit for its fifteenth-century altar piece of St Stephen. There are several local crafts shops in the village; in fact the GR 4 emerges suddenly in Gréolières opposite Dick Le Tisserand a handweavers' shop.

Gréolières-les-Neiges
Situated on the north side of the Cheiron mountain, it is 11.2 miles (18km) from Gréolières by road and has the distinction of being the closest ski-resort to the Mediterranean. There are 10 lifts onto the Cheiron, one chair-lift operating during July and August to the summit of the mountain. It is mainly a centre for cross-country skiing.

ROUTE

From place Merle in the centre of Gréolières, take the red/white waymarked route which passes through an alleyway, leads up to a bus shelter and public telephone, and heads up towards Haut-Gréolières, which is mainly in ruins. Turn right at the road at a hairpin bend (GR 4 sign). Just after this bend take a path off to the right, pass to the right of the chapel in the "haut" (upper) village and continue the ascent. Just above the ruined buildings a spring is reached, where the water is probably safe to drink. The ascent of the Barres du Cheiron is on a clear well graded path, an ancient route over the mountains. The path winds its way through scattered scrub and rocks, and provides distant views of the Alps of High Provence.

At the top of the ridge the route reaches a wide bulldozed track. Turn right on this, starting a gentle descent, but leave the track after a few hundred metres by taking a thin path down to the right which descends to a road at a small wayside calvary (Notre Dame des Neiges) and wooden signpost (GR 4). To the right lie the buildings of Gréolières-les-Neiges, a winter ski-resort. Cross the road to a second signpost, indicating Vegay and Aiglun.

Follow this route, soon bearing off to the left on a footpath through pine trees. The path climbs over the small ridge ahead and then descends through trees, steeply down into the gorge below. At Vegay (in ruins) there is a multi-footpath signpost indicating l'Esteron and Aiglun ahead on the GR 4 (there is also an an *Intineraire Pedestre* waymarked in yellow from here to Taulane and the Crête de Fourneuby). Continue downhill on the GR 4 on the centuries old path/track which once served the hamlet. After 10 minutes or so of descent, a stream is reached on the left-hand side. Whilst on this descent, the village of Aiglun comes into view, clinging to the hillside on the other side of the River l'Esteron. The path descends to a track just above the river (signposted left to Aiglun and Les Tardons, GR 4, and right to Pont de Vegay and Vascognes on the *intineraire pedestre*). Turn left on the GR 4. The track leads to an old bridge over the River Gironde, 100 metres after which there is another wooden signpost. Turn left to resume the GR 4, but for Aiglun, which is seen above, continue straight ahead.

DAY 3
AIGLUN TO AMIRAT

	DISTANCE:	8.0 MILES (12.9km)
	TOTAL ASCENT:	3895ft (1188m)
	TOTAL DESCENT:	3049ft (930m)
	TOTAL ESTIMATED TIME:	5 HOURS

| | Height Above Sea Level | | Distance | | | | Est. Time | |
| | Sea | Level | Sect. | | Cum. | | Sect. | Cum. |
	ft	m	mile	km	mile	km	hr m	hr m
AIGLUN	2046	624						
LA CLUE	2623	800	1.6	2.5	1.6	2.5	1.15	1.15
CRETE DE CHARAMEL	3786	1155	0.7	1.1	2.3	3.6	0.50	2.05
LES MUJOULS	2646	807	3.0	4.9	5.3	8.5	1.35	3.40
COLLONGUES	2059	628	0.2	0.4	5.5	8.9	0.10	3.50
AMIRAT (LES AGOTS)	2891	882	2.5	4.0	8.0	12.9	1.10	5.00

FACILITIES
Accommodation
The *gîte d'étape* of Amirat (GTA), is actually in the adjoining village known as Les Agots, a few hundred metres to the south of the GR 4. The *gîte* is run by the mayoress of the village, from whom the keys may be obtained if the building is locked (her house is a few metres past the *gîte* on the left).

Note that the *relais d'étape* in Collongues closed several years ago and there were no plans to open another one.

Those wanting hôtel accommodation will have to combine Days 3 and 4 to reach Entrevaux.

Restaurants/Cafés/Bars
There is a bar/restaurant below and on the outskirts of Collongues, a few metres from where the GR 4 emerges at the road.

There are no restaurants at either Amirat or Les Agots, but the mayoress will sometimes provide meals if ordered in advance or on arrival (these are cooked in her own house and brought over to the *gîte*). Otherwise food must be bought earlier and carried to the gîte, where there is an adequately equipped kitchen. A good alternative is to eat in the restaurant in Collongues before continuing to the *gîte* for overnight accommodation.

Shops
Honey (in French *miel)* is usually for sale at the hamlet of La Clue.

The owner of the bar/restaurant in Collongues will usually sell bread, ham, cheese and the like. There is also an *épicerie* in Collongues.

SUMMARY
The route continues north-westwards over the Montagne de Charamel to Collongues and on to the village of Amirat. As this is another short day, there is plenty of time to rest and admire the scenery. There are particularly good views from the vicinity of the hamlet of La Clue back towards Aiglun. Note also the impressive, large and prominent limestone face when climbing above La Clue. There are several sections of woodland on today's route, and these will be particularly appreciated if the sun is burning fiercely. The golden brown, yellow and red tints of the turning leaves in autumn are particularly attractive.

A number of large, well made, wooden, numbered signposts are a feature of this section. The Trail now passes through Les Mujouls, but note that the original GR 4 avoided this small village by keeping to the east, aiming directly for Collongues. The GR 4 joins the GR de Pays called the GR de Huit Vallées (Eight Valleys). The two trails share the same route to Amirat.

ROUTE
Return to the GR 4 signpost below Aiglun. Take the path signposted to Les Tardons, Adom and Les Mujouls. Thus begin the long climb (nearly 2300ft [700m] of ascent) to the Crête de Charamel. First climb to the D10 road, where turn left, continuing gently uphill passing another signpost to Les Tardons. At a hairpin bend (telephone box) at Les Tardons take a path on the left signposted to Les Mujouls and Collongues (ignore the sign to Le Mas par la Gironde). Climb to the road (signpost No. 96), cross and continue on a path which leads to a road at the hamlet of La Clue. The path climbs to the left of a building to a second track, where turn left, but after 60 metres turn right up a footpath. Continue on this clear, well waymarked path which climbs and zig-zags all the way to the Crête de Charamel.

Descend to a signpost (No. 97) indicating the GR 4 to the right (l'Esteron, Pont de Mujouls and Collongues). Continue to Abdoun (sign on rock) or Adom (signpost and map). Follow the thin path heading west (take care here not to follow the track heading to the building over to the right). The path descends through trees, crosses a dried-up river and ascends very slightly before resuming its descent. Be sure to follow the waymarks carefully here, down to a wide, bulldozed track at a hairpin bend. Continue downhill on this track to a T-junction of tracks, where turn right. Cross over a wooden bridge spanning the river to reach another track at a T-junction where turn right. Soon reach another signpost (No. 63) which indicates Collongues ahead (to the right lies the "Circuit du Bourillon"). Take the GR 4. In 150 metres there is another signpost (left to

"Gars par les Cougourdieres", waymarked in yellow). Continue on the dirt track signposted to Les Mujouls until it curves gently to the right: here take a footpath off to the left (GR 4 signpost). The path climbs between hedges to reach a wooden signpost (No. 67) by a house. Turn right climbing on the path/track to Les Mujouls (ignore the "intineraire pedestre" ahead) on the GR 4. Bear to the left at Les Mujouls to pick up the GR 4 waysigns and reach signpost No. 59, which indicates the way to Collongues down to the left. Descend on a narrow confined footpath to signpost No. 58 at the road below Collongues. Turn left for the GR 4, but for a visit to the village of Collongues turn right on the road, walk over the bridge and turn left on the D86.

Return to signpost 58 and follow this in the direction indicated to Amirat, Les Agots and Chapelle Saint Jeannet. Continue on a road for about 0.7km, climbing gently to a footpath sign (No. 57). Turn right leaving the road for a track through trees (yellow waymarking accompanies the red/white of the GR). The track reaches a road at a GR 4 and S.D.2 signpost (the latter trail accounts for the red/yellow waymarking). Turn right walking downhill on the road (ignore the red/yellow waymarked route to Les Agots which takes a track to the left). Continue on this poorly surfaced lane climbing to some buildings and trees. Keep to the right of these on an earthy track. Pass under high tension electricity cables near a pylon and remain on the track as it bends to the left and climbs to the village of Amirat. Locate a wooden signpost indicating the way to the *gîte d'étape* (600 metres further on in Les Agots). Continue ahead on the D83. After about 400 metres the GR 4 heads off to the right (signposted to the Col de Trebuchet and l'Ubac d'Amirat). The *gîte d'étape*, however, will be found ahead on the left-hand side of the road.

DAY 4
AMIRAT TO ENTREVAUX

DISTANCE: 6.6 MILES (10.5km)
TOTAL ASCENT: 2065ft (630m)
TOTAL DESCENT: 3390ft (1034m)
TOTAL ESTIMATED TIME: 3 HOURS 35 MINUTES

| | Height Above Sea Level | | Distance | | | | Est. Time | |
| | Sea | Level | Sect. | | Cum. | | Sect. | Cum. |
	ft	m	mile	km	mile	km	hr m	hr m
AMIRAT (LES AGOTS)	2891	882						
CRETE DE CHADASTIER	3770	1150	1.2	2.0	1.2	2.0	0.50	0.50
L'UBAC D'AMIRAT	3082	940	0.8	1.2	2.0	3.2	0.25	1.15
CASTELLAT-SAINT-CASSEIN	2790	851	0.8	1.2	2.8	4.4	0.25	1.40
LA BATIE NEUVE	3770	1150	1.4	2.2	4.2	6.6	0.45	2.25
ENTREVAUX	1567	478	2.4	3.9	6.6	10.5	1.10	3.35

ALTERNATIVE ROUTE
The recommended route from Castellat-Saint-Cassein to Entrevaux, as described below, is a variant of the standard route of the GR 4. The latter heads west from Castellat on the D10 road, before swinging north to the Col de Félines (3049ft; 930m) on the D911 road. It then follows the line of this road, crossing and following it on several occasions as it heads north-east down to Entrevaux. The standard and variant routes are of approximately the same length, but the view of Entrevaux on the descent is much finer on the variant than on the standard GR 4. Note that whereas the latter is waymarked with red/white stripes, the variant does not carry these marks, but it is waymarked with both orange and yellow single stripes.

FACILITIES
Except for a bench and telephone box in Castellet-Saint-Cassein, there are no facilities until Entrevaux.

Accommodation
For a town which is such a magnet for tourists, Entrevaux has little choice of hotel accommodation. However, the town is very small (pop. 700) and most tourists tend to visit only for the day, as will be witnessed by the number of tourist coaches in evidence during the main season. There are two hotels: Hôtel

AMIRAT TO CASTELLANE VIA ENTREVAUX
(Days 4 - 6)

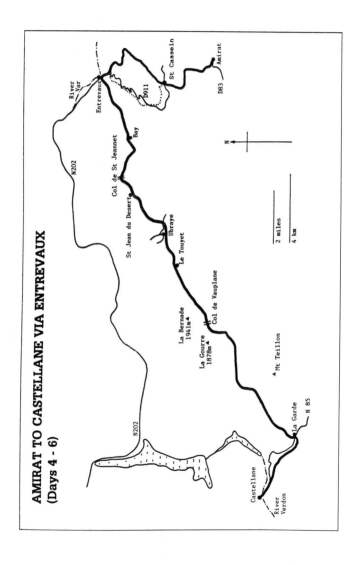

du Var (tel. 93.05.46.80) and Hôtel Vauban, south of the river (tel. 93.05.42.40).

The *gîte d'étape* communal is situated behind the public washing area, near to the aqueduct. There were plans for a new *gîte d'étape* in the town (all enquiries to the mairie in the central square in the main town).

There is camping in Entrevaux. This will be found on the right just before entering the old town, ie. just after the road sign indicating the outskirts of Entrevaux.

Restaurants/Cafés/Bars
The following are all in Entrevaux:

The restaurant l'Echauguette, in place Saint-Martin in the old town, can be recommended, although it is a little expensive. The Hôtel du Var is also a restaurant which serves meals to non-residents. The Bar au Pont-Levis (opposite the drawbridge) and Le Planet in the place de la Mairie both provide snacks and drinks.

Shops
Entrevaux has *épiceries, boulangeries*, a *charcuterie*, and a *pharmacie*. A local speciality, a dried beef sausage *(secca de boeuf)*, eaten with lemon and olive oil, is available from the *charcuterie*.

Public Transport
The railway station (SNCF) is a little downstream of the drawbridge, on the south bank of the River Var. There are trains to both Nice and Digne, stopping at a number of intermediate stations.

Local bus services (eg. between Nice, Guillaumes and Entraunes) also stop at Entrevaux (tel. 93.80.94.91 for information).

Miscellaneous
There is a *Syndicat d'Initiative* near to the bridge (open during the main summer season only). Entrevaux has a post office (PTT) and a bank (Crédit Agricole), although the latter is open only four days per week and then for only a couple of hours (either morning or afternoon) on these days.

An annual two-week festival of baroque music is held every August in Entrevaux.

SUMMARY
A pleasant walk, mainly along woodland tracks and paths, over the ridge (the Crête de Chadastier) north of Amirat and down to the hamlet of Castellat-Saint-Cassein. From here there is a choice of route to Entrevaux. The described route is not the main GR 4 trail, but is recommended in preference to the latter, as it does not meet a road until just before the town, and offers better views on the approach to Entrevaux. From Castellet-Saint-Cassein the "variant" follows

a track which climbs to a deserted building; a path then skirts the mountainside, before turning to reveal Entrevaux in the Var valley below.

Entrevaux

The small fortress town of Entrevaux is one of the highlights of the walk. Built on the site of a Roman settlement on the north bank of the River Var, the town became an important border post on the frontier between Provence and Savoy. The ramparts, which remain intact, were built during the seventeenth century by the military engineer Vauban, under instructions from Louis XIV. The approach to the old town is over a single arched drawbridge spanning the River Var and through the main gate in the town walls. Inside there are numerous buildings dating from the middle ages. The church is interesting in that its right side is built into the town walls and its towers are crenellated. The Porte d'Italie, behind the church, leads to a pleasant riverside walk. A series of nine ramps, again built by Vaudan, lead up to the château or citadel (insert coins to get through the turnstile allowing access to the ramp) from where, 443ft (135m) above the river, there is a grand view of the surrounding countryside. There is also a small motor museum in Entrevaux, a rather unlikely venue for such an exhibition.

Entrevaux, with its moat and drawbridge approach, fortified walls and lofty citadel, has a rather fairy tale like appearance, and a visit here, preferably out of main season, is to be recommended.

ROUTE
Return along the road to rejoin the GR 4 (there is also a signpost here indicating the "Col du Buis par les Crouisses") to climb on a surfaced drive which soon becomes a gravel track leading to signpost No. 52, where turn left (ignore the path ahead to the Col de Trebuchet). Climb on a path through trees (the route is also waymarked with yellow dots) to signpost No. 48, where turn right, signposted to Castellat-Saint-Cassein (ignore the path to the left to the Col du Buis). The top of the climb is soon reached on the Crête de Chadastier. Follow a path and then track downhill to the hamlet of l'Ubac d'Amirat.

Pass amongst the buildings to locate a footpath heading down to the left to enter woodland. Continue on this path taking care not to emerge on a grassy pasture half-way down (there are many branching paths in the area and care should be taken to follow the somewhat sparsely placèd waymarks). Descend to cross a bridge over a stream and then take a track across pasture. Where this track swings to the left at a solitary tree, turn right on a grassy track climbing up towards the buildings. The track leads to a château-farm and the D10 road at the hamlet of Castellat-Saint-Cassein, where there is a bench and telephone box.

The standard route of the GR 4 turns left at the telephone box on the D10 heading south-west, but for the variant, recommended and described here,

The houses of Entrevaux with its citadel perched high on a rocky outcrop

walk to the north, downhill on the D10. Note that the route from here to Entrevaux is not waymarked with red/white paint stripes. Soon after passing a wayside shrine, cross an old Roman bridge. 20 metres after the bridge, turn left on a track (there should be a small cairn at this point). The track is at first surfaced up to a house on the right, but then continues climbing ahead as a stony, dirt track. This route through woodland is waymarked with single orange paint stripes and arrows. On reaching the pass near the top of the climb, turn left to pass under the high tension electricity cable and head towards a ruined building (daubed with several orange waymarks). A superb panorama opens up here of the mountains over the other side of the valley.

Pass to the left and then to the back of the ruined buildings, following the direction of an orange arrow on a tree ie. towards the right at the back of the buildings (note that yellow stripe waymarkings now accompany the route). Continue on a narrow path with a ravine down to the right. After nearly a kilometre the path swings very sharply round to the left and descends more steeply (yellow waymarkings now predominate). The path, steep in places, leads to a first-rate viewpoint of the small town of Entrevaux in the valley of the Var below. Note the château (the citadel) on the hill above the town. The route now soon reaches a minor road, where turn left. Descend on this lane to the D911, where turn right. The descent continues to enter Entrevaux by the drawbridge over the River Var.

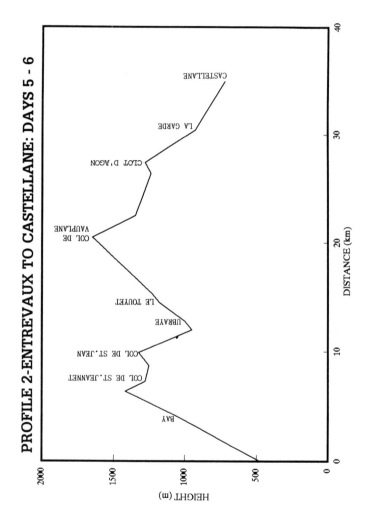

PROFILE 2-ENTREVAUX TO CASTELLANE: DAYS 5 - 6

DAY 5
ENTREVAUX TO LE TOUYET

DISTANCE:	9.5 MILES (15.3km)
TOTAL ASCENT:	4252ft (1297m)
TOTAL DESCENT:	1787ft (545m)
TOTAL ESTIMATED TIME:	5 HOURS 15 MINUTES

	Height Above Sea Level		Distance				Est. Time	
			Sect.		Cum.		Sect.	Cum.
	ft	m	mile	km	mile	km	hr m	hr m
ENTREVAUX	1567	478						
BAY	3560	1086	2.7	4.3	2.7	4.3	1.40	1.40
COL DE SAINT JEANNET	4216	1278	1.9	3.0	4.6	7.3	1.05	2.45
CHAPELLE SAINT JEAN DU DESERT	4101	1251	0.8	1.4	5.4	8.7	0.25	3.10
COL DE SAINT JEAN	4347	1326	0.7	1.2	6.2	9.9	0.20	3.30
UBRAYE	3278	1000	1.8	2.9	7.9	12.8	1.00	4.30
LE TOUYET	4032	1230	1.6	2.5	9.5	15.3	1.15	5.15

FACILITIES
There are very few facilities available between Entrevaux and Castellane, a distance of some 35km (22 miles) across mountain country, which will take most walkers two days to accomplish. This should be borne in mind when planning this section of the walk.

Accommodation
The major problem with this stage of the walk, now that the *gîte d'étape* in Ubraye has closed, is the lack of suitable overnight accommodation between Entrevaux and Castellane (the *gîte* closed in August 1988, and there were no plans to re-open it). Until a new *gîte d'étape* is opened, the walker who is not carrying a tent has a problem, but not one that is unsurmountable. Firstly, a very fit walker, with an early start, could make La Garde (see Day 6) or even Castellane in one day's march. However, such a walk should not be underestimated; there is considerable ascent and descent and the area is remote. Secondly, a polite request for a *grange* for the night in Le Touyet, should produce a warm and dry hay barn for only a few francs. It is assumed that most walkers will exercise this option. The accommodation situation may well change for the better in the future, and it is advisable to enquire in Entrevaux before setting out. There are public telephone boxes in both Ubraye

and Le Touyet, if a taxi is required.

Near the small shrine at the Col de Saint Jeannet there is a good, flat area, suitable for wild camping, although there is no obvious sign of water here.

Restaurants/Cafés/Bars
No such establishments will be passed today, the first place to purchase food and drink after Entrevaux being at La Garde, near the end of tomorrow's stage.

Shops
There are no shops between Entrevaux and La Garde, a little before Castellane. Therefore it is essential that sufficient food and drink is carried from Entrevaux. Cheese can be bought from one of the houses in Ubraye.

Public Transport
There is none until La Garde (see Day 6).

Water
It is essential, because of the relative remoteness of the area, to top up with supplies wherever possible. There is a good water supply at a small, ornate fountain located alongside the track, half-way between the Col de Saint Jeannet and the Chapelle Saint Jean du Désert. There is a water fountain in Ubraye.

SUMMARY
The GR 4 now changes direction to head south-east, climbing back into the mountains to the tiny communities of Bay, Ubraye and Le Touyet, before traversing the flanks of the Bernarde and Teillon massifs to reach the Route Napoléon to the east of Castellane. This is a two-day expedition, which requires careful planning with respect to food and water provisions, and accommodation (see above).

Much of today's route is through the well established oak and pine forests characteristic of the area. Walkers visiting the region in September and October will enjoy the rich autumnal colours of the turning leaves.

The section of today's route between Entrevaux and the Chapelle Saint Jean du Désert is shared by a regional trail which has been developed and signposted by an organisation know as "ADRI 04" - the Comité Départemental de la Randonnée Alpes-de-Haute-Provence. Small white discs, bearing a design of a mountain silhouette, will be seen on several signposts

Several small shrines will be encountered along today's path, most notably at the Col de Saint Jeannet and at the Col de Saint Jean (labelled as either "orat." or "oratoire" on the maps).

Ubraye is a picturesque village in a superb mountain location, perched on a hillside, offering excellent views of the sun-baked hills all around. Note the communal oven on the right-hand side on entering the village. These were once common in the villages of Provence and the Massif Central, being used until quite recent times to bake bread and other items for the whole community. Such ovens are nowadays mainly used during the time of the annual village fête.

This area of France is characterised by deeply cut wooded valleys, with isolated villages hidden away down these valleys or perched on hilltops. Be sure to look back towards Ubraye on the ascent out of the village; its gorgeous mountain setting will then be fully appreciated. On the latter stages of today's walk, several high, shapely mountains will come into view: these will be encountered at much closer range tomorrow, when there will be possibilities to make optional ascents of several of these peaks.

ROUTE
From the bridge outside the main gate of the old town, take the D610 signposted to Bay, Le Champ and Villevieille. After about 100 metres, at the first bend, turn right on a footpath passing to the left of a house. Just after the house keep to the left and straight ahead, ie. do not cross the small gully to the right. The waymarks in this region are rather poor. Meet and cross the road and continue uphill. On meeting the road for a second time, follow a drive up towards a house, leaving the drive on the left after the building, but rejoining it near a group of houses. Where the track loses its surface, turn left along a footpath which climbs to meet a road, where turn right. After 100 metres turn right, now following small white discs bearing a "black mountain peaks" logo. The path climbs by a series of zig-zags before levelling out and heading towards the south-west and the hamlet of Bay. The route traverses pleasant oak woods. Take care not to miss a turning on the right. When the path reaches a road, turn right along it, but take a track off to the right at the building ahead. This track runs parallel with the road and soon rejoins it. Follow the road into Bay.

Climb to the Chapelle Saint Claude (restored in 1989) and from here continue the ascent on a poorly surfaced road. After about a kilometre turn right on a track (just before a building over to the right). Climb on this path amidst oak woodland to the top of the ridge which is also covered in trees. Descend through coppiced beech woods to a clearing at the Col de Saint Jeannet, where there is a small shrine. Turn left at this point and continue in a south-westerly direction, downhill, with good views over to the right. After about 10 minutes of walking, pass a small ornate "fountain". Cross an old landslip and then pass a small wayside shrine, before reaching a wooden signpost and a trail junction, with the buildings of the Chapelle de Saint Jean du Désert over to the right. A regional route, signposted with red/yellow flashes, goes to the right (Annot-Digne), but our route takes the GR 4 to the left, signposted to Ubraye and Castellane. At this point the white disc waymarking (ADRI 04) for the GTPA route is left behind.

Climb on a path soon with a ravine down to the right. The path bends slightly to the right to reach the Col de Saint Jean, where there is another small

The mountains rising behind the village of Ubraye

shrine. This is a good spot for lunch. Turn left at the col heading downhill through the trees still heading in a south-westerly direction. Descend on a path and later a track down into a wide, lush valley. Pass a small chapel on the left and then cross over a very old, dilapidated wooden bridge, to reach a road, the D10, where turn right. About 0.5km along this road cross a bridge and 30 metres after this take the second track on the left (GR 4 sign). Climb to the picturesque village of Ubraye.

Follow the road around the church and 50 metres before the roadsign indicating the limit of the village, turn left along a drive. Take the gravel track to the right of a small iron cross, which leads to a group of buildings. Follow a grassy slope up between these buildings to reach a confined footpath which climbs steeply to a road. Turn left. Leave the road on the left, 50 metres later at the hairpin bend. Climb steeply on a path which eventually levels out to skirt around the mountainside. Climb again to reach a small metal cross on the right-hand side of the path. The small village of Le Touyet comes into view at the top of the climb. The path continues to contour the mountainside (good views of the shapely, 6035ft [1841m], Picogu) to reach the road at Le Touyet. Turn left.

DAY 6
LE TOUYET TO CASTELLANE

DISTANCE:	12.1 MILES (19.6km)
TOTAL ASCENT:	1705ft (520m)
TOTAL DESCENT:	3377ft (1030m)
TOTAL ESTIMATED TIME:	5 HOURS 50 MINUTES

| | Height Above Sea Level | | Distance | | | | Est. Time | |
	Sea ft	Level m	Sect. mile	km	Cum. mile	km	Sect. hr m	Cum. hr m
LE TOUYET	4032	1230						
COL DE VAUPLANE	5409	1650	3.2	5.2	3.2	5.2	1.40	1.40
CHAPELLE DE SAINT BARNABE	4527	1381	1.2	2.0	4.4	7.2	0.50	2.30
CLOT D'AGNON	4196	1280	3.0	4.9	7.4	12.1	1.30	4.00
LA GARDE	3039	927	1.9	3.0	9.3	15.1	0.45	4.45
CASTELLANE	2360	720	2.8	4.5	12.1	19.6	1.05	5.50

OPTIONAL EXCURSIONS: ASCENTS OF NEIGHBOURING PEAKS
1. **Sommet de la Bernade (6363ft; 1941m) and the Sommet de la Gourre (6157ft; 1878m)**
The footpath leading to these two peaks, separated by a long ridge, the Crête de Bernade, leaves the GR 4 between the Col de Vauplane and the D102 road. The route is waymarked with single blue paint stripes.

2. **Le Teillon (6206ft; 1893m)**
A trail to the summit leaves the GR 4 a little before La Garde. The official time given for the ascent and descent from La Garde (3167ft; 966m of ascent) is 5 hours.

3. **Sommet de Destourbes (5058ft; 1543m)**
The official time for the round trip to the summit from Castellane is 5 hours.
    The point at which the footpaths leading to these summits leaves the Trail is given in the route description. As the day is not over long, it may be possible for the fit walker to include some of these summits on his or her itinerary. None of the summits are particularly difficult to attain, provided that the standard waymarked routes are followed.

FACILITIES
Note that there are no facilities available until reaching La Garde on the Route

Napoléon (with the exception that during the winter skiing season only, the Stade de Neige on the Col de Vauplane will be open).

Accommodation
La Garde: The Auberge du Teillon (tel.92.83.60.88) a 2-star Logis de France, is opposite the point where the GR 4 emerges onto the Route Napoléon. The small *gîte d'étape* in La Garde has a doubtful future.

Castellane: Directions to the *gîte d'étape* La Galoche are given at the beginning of the "Route" section for Day 7. See also Appendix 1.
   There are several 2-star hôtels in Castellane eg. Ma Petite Auberge (8, boulevard de la République, tel. 92.83.62.06), Grand Hôtel du Levant (place Marcel Sauvaire, tel. 92.83.60.05), Hôtel du Verdon (boulevard de la République, tel. 92.83.62.02), Hôtel Restaurant du Roc (place de l'Eglise, tel. 92.83.62.65). Ma Petite Auberge can be recommended. The most expensive is the Hôtel du Commerce in place Marcel Sauvaire (tel. 92.83.72.14).

Camping: The region in and around Castellane is popular with French campers, and consequently there are many campsites, of varying degrees of sophistication and price, in the vicinity. There are said to be twelve within 3 km of the town. The closest to the centre of Castellane is the 2-star Le Frederic Mistral (tel. 92.83.62.27). This is by the river on the Route des Gorges de Verdon (100 metres from the centre of Castellane). For all mod cons there is the 4-star Camping International (tel. 92.83.66.67) 1km from the town centre (follow the signposted arrows along the Route Napoléon in the direction of Digne). A basic but good *camping à la ferme* site is passed on the GR 4 between La Garde and Castellane (see "Route"). There is a shower and telephone here.
   Note that during the height of the summer season, Castellane caters for a large number of tourists, and finding accommodation can be difficult. It is recommended that at such times accommodation is booked ahead by telephone (phone the tourist office if you cannot speak French - see below).
   There are several opportunities for wild camping, but only before La Garde. An attractive site would be somewhere close to the Chapelle de Saint Barnabé (4527ft;1381m), above the D102 road.

Restaurants/Cafés/Bars
The food at the Auberge du Teillon in La Garde can be recommended. It will no doubt be welcome after the austerities of the previous night. The GR 4 re-emerges on the N85 before Castellane at Le Grillade, a buffet open 12 hours a day and offering snacks, drinks and small meals.
   There are plenty of restaurants, cafés and bars in Castellane. The food at the Hôtel-Restaurant du Roc and at La Forge, both in the place de l'Eglise, is reasonable.

Shops
The first shop selling food since Entrevaux is a small shop in La Garde (off the Route Napoléon) selling "products of the farm", viz. honey, cheese, yoghurt, paté. There is also another shop in the vicinity of the *camping à la ferme* between La Garde and Castellane.

All types of food shops will be found in Castellane. Gift shops also abound.

Public Transport
There are daily bus services (1 bus per day throughout the year) from the main square in Castellane to Grasse, Cannes and to Digne, Sisteron, Grenoble and Geneva. These buses also stop at La Garde (bus stop opposite the Auberge du Teillon). There are also daily buses (1 bus per day from the beginning of July until the middle of September) to Rougon, La Palud, Moustiers, Roumoules, Riez, Gréoux-les-Bains (see Days 7 to 11) and on to Aix and Marseille (tel. 42.67.60.34 or 92.78.03.57).

For taxi services in Castellane phone 92.83.63.27 or 92.83.62.08 or 92.83.61.62.

Water
The stream that is crossed on the climb from Le Touyet to the Col de Vauplane is a good source of water. Another stream is crossed on the descent from the Col to the D102.

Miscellaneous
There is a tourist office in Castellane in the rue National (tel. 92.83.61.14). English is usually spoken here. The office will make hôtel and even campsite reservations, and provides a number of free leaflets and booklets, including a useful annual publication entitled *Bienvenue à Castellane,* which lists all facilities in the area. The latest information on all the *gîtes d'étape* in the Verdon area will also be available from the tourist office.

Castellane has a number of outdoor shops, selling all manner of gear for walking and climbing. These might be useful to replace a broken or lost piece of equipment.

There are banks and a post office in Castellane.

SUMMARY
The second part of the walk between Entrevaux and Castellane traverses high mountain country. The Col de Vauplane, the crossing of which holds the key to the route across the mountains to the valley of the Verdon, is, at 5409ft (1650m), the highest point reached on the Trail in the Préalpes. Indeed only the mighty Mont Ventoux (see Day 17) attains a greater height on the entire journey to the Cévennes. Many of the principal peaks in the region (La Bernade [6363ft; 1941m], La Gourre [6157ft; 1878m], Picogu [6035ft; 1841m], Le Teillon

[6206ft; 1893m] and Destourbes [5058ft; 1543m]) are on view from the Trail, and there are possibilities to ascend some of these from the GR 4, as indicated in the "Route" section below. If time is available, an extra day in this area can be recommended, to provide additional time to climb some of these mountains. The Sommet de Destourbes is easily achieved from a base in Castellane, and with a little more effort, so too is Le Teillon, with its most impressive sheer rock face, seen to good effect from the GR 4 and from the Route Napoléon in La Garde.

After leaving Le Touyet, a well graded path provides a superb walk beneath the crags of Picogu, leading to the broad Col de Vauplane, where there is a small ski complex, with associated paraphernalia. The ski complex is the relatively new "Stade de Neige de Soleilhas - Vauplane" and, compared with many in the high Alps is a relatively unobtrusive affair. Hopefully it will not be further developed in the future, as this would do much to rob the area of its remote character.

Good walking on an old Roman road provides views down towards the artificial lakes of Castillon and Chaudanne and the approaching Verdon valley, reached at the small village of La Garde, which is worth a few minutes exploration to see its narrow main street bordered with ancient houses (the village [pop. 80] dates from the twelfth century). There is the church of Notre-Dame des Ormeaux, the chapel of Sainte-Anne and the vestiges of the ruined château. The main attraction for many, however, will probably be the first restaurant encountered since leaving Entrevaux.

Castellane

Castellane, a Sous-Préfecture of the Alpes-de Haute-Provence, is the nearest town to the entrance of the Verdon Gorges (the town is dubbed the "Gateway to the Gorges"), and is consequently a frenetic tourist resort during the summer months. It can, however, be surprisingly tranquil both early and late in the season. The natural feature which dominates the town, and which will soon become evident to the walker approaching the town on the GR 4, is the hugh edifice of rock known as the "Le Roc". It is possible to reach the chapel of Notre-Dame-du-Roc, on the summit of this outcrop, by climbing a tortuous path that starts from behind the church in the place de l'Eglise. There is a fine view of the surrounding mountains and the distant gorge. Also of note in the town is the fifteenth-century bridge, sections of the old ramparts including the Tour Pentagonale, and a picturesque fourteenth-century clock tower. Winter walkers may witness the festival (Fête des Pétardiers) which takes place every 31st of January, to commemorate the successful resistance of a siege on the town led by Huguenots in 1586.

Castellane is a good base for mountain walking and for touring the Verdon Gorges. Those wanting to plan a few day walks from here are recommended the Destourbes and Teillon peaks. Also consult the *Bienvenue à Castellane* publication, available from the tourist office, which describes a number of short walks in the area. For more extended day trips mountain bikes can be hired from a number of establishments in and around Castellane. A trip to the Lac de Castillon can be recommended, particularly to those who enjoy sailing, canoeing, swimming or windsurfing (all equipment can be hired). There are also possibilities for river rafting and for guided walks in the area, including guided tours along the Verdon Gorges. The hire of a bike would also allow a visit to the rather unusual religious centre of La Mandarom, 3.1 miles (5km) from Castellane at La Baume (leave Castellane on the road to St André, turning off to the left at the Col de Cheiron). It is possible to partake in meditation courses at this retreat, which caters for both western and eastern religions (there is a large, ornate buddha on show).

ROUTE

Continue along the road in Le Touyet to the last group of houses where turn left on a dirt track signposted GR 4 (note that road building in the area may change these details slightly in the future). The track passes to the left of a small shrine. Ignore a track going down to the left, but continue uphill on a broad track. When this track swings to the right, leave it by turning left on a footpath at the GR 4 sign and cairn. Cross a stream (La Bernade) and climb quite steeply on a good mountain path following the red/white waymarks heading towards the Col de Vauplane. The route passes below the crags of Picogu (6035ft; 1841m) over to the left. The path levels for a while, passes to the left and above a small stone hut and continues the climb up to the col.

On reaching the broad Col de Vauplane (5409ft; 1650m) head over to the right to the large white building. A road is reached here by a small shrine to the Virgin Mary, the Notre Dame des Neiges et des Bergères, erected in 1987/88. Descend on this road from the "Stade de Neige" complex. Just before a bend in the road, in line with the edge of the trees on the hillside to the right, take a footpath off to the right. After only 15 metres, take the left fork going downhill. Descend into a ravine passing a signpost indicating the route to the right to the Sommet de la Gourre (6157ft; 1878m) and the Sommet de la Bernade (6363ft; 1941m). From here on the red/white of the GR 4 is accompanied by single blue paint stripe waymarking. On reaching a cross-track at a T-junction turn right for 30 metres and then left on another track (yellow waymarks are now also encountered; "GR 4" is painted in yellow on a rock). 80 metres later turn right on another path ("GR 4" painted in yellow on a tree) to pick up the red/white waymarks once again (care should be taken in this area to avoid navigational errors). After crossing a stream and a marshy area, a small stone chapel is reached, the Chapelle de Saint Barnabé, in a delightful location at a height of 4527ft (1381m).

Leave the track just below the chapel, taking a thin footpath off to the right. Soon pick up a track descending to the road, the D102. Take the track opposite which follows the line of the road at first. Cross under telegraph wires and enter

The Pic de Teillon seen from La Garde

trees. Remain on this clear track for several kilometres. After just over a mile (1.6km) an excellent view opens out of the village down to the right (Demandolx), the upper and lower lakes (both reservoirs) and the mountains beyond (this is a good spot for a picnic). Eventually leave this good track by taking a narrow footpath off to the left at a point where the track curves to the right descending to a hollow. Cross over a stream bed and continue on the path to meet a track at a hairpin bend. Turn left on this pleasant track through trees (note: the footpath to the left of this track follows it for a while, eventually rejoining it). Remain on this track until it emerges into an open area at a pylon at the Clot d'Agnon.

At the pylon with the small building next to it, take the track on the left-hand side, heading downhill (magnetic compass bearing of 205 degrees) ie. do not take the track over to the right. Descend to a second pylon at a point where the power cables change direction abruptly, heading downhill to the right. An old variant route follows the pylons down to the valley, but for the main route to La Garde remain on the track, which within 50 metres becomes a narrow footpath. This pleasant path through woodland is also waymarked with orange and yellow and some blue paint stripes. During the descent to the road (N85, Route Napoléon) at La Garde, there are views of the impressive mountain wall of Le Teillon (6206ft; 1893m). This peak can be attained by following a waymarked route (5 hours there and back form La Garde).

The path emerges on the N85 opposite the Auberge du Teillon. Turn right and walk out of La Garde on the main road (or better explore the village to the south of the N85 and then follow the principal village street out until it meets the main road). 100 metres after the small chapel on the left of the N85, turn left down a narrow footpath which descends, steeply in places, to a track where turn left. Continue the descent on the track which passes a *camping à la ferme* establishment within 150 metres and continues to cross a bridge over a stream. Where the track emerges at the N85 at "Le Gailladin", turn left on the main road to walk into the town of Castellane. The road is a busy one, particularly during the holiday season, but a gravel footpath can be followed on the right-hand side of the road for much of the way. Before entering Castellane notice the footpath off to the left, waymarked in yellow, to the Sommet de Destourbes (5058ft; 1543m). It is 3 hours 30 minutes to the summit from this point. Cross the river on the road bridge to reach the main square of Castellane, where several hôtels will be found. For directions to the *gîte d'étape* and two other hôtels, see the route description for Day 7.

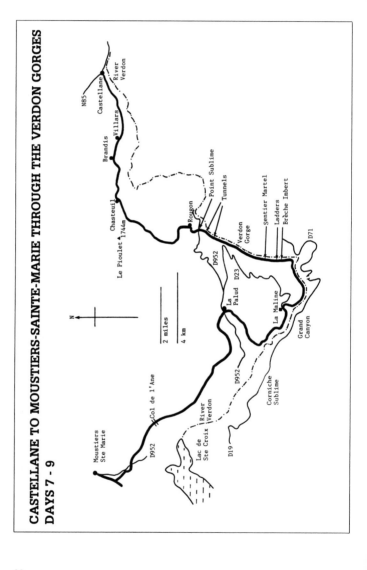

CASTELLANE TO MOUSTIERS-SAINTE-MARIE THROUGH THE VERDON GORGES
DAYS 7 - 9

PROFILE 3 - CASTELLANE TO MOUSTIERS-SAINTE-MARIE THROUGH THE VERDON GORGES: DAYS 7 - 9

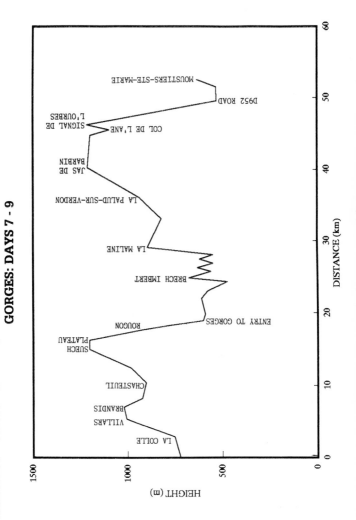

DAY 7
CASTELLANE TO POINT SUBLIME (ROUGON)

DISTANCE: 11.4 MILES (18.2km)
TOTAL ASCENT: 2262ft (690m)
TOTAL DESCENT: 2042ft (623m)
TOTAL ESTIMATED TIME: 4 HOURS 55 MINUTES

	Height Above		Distance				Est. Time	
	Sea	Level	Sect.		Cum.		Sect.	Cum.
	ft	m	mile	km	mile	km	hr m	hr m
CASTELLANE	2360	720						
LA COLLE	2478	756	1.7	2.8	1.7	2.8	0.40	0.40
VILLARS	3291	1004	1.6	2.5	3.3	5.3	0.35	1.15
BRANDIS (RUINS)	3344	1020	1.0	1.6	4.3	6.9	0.25	1.40
CHASTEUIL	2950	900	2.1	3.4	6.4	10.3	1.00	2.40
SUECH PLATEAU	3934	1200	2.9	4.6	9.3	14.9	1.15	3.55
ROUGON	3049	930	1.7	2.7	11.0	17.6	0.40	4.35
LA VIGNE	2688	820	0.2	0.3	11.2	17.9	0.10	4.45
CHALET DU POINT SUBLIME	2580	787	0.2	0.3	11.4	18.2	0.10	4.55

OPTIONAL EXCURSION
An ascent from Villars can be made to the Crête de Colle Bernaiche and on to the Cadières de Brandis, the impressive serrated cliffs above and to the north of the ruined hamlet of Brandis. This most worthy excursion would add about 3 hours to the length of the day.

FACILITIES
Accommodation
There is plenty of accommodation, of all types, along this section. The major problem is finding everywhere full during the main season. The stage is designed to end at the Point Sublime overlooking the Couloir Samson at the entrance to the gorge, where there is a 1-star hôtel, the Auberge du Point Sublime (tel. 92.83.60.35) which has 14 double rooms. It is in an ideal position for the walk through the gorges on the following day. The proprietor organises a taxi service to La Mâline for those who wish to walk through the gorges in the opposite direction to that described in this book, so ending the day back at the Auberge du Point Sublime where a second night is spent. This may appeal to those not wishing to carry a pack through the gorges. A taxi to La Mâline, or to La Palud, could be taken on the following day to resume the walk.

The River Verdon at Castellane

If the hôtel is full, the only alternative, unless a taxi is taken to another hôtel, is the *relais d'étape,* La Vigne, on the hillside behind Point Sublime (directions to this are given in the "Route" section). Although basic (see details in Appendix 1), it is possible to have dinner in the hôtel-restaurant below and only return up the hillside to sleep the night at La Vigne (a torch is useful for the re-ascent of the hill in the dark).

Between Castellane and Rougon on the GR 4, there is a hôtel-restaurant Moulin de la Salaou on the D952, a mile to the west of Castellane, a large 4-star campsite (Camp du Verdon) located at the point where the C8 meets the D952, west of Castellane, and another campsite (2-star) in the village of La Colle (this closes by the middle of September). Finally there is another *gîte d'étape* in the hamlet of Villars, between Le Colle and the ruins of Brandis.

Restaurants/Cafés/Bars
A restaurant (Moulin de la Salaou - see above) is passed shortly after leaving Castellane (note that mountain bikes can be hired from this establishment; rafting trips along the Verdon can also be arranged from here). There is a buvette serving drinks and snacks in Chasteuil (open during the main summer season only). Good food is served in the Auberge du Point Sublime.

Shops
There is a small *alimentation* in Rougon. This is very useful as it is the only food shop between Castellane and La Palud (Day 9).

Public Transport
A once daily bus service stops in Rougon during the main summer season (see Facilities for Day 6). For a taxi service in Rougon phone 92.83.65.38 or 92.83.68.06.

Water
There is a source of water in the hamlet of Villars (an arrow on a tree points the way). Rougon has a water fountain. There is a water source at La Vigne and another just outside the Auberge du Point Sublime.

Miscellaneous
Rougon possesses a sub-post office and telephone.

SUMMARY
Walkers anxious to get to grips with the Verdon Gorges, which now seem so near, should curb their impatience, for today's section over the hills to the north of the deeply cut valley of the Verdon, offers some of the best mountain walking on the entire journey. After a gentle but rather pleasant start, leaving Castellane along a quiet backstreet past a number of attractive villas and private gardens, the route takes to the mountains to visit the hamlets of Villars (where there is a fine *gîte d'étape)* and Brandis, now a collection of sad ruins.

Some of the finest, most dramatic, natural scenery in all France will be seen in this area: twisted and convoluted rock strata, dramatically tilted, cone-shaped peaks and towering cliffs. This is limestone country par excellence. Perhaps the most striking natural feature is the Cadières de Brandis, a series of vertical limestone rock pinnacles towering above the ruins of Brandis. These are seen to good effect from the little veranda of the buvette at Chasteuil, a small picturesque mountain village, home of a number of local craftsmen, especially potters. The deeply cut and twisting valley of the Verdon is often visible whilst on the walk, steeply down to the left; one can marvel that the tiny green river seen far below has sculptured such an enormous gorge and valley system. The river under most lighting conditions really does appear a deep green colour (the reason for the name given to the river - ie. Verdon). The Pic de Tailoire with its summit chapel, above the hamlet of the same name on the opposite bank of the Verdon, is one of a number of shapely peaks on view during the walk. Some of these summits and surrounding ridges can be reached by detours from the Trail (eg. a waymarked route from Villars leads to the Crête de Brandis - see "Route" section). For those with more time available in the area a number of extended excursions on foot are possible. In particular the climb to the Cadières de Brandis, the ascent of the Mourre de Chanier (6239ft; 1903m) from Rougon, and to the Sommet du Robion (5439ft; 1659m), south-west of Castellane, can all be recommended for superb all round views of the area. Details of more walks in the area will be found in the publication *Guide des Sentiers du Verdon* by Franck Ricordel, which should be on sale locally.

Romantics will no doubt fall immediately in love with picturesque Rougon, whose ancient red-roofed houses are perched so dramatically on the hillside overlooking the huge cleft in the cliff face opposite that marks the entrance to the Verdon Gorges. Few of the many tens of thousands of tourists who visit these world famous gorges every year proceed past the Point Sublime. Once here the privileged walker will be full of anticipation for the walk through the gorges on the morrow. The gigantic Couloir Samson is certainly most awe inspiring from here. From the canyon rim down to the tiny river the immense vertical walls are over 1300ft (397m) high at this point. Be sure to walk out to the Belvédère at the Point Sublime. Here there is a small memorial to Isidore Blanc (1873-1932) who, with the geologist and speleologist E.A.Martel (1859-1938), undertook the first exploration of the gorge, completed in August 1905, and to Albert Blanc (1905-1952) who continued his work.

ROUTE

From the place Marcel Sauvaire in Castellane, turn down the side road by the Hôtel du Verdon to reach the river, where turn right. The *gîte d'étape* La Galoche will be found about 250 metres along here, on the left-hand side, about 100 metres after another two hôtels. Continue along this flat and straight road, with pleasant houses and gardens on both sides, to a T-junction, where turn right. On reaching the main road (D952) at the Moulin de la Salaou, turn left for about 150 metres to turn right near the Camp du Verdon, on the C8 signposted to Villars-Brandis, La Colle and Brayal. Climb on this minor road to the village of La Colle, where there is another campsite.

Walk through La Colle on the C8. Near the far end of the village turn left on the GR 4 to cross a bridge over the river (signpost to Villars, *gîte d'étape).* Climb on a poorly surfaced road which, after a few hundred metres, becomes a gravel track. The route skirts the side of the mountain above the road and River Verdon, down to the left. After about one and a half kilometres leave the track by taking a track climbing to the right. This leads to a lane at a hairpin bend, where turn left. The first building reached on this climb is the *gîte d'étape* at Villars. Continue up the road/track until the last house of the village is reached. Locate arrows on a tree pointing to the left to a water source and to Brandis. The source of water will be found just behind the buildings. Climb the hill behind Villars to reach a small building and a signpost indicating to the right the Colle Bernaiche, a 400m (1311ft) climb in 1 hour 45 minutes, and the Cadières de Brandis, the most impressive cliffs above and to the north of the ruined hamlet of Brandis. This route into the mountains is waymarked with red flashes. However, for the GR 4 turn left at the signpost. Climb a little further before contouring on a footpath around the mountainside. The views of the surrounding mountains and down to the River Verdon are first-rate from here. The path reaches the sad ruins of Brandis. Locate a path which descends to the left of the

Jagged, tilted peaks above Chasteuil

buildings to reach a T-junction where turn right on a narrow path which contours around the mountainside and climbs very gently to the Col de la Chapelle Saint Jean (small shrine). Continue on this good mountain path (a Roman road) heading for the village of Chasteuil seen on the hillside ahead. The next destination, a col at 3934ft (1200m) is visible to the left of the village, amongst trees.

The path contours to reach the village of Chasteuil, where there is a snack bar. The tables outside this buvette provide a good spot from which to admire the vertical rock towers of the Cadières de Brandis. Walk up through the village continuing on the good track which climbs gradually through trees, emerges from these and then zig-zags all the way up to the col at 3934ft (1200m), where there is a ruined building. The Trail continues across a flat, massive plateau, heading towards the far end of a line of telegraph poles. On reaching the edge of this plateau, join a track which passes under high tension electricity cables and which follows the line of telegraph wires for a time. The Verdon Gorges down to the right have by now become visible as well as the next destination, the village of Rougon. Remain on the wide, zig-zagging path descending towards Rougon. On reaching a small shrine before the village, leave the track by taking a path on the left down through trees. This emerges in the village opposite a small *alimentation*. Turn right to descend to a communal washing place, fountain and car park. Take the track leading down from the car park with gardens either side, heading down towards the mouth of the gorge. At the end of the garden on the right, turn right on a path going downhill. Just after an enclosed section of this footpath, a sign is reached indicating "Rougon-relais d'étape, La Vigne" to the right. In 100 metres this leads to an area of erected tents (see Facilities). However, ignore this detour if seeking the hôtel in preference to this rather basic accommodation, and continue downhill on the path to emerge at a road where turn left to reach the Auberge du Point Sublime.

DAY 8
POINT SUBLIME (ROUGON) TO LA MALINE
THROUGH THE VERDON GORGES

DISTANCE: 6.7 MILES (10.8km)
TOTAL ASCENT: 2295ft (700m)
TOTAL DESCENT: 1947ft (594m)
TOTAL ESTIMATED TIME: 6 HOURS 10 MINUTES

| | Height Above Sea Level | | Distance | | | | Est. Time | |
	ft	m	Sect. mile	km	Cum. mile	km	Sect. hr m	Cum. hr m
CHALET DU POINT SUBLIME	2580	787						
ENTRY TO GORGES	1967	600	0.4	0.7	0.4	0.7	0.20	0.20
END OF SECOND TUNNEL								
(TUNNEL DE TRESCAIRE)	1934	590	0.6	0.9	1.0	1.6	0.20	0.40
BRECHE IMBERT	2213	675	3.1	5.0	4.1	6.6	2.00	2.40
START OF MAJOR CLIMB								
(PATH JUNCTION)	1803	550	2.0	3.2	6.1	9.8	2.10	4.50
LA MALINE (CAF)	2927	893	0.6	1.0	6.7	10.8	1.20	6.10

OPTIONAL EXCURSIONS

1. A five minute stroll from the Chalet du Point Sublime to the Point Sublime Belvédère (viewpoint) is recommended for a close up view of the Couloir Samson and the entrance to the Gorges du Verdon. Follow the green arrow waymarks.

2. There are a number of other short waymarked walks that can be taken from the Point Sublime, which provide views of the Gorges. Details of these should be shown on a map at the back of the kiosk at Point Sublime. Alternatively, ask in the auberge for details. They are waymarked with green paint flashes.

3. For those wishing to walk through the Verdon Gorges with only a daysack and return for the night to the Auberge du Point Sublime, it is possible to hire a taxi from Point Sublime to La Mâline, and then walk back through the Gorge to the Couloir Samson and Point Sublime. This is a popular excursion undertaken by many walkers during the main season. Enquire at the Auberge du Point Sublime for details. It is also possible to join a guided walking party during the summer months. The La Mâline to Point Sublime route is the favoured direction for many day walkers as there is less climbing involved.

FACILITIES
Accommodation
The stage ends at the CAF Refuge of La Mâline, perched on the rim of the gorge. Dinner, lunch and breakfast are all available here. The main building is closed during the winter months, but at these times the adjacent winter refuge is left open. Those looking for hôtel accommodation will have to continue into La Palud-sur-Verdon, where there is also a youth hostel (see Day 9).

Restaurants/Cafés/Bars/Shops
There are a few kiosks selling drinks, chocolate, ice-cream and souvenirs at the Point Sublime, and there is a small snack bar (the Buvette Samson) located 100 metres to the left at the GR 4/49 path junction. After this there are no shops, cafés, restaurants, or any other facilities anywhere along the Gorge between the entrance below Point Sublime, and La Mâline at the end of the day. Therefore be sure to take a good packed lunch.

Public Transport
There is usually a mini-bus service operating daily between Point Sublime and La Mâline. Alternatively, the local taxi services only too eagerly offer transport between Point Sublime, La Mâline and La Palud-sur-Verdon.

Water
The gorge can become intensely hot during the summer months, but with the River Verdon always close at hand lack of water is never a problem (water purifying tablets are advisable; some people may prefer to carry their own water for the day. Keep well away from the water if it is in flood).

Miscellaneous
Remember that in order to negotiate the dark tunnels at the start of the gorge, a *torch* is an *essential* item of equipment.

SUMMARY
Of all the many highlights on this walk across southern France, the Sentier Martel through the Grand Canyon du Verdon, will probably be the one most remembered. There can be many hundreds of people walking through the gorges during the main summer season, in large and small groups, guided or unguided, in pairs and alone. Even out of season you are unlikely to pass through the gorges without meeting several other walkers. La Mâline to Point Sublime is the popular direction to walk the canyon, as this involves a long descent at the start of the day, rather than a tiring climb out of the gorge at the end of the day, if heading towards La Mâline. Hence GR 4 walkers in July and August are likely to pass many others heading in the opposite direction.

The River Verdon is the most important tributary of the River Durance, the major river in the southern French Alps. Of its 109 miles (175km) it is the section from Castellane to the artificial Lac de Sainte-Croix, through the mighty defile of the limestone Grand Canyon, that is the most well known. The gorge was not fully explored until the beginning of the present century, principally by the French speleologist Edouard Martel, after whom the main footpath through the canyon is named. The "Sentier Martel" is the work of the Touring Club de France (T.C.F.). The artificial dammed lakes in the region, operated by the French Electricity board (Electricité de France [E.D.F]) control the rate of flow of water in the Verdon; the rate now generally varies between 5 and 30 cubic metres per second, whereas some 30 years ago, before the dams were built, the rate was as high as 800 cubic metres per second when the winter snows were melting! Nevertheless care should be taken when in the vicinity of the water as the level and speed of the torrent can vary greatly, depending on the operation of the sluice gates in the dams higher up stream. The river finally leaves the gorge to empty into the vast artificial Lac de Sainte-Croix which will be seen on Day 9.

After negotiating the tunnels which are the only way past the Couloir Samson into the heart of the gorge, the footpath clings to the side of the canyon, sometimes dropping to the river, at other times climbing tortuously to avoid yet another natural obstacle. It must be said that this stage through the Verdon Gorge is more difficult than any other on the walk (although it does not have the amount of ascent/descent found on many of the mountain stages). There are inky dark tunnels to negotiate at the start of the Trail at the Couloir Samson, and very steep ladders to contend with to reach the Brèche Imbert at the half-way stage. However, there are no real technical difficulties and, as the gorge is so confined in most places, few opportunities to make navigational errors. All but the most timid of ramblers should be able to tackle the walk, providing that the weather is fine and settled, and that care and common sense is practised at all times. However the first tunnel, which is long and "S" shaped, is no place for the claustrophobic. Also, anyone suffering from vertigo would find the Brèche Imbert ladders somewhat daunting, although they are more like steep stairways than ladders, with rails on both sides, giving a feeling of security. If there is any doubt at all, it should be possible to join one of the many guided tours that pass through the gorge on most days during the main season and at weekends during the spring and autumn.

It is possible to remain in the gorge below La Mâline and continue along it all the way to Mayreste, west of La Palud. However, this is a more serious journey, involving river crossings and requiring specialist equipment. It must not be attempted by the inexperienced, unless accompanied by one of the official local guides (it is possible to join a guided party - see below).

There are several outdoor pursuits that can be enjoyed in the Verdon gorges, including climbing, white water rafting, canoeing, hydrospeeding and "adventure walking" along the floor of the gorge. Official guides can be hired at the Refuge de La Mâline and at La Palud-sur-Verdon for all these activities.

Some of the sheer rock walls found in the Verdon Gorge

A guide for an exploration of the floor of the canyon costs about 180FF per person for half a day and 360FF for a full day (3 persons minimum). This is for the adventurous only as it involves wading, often in quite deep and fast water (participants are roped together), and sometimes negotiating awkward cave systems and climbing over rock obstacles in the gorge. It is nevertheless an exciting way to spend a day-off from the walk. Note that because of the activities of the E.D.F. these trips are not always possible (ie. when the river is in torrent after the opening of the dam sluice gates). Walkers wishing to spend a less thrilling day-off from the GR 4 in this beautiful area, may be interested in purchasing a large scale map of the Verdon Gorges and environs; such a map showing all the trails in the locality is usually for sale at the La Mâline refuge. Finally, if a car or bicycle is available, do not miss the 81-mile (130km) drive around the perimeter rim of the gorges on the Corniche Sublime (D71) along the southern edge, and the Route des Crêtes (D952) which follows the northern edge. There are many stopping places (bélvèderes) along this tourist trail which provide fine viewpoints down into the canyon.

There should be plenty of time on this section to relax and enjoy the experience of wandering through this magnificent gorge. It should not be hurried. The undergrowth that the Sentier Martel passes through on the floor of the gorge may be appreciated for the shade it provides on a fiercely hot day. Take time to gaze up at the sheer cliffs and try to spot climbers high up on the limestone walls, and tourists peering down into the gorge from the various viewpoints on the road high above along the rim of the gorge (binoculars are useful). A picnic by the riverside can be recommended, and perhaps go for a paddle in the deliciously cool, crystal clear water (but watch for sudden changes in water speed and level). There are many limestone cliffs and pinnacles to admire and caves to inspect (from a distance; do not leave the marked Trail). This is surely one of the classic walks in Europe and a day in the gorge should provide memories for many years to come.

The refuge of La Mâline occupies a superb location on the rim of the canyon, and is the perfect place to spend an evening after a day in the gorge. Here tired walkers can mingle with the rock gymnasts who spend their summers scaling the sheer walls of this mecca of the rock climbing world. The view from the terrace down the length of the gorge is breathtakingly beautiful - sometimes a blanket of cloud hangs low in the gorge, leaving the rim bathed in sunlight. British walkers may be somewhat amused by the notice board outside the refuge, which gives Important Advices *(sic)* in English. The level of English is little better in the *Complete Guide of the Grand Canyon* booklet, which is on sale locally and which supplies interesting facts about the gorge.

A final word of warning. The region is, unfortunately, a popular haunt of thieves. Do not leave your valuables unattended in *gîtes*, refuges, unlocked hôtel rooms, etc.

ROUTE

From the Auberge du Point Sublime turn left down the road, but after 100 metres take the path descending to the left (the route is accompanied by green arrow waymarks). Eighty metres along this path is the junction of the GR 4 and the GR 49. The latter, together with the green arrows, goes off to the left, but for the GR 4 and the Sentier Martel take the right fork. Follow the path beneath red and grey cliffs to the road (D234), car park and viewpoint at the mouth of the gorge.

At the car park take the path down to the left of the notice board. Walk down concrete steps to a footbridge. Climb the few steps and continue on the path ahead, ie. do not descend to the river on the left immediately after the bridge. It is important not to descend to the river at this point, as the dams further up the river release water from time to time, causing flash floods. Climb a further flight of concrete steps leading to some wooden steps and the entrance to the first tunnel (Le Baou: 670 metres long with a diameter of 3 metres). A torch will be required from hereon. After about 150 metres into the tunnel, two "windows" are reached on the left-hand side, providing views of the river. From this point the tunnel becomes very dark. After 400 metres into the tunnel a "hole" is passed (about 2ft across with a view down to the river) before a third window is reached. Here a detour down to the River Verdon is possible by taking a steep stairway down to a cave mouth (the Baume aux Pigeons). This detour can be recommended, providing a break from the confines of the tunnel. A further 250 metres or so of darkness leads to the tunnel exit and welcome daylight (take care not to walk into a large rock inside the first tunnel just before the exit). The second tunnel (the Tunnel de Trescaïre) is only about 100 metres long and is straight, the light at the exit being reassuringly visible from the entrance. After emerging from this tunnel the torch can be returned to the rucksack as there are no further tunnels to negotiate (note that there are more tunnels in the gorge, but these are in a dangerous condition, do not form part of the Sentier Martel and must not be entered).

On reaching the entrance to the third tunnel take the steps down to the left. Continue along the obvious path on the right bank of the river, looking out for climbers on the cliffs far above. The route through the gorge is straightforward and well waymarked and so there is little chance of making navigational errors. After about 2 hours of moderately paced walking from the entrance of the gorge, the path leads down to a stony beach on the banks of the river. This is an excellent spot for lunch. From the beach climb back up the 20 metres to the footpath and turn left to continue through the gorge. The path soon climbs steeply to avoid a rock face, over a few easy rock steps and beneath an overhanging cliff. Ascend for about 650ft (198m) above the river and then begin a gradual descent on a balcony path below overhanging crags. The path starts to climb again to reach the foot of a series of metal ladders. Although steep there are banisters either side and the climb up the rock face is relatively easy and safe. The ladders climb a steep cleft or gully between the cliff face on the right and an isolated crag on the left. After the first ladder the stairways increase in steepness. The climb leads to a narrow gap in the rocks, the Brèche Eiwan Imbert, where a few moves to the left lead to a viewpoint for uninterrupted views back down the gorge and of the famous cliff faces beloved of climbers. There is also a view across the gorge to Le Relais des Balcons, the viewpoint on the road high above.

Soon after beginning the descent from the Brèche Imbert, pass a signpost indicating the mid-point of the Sentier Martel (3 hours ahead to La Mâline and 3 hours back to the Point Sublime). This is the point at which the River Verdon changes direction sharply, from north-south to approximately east-west, and hence views further up the gorge open out here. Another enormous and sheer rock face comes into view. The route passes the Mescla (=mixing) the point where the Rivers Verdon and Artuby converge. The path descends to the river again, but soon climbs with the aid of a fixed cable and some more ladders (less steep than the Imbert stairways, and fewer of them). The path meanders up and down for well over a mile before finally beginning the ascent out of the gorge. Eventually a signpost is reached at a path junction. The Sentier TCF to Estellie (15 minutes) and Imbut (2 hours 30 minutes) takes the left fork to cross the river by a footbridge and continue further along the gorge (the GR 99, also waymarked with red/white flashes) but the GR 4 turns right to climb steeply away from the river. The steep zig-zagging path leads to another step ladder at a rock face (a chain is provided for assistance). The climb continues above this obstacle and provides an exhausting finale to a memorable day in one of the most dramatic gorges in the world. During the latter stages of the ascent the Chalet Refuge of La Mâline comes into view on the road up ahead. The path climbs away from the hut at first before contouring around the hillside to reach the road at a small car park. Here turn left to reach the entrance to the CAF refuge.

DAY 9
LA MALINE TO MOUSTIERS-SAINTE-MARIE VIA
LA PALUD-SUR-VERDON

DISTANCE:	14.5 MILES (23.5km)
TOTAL ASCENT:	1964ft (599m)
TOTAL DESCENT:	2823ft (861m)
TOTAL ESTIMATED TIME:	7 HOURS 40 MINUTES

	Height Above Sea Level		Distance				Est. Time	
			Sect.		Cum.		Sect.	Cum.
	ft	m	mile	km	mile	km	hr m	hr m
LA MALINE (CAF)	2927	893						
LA PALUD-SUR-VERDON	3059	933	4.3	7.0	4.3	7.0	1.50	1.50
JAS DE BARBIN	3967	1210	2.6	4.2	6.9	11.2	1.40	3.30
COL DE PLEIN VOIR	3914	1194	2.8	4.5	9.7	15.7	1.10	4.40
COL DE L'ANE	3590	1095	0.5	0.8	10.2	16.5	0.20	5.00
SIGNAL DE L'OURBES	3977	1213	0.4	0.7	10.6	17.2	0.30	5.30
ROAD (D957)	1728	527	2.0	3.3	12.6	20.5	1.10	6.40
MOUSTIERS-SAINTE-MARIE	2069	631	1.9	3.0	14.5	23.5	1.00	7.40

FACILITIES
There should be few problems with finding facilities along the Trail for the next few days as the GR 4 passes through several towns and villages.

Accommodation
The youth hostel (AJH) of La Palud is about 0.5km before the town at the point where the GR 4 leaves the D23 road at a bend. It is also possible to camp here, using the indoor facilities of the hostel, but for more luxury a 3-star hôtel-restaurant (Les Gorges du Verdon, tel. 92.74.68.26) is just 200 metres away to the right. There are other hôtels in La Palud including Le Provence (a *Logis de France* - 2-star, tel 92.74.68.88) and L'Auberge des Crêtes (1km east of La Palud, tel. 92.74.68.47).

There are other *gîtes d'étape* in the vicinity (see Appendix 1) and two campsites, viz. the Camping Municipal, a little to the west of La Palud (2-star, tel. 92.74.68.13) and the more basic Camping Bourbon (a 1-star *camping à la ferme*). The latter is 1km off-route (turn right off the D23 before reaching La Palud, at the signpost for the campsite).

The several hôtels in Moustiers-Sainte-Marie tend to be somewhat more expensive than those in the less touristy areas visited so far on the Trail. Try the Hôtel Bélvèdere or La Bonne Auberge or Le Relais (tel. 92.74.66.10).

The *gîte d'étape* is a little way out of Moustiers, but is close to the GR 4 (see "Route" section below).

There are several campsites in the vicinity of Moustiers, some of which are passed en route. The 2-star campsite Saint Clair is located at the point where the D952 meets the D957, 1.6 miles (2km) south of Moustiers. The Camping de Peyrengues is 0.5km further along the Trail. Another campsite, closer to Moustiers, is passed on the walk between the *gîte d'étape* and the town centre (see "Route").

Restaurants/Cafés/Bars

La Palud has at least two bar-restaurants (Lou Cafetié and Chez Maurel), and a crêperie, pizzeria and a snack bar.

There are many restaurants and cafés in Moustiers-Sainte-Marie, but the prices tend to be rather high. The courtesy that you may have come to expect is also not very evident in this tourist centre. The Restaurant de la Ferme Rose, adjacent to the *gîte d'étape*, is convenient for those not wishing to make the detour into Moustiers.

Shops

There are *boulangeries, épiceries,* small supermarkets, *pâtisseries* and *boucheries* in both La Palud-sur-Verdon and Moustiers-Sainte-Marie. There are many souvenir shops, especially those selling local pottery, in Moustiers.

Public Transport

See "Facilities - Day 6". A taxi service around the Gorge operates from here. For a taxi in Moustiers phone 92.74.66.87.

Miscellaneous

La Palud is *the* centre for outdoor activities on and around the River Verdon. Enquire at Le Cabanon du Verdon for guided adventure tours along the bottom of the gorge and courses on climbing, rafting and canoeing. Other similar establishments compete for business. There is also a Club Equestre for horse riding tours of a few hours to several days in duration. All the necessary gear for these activities is available for hire. There are also several shops selling walking and climbing equipment. This is the last place on the entire Trail where good quality replacement outdoor gear can be purchased.

Moustiers boasts a bank (Crédit Agricole - limited opening) and a post office. If the bank is closed there is a money exchange in the *boulangerie*(!) opposite the Hôtel-Restaurant La Bonne Auberge. The post office will cash Eurocheques. The *Syndicat d'Initiative* in Moustiers (tel. 92.74.67.84), housed in the Mairie, is open from mid-June to mid-September.

Lac de Sainte-Croix

SUMMARY

The day starts with a section of road walking to La Palud-sur-Verdon. However this is not unpleasant as the minor D23 road is generally fairly quiet (at least outside of the main summer season and particularly if an early start is made from the refuge). Moreover there are good views for much of the way down to the Gorge bottom. Low flying military aircraft may accompany you on this section (indeed you may have noticed them yesterday whilst in the gorge). These are from the Camp de Canjuers, a nearby military training area.

La Palud is the closest town to the Verdon Gorges and is particularly popular with young outdoor types. It is a good place to stop for elevenses, or to book onto a guided tour or course, but otherwise holds little attraction. Whilst in the town search out some of the postcards on sale depicting La Palud as it appeared before all the commercialism of the late twentieth century - it was in those days merely a château and a church!

The GR 4 climbs into the hills once more after La Palud, first on an old track which leads into forest, where care with navigation is required. There have been extensive forestry operations in the area, tree felling and the formation of wide bulldozed tracks, with consequent loss of red/white waymarks, and so particular attention should be paid to the route description and to the map and compass. The route through this area might be re-waymarked in the future, in which case the difficulties should largely disappear. The Trail eventually emerges onto open hillside and leads to the Col de Plein Voir, from where there is a first rate view of the immense Lac de Sainte Croix, and the first glimpses of the distant Lure mountains and the Lubéron, the destination of the GR 4 after the Durance valley. Keen eyes may even be able to pick out Mont Ventoux, the highest point in Provence, and the principal highlight of the walk after the Lubéron. This is a good spot for lunch. From here the Trail follows the edge of a fine rocky escarpment, climbing amongst scrub to its highest point (the Signal de l'Ourbes, 3977ft; 1213m) before commencing a long, steep and zig-zagging descent down a rocky cleft, amidst admirable scenery of jagged limestone. The GR 4 does not actually pass through Moustier-Sainte-Marie, but a short detour soon leads up to the town.

Moustiers-Sainte-Maire

It is difficult to recommend the "Cité de la Faïence" (town of pottery) as, during the main summer season it is seething with tourists browsing amongst its many local craft shops. Furthermore services in the town are relatively expensive and people are not as friendly as is often the case in southern France. However, Moustiers is certainly an attractive town, its houses huddled dramatically beneath two enormous towering cliffs, and its narrow streets can be a pleasure to wander around during the relative tranquillity of spring and autumn. The red glow of the setting sun on the roofs of the town and the surrounding crags (well seen on the approach walk from the *gîte d'étape*) is a beautiful sight.

Moustiers has one curious feature, a star suspended high above the houses on a long chain between the two crags which dominate the town. This is associated with a legendary story dating from the crusades, although the present star and chain were erected as recently as 1957. Water tumbles down from the gorge between the two crags by a series of small waterfalls to rush through the town. Some of the houses are built into the rock alongside the river. The sound of running water is never far away, the town containing a multitude of water fountains.

The pottery industry in the town dates from the late seventeenth century, when it was started by one Antoine Clérissy making use of the abundant local clays. It reached its height by the end of the eighteenth century, but declined in the following century with competition from the north of Europe. However, the industry revived after the First World War and today thrives on rather cheap and poor quality products which its sells to the many tourists who invade the town every year. Moustiers pottery is characterised by its ornamentation which is often of scenes from classical mythology. The Museum of Pottery (closed on Tuesdays) contains some notable items and tells the story of pottery making in Moustiers. Note that even the street signs in Moustiers are made from glazed pottery!

The romanesque church has a rather fine bell tower, and is worth a visit. If further exercise is sought then a walk up to either the twelfth-century chapel of Notre-Dame-de-Beauvais, or the Château de Trigance will pleasantly while away some time.

ROUTE
The GR 4 takes the D23 road all the way from La Mâline to La Palud-sur-Verdon. Turn left outside the refuge along the road which follows the rim of the gorge.

The road, which is generally fairly quiet in the early morning, except in the height of the summer season, provides good views down into the gorge. Pass the Belvédère du Baucher and the Belvédère du Maugue and a number of other viewing points provided for motorists driving around the rim. There is another viewing platform at L'Imbut. The gorge narrows quite dramatically in this area, the sheer walls rising abruptly from the river. Shortly after L'Imbut the road leaves the canyon, climbing gradually towards the north-east to La Palud. The GR 4 leaves the road at a bend in the latter, about 0.5km before reaching the town, where the Youth Hostel of La Palud is situated. Take the grassy path straight ahead at the hostel, continuing to re-join the road to enter the town, ie. this path merely short-cuts the D23.

From the centre of La Palud take the D123 signposted to Châteauneuf. After about 300 metres, where the road bends to the right, turn left on a poorly surfaced narrow road at a small shrine ("no through road" sign). Where this bends to the right towards a house in about 100 metres, go ahead up 3 steps to join a footpath. This clear, easy to follow path climbs the hillside behind La Palud. Cross a track and continue to climb on the footpath. An extensive view opens out behind La Palud to distant mountains, and there are also some last glimpses of the Verdon Gorges over to the left, which from this angle looks rather like a giant "unzippered" zip. When the path levels out amongst trees, over an hour from La Palud, be sure to take a left fork downhill through trees. This comes down to a wide, bulldozed track, where turn left, following it around a hairpin bend, but 80 metres after the bend, locate a path on the left leading downhill through the forest (there should be a cairn at the point at which the path leaves the track). Care is required in this area, as forestry operations are affecting the footpaths and waymarking. Further down the path avoid a turn to the right (at a point where a ruined house is visible through the trees - the Jas de Barbin). Soon bear left on a track, but about 400 metres later ignore another track up to the left. Later cross a wider track (at "tree number 413"). One hundred and fifty metres later, at another wider, gravel track, turn right to walk around a left-handed right-angled bend and climb on the track. Ignore a track to the left at the top of this short climb, but continue ahead slightly downhill. A little later, at a signpost to Moustiers-Sainte-Marie, turn right off the main track onto another track passing through pine trees. This track eventually emerges from the trees as a path contouring the mountainside, with extensive views of the surrounding mountains.

The path continues to the Col de Plein Voir, where yellow paint stripe waymarked paths descend to both left and right. The best spot for lunch is not here but another few hundred metres farther on along the GR 4, at a pylon carrying a high tension electricity cable. Here there is an outstanding view to the left, of the Lac de Sainte Croix, a huge, turquoise coloured reservoir. From this viewpoint take the path descending just to the right of the pylon. Pass under a second pylon to reach the Col de l'Ane, the Col of the Donkey. Here there are

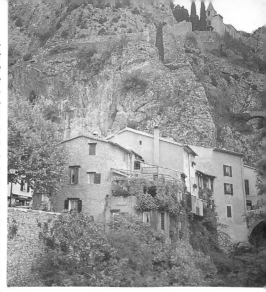

Houses perched at the water's edge and beneath the crags at Moustiers-Sainte-Marie

paths (waymarked with orange stripes) down to the left to the lake and also off the crête to the right. However, the GR 4 remains on the ridge, climbing the hill ahead. The ascent to the Signal de l'Ourbes (3977ft; 1213m) is a little overgrown and rather confusing, with many narrow paths, but perseverance will lead you to the top (if in doubt always aim for the edge of the escarpment).

Continue along the red and white waymarked path along the cliff edge. The path descends the ridge to a lower plateau at the end of which take a right fork (red/white and yellow waymarkings) to begin the descent to the wide valley floor seen below. A stony path zig-zags down beneath a huge cliff face, finally descending to the D952 road, the Route des Gorges, at a small bridge. Turn right at the road, but in less than a 100 metres, at the hairpin bend, continue ahead on a footpath. This soon rejoins the road which is crossed to take the footpath opposite, descending to meet the road for a third time, at another small bridge. Turn left, but in a few metres turn right on the D952 road heading north (there is a campsite here at Saint Clair). Continue along the road for about 0.5km until, about 250 metres after a chapel on the right, at the Aire Naturelle de Camping de Peyrengues, turn left along a track. This bends to the left and then to the right to cross a stream; 20 metres further, at a T-junction, turn right for the GR 4 (take the left-hand fork for the campsite). Continue on the earthen track to a cross-tracks (stream over to the right). The GR 4 to Riez (see Day 10) takes the left fork here, but to reach Moustiers-Sainte-Marie turn right. Those requiring the *gîte d'étape* should continue ahead on the track: after a further 400 metres take the left fork signposted "La Cavalier" and restaurant. The *gîte* is situated behind the restaurant.

To reach the town of Moustiers from the *gîte d'étape,* turn left on the minor road outside the *gîte* to a T-junction where turn right. At the main road, the D952, turn right but in about 150 metres turn right again (campsite). This lane leads to the centre of Moustiers.

DAY 10
MOUSTIERS-SAINTE-MARIE TO RIEZ

DISTANCE:			11.2 MILES (18km)					
TOTAL ASCENT:			1000ft (305m)					
TOTAL DESCENT:			1338ft (408m)					
TOTAL ESTIMATED TIME:			4 HOURS 40 MINUTES					

	Height Above Sea Level		Distance				Est. Time	
	Sea ft	Level m	Sect. mile	km	Cum. mile	km	Sect. hr m	Cum. hr m
MOUSTIERS-SAINTE-MARIE	2069	631						
PLATEAU (TOP OF CLIMB)	2524	770	2.4	3.8	2.4	3.8	1.10	1.10
ROUMOULES	1918	585	6.1	9.9	8.5	13.7	2.20	3.30
RIEZ	1731	528	2.7	4.3	11.2	18.0	1.10	4.40

FACILITIES
Accommodation
The old Hôtel des Alpes (1-star) in the centre of Riez is rather run-down, but there are plans for improvements to the establishment. The food is excellent. There is a much more expensive, modern hôtel some distance from the centre of town. The Gigalou is a medium priced hôtel about 1.2 miles (2km) from Riez.

Restaurants/Cafés/Bars
Roumoules boasts two cafes, but the larger Riez has several bars and restaurants (eg. Les Abeilles).

Shops
There is an *épicerie* next door to the Café du Midi in Roumoules (open every day, but closed 1 to 4pm).

Riez has a large variety of shops. There is a large supermarket on the outskirts of the town. Honey is for sale at the bee museum in Riez.

Public Transport
There is a twice daily bus service between Riez and Marseille stopping at Saint Martin-de-Brômes, Gréoux-les-Bains and Aix-en-Provence (tel. Autocars Sumian 42.67.60.34). See also "Facilities - Day 6".

Water
There is a water fountain in Roumoules and another in Riez.

Miscellaneous
Roumoules has a small post office and public telephone. Riez has banks and a larger post office.

SUMMARY
There is now quite a sudden and dramatic change in the landscape. The walk thus far has threaded its way over mountains and through deep gorges, but now the route traverses high plateau land where lavender is grown commercially on a large scale. It is a crop quite alien to British eyes and so will add interest for British walkers. Those walking the Trail during the early summer when the flowers are in full bloom will find the region particularly attractive. Although now left behind, the mountain range that has been recently traversed will be on show for much of the early part of today's walk. Moreover the hills of the Lubéron on the other side of the Durance valley, the next major objective, will begin to appear more prominent as the walker heads further to the west.

From the stream at the foot of Moustiers, a steep track leads up through trees to reach a flat plateau, where the route is through lavender fields all the way to the village of Roumoules, which has nothing of note except for a welcoming café. A futher climb leads to more lavender fields, before the route finally descends to the ancient town of Riez. Strong walkers may wish to continue further along the trial without an overnight stop in Riez, but it would be a pity to miss the several attractions of this pleasant town, which is a world

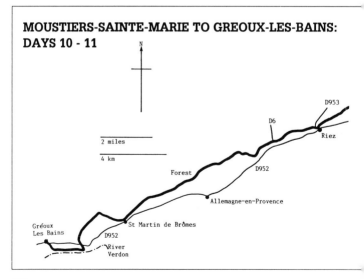

MOUSTIERS-SAINTE-MARIE TO GREOUX-LES-BAINS: DAYS 10 - 11

apart from the tourist bustle of nearby Moustiers.

Riez

Of Roman origin, Riez is said to be the oldest town in the Alpes-de-Haute-Provence. It has the atmosphere of a town that has seen better times, as will be witnessed by its several rather faded Renaissance buildings. Riez has been surprisingly, and thankfully, more or less untouched by modern tourism. It survives instead on the lavender industry and to a lesser extent on pottery and apiculture.

As the day's walk is a short and easy one, there should be plenty of time available to visit some of the attractions of the town:

1. The Roman Columns. These are located in a field to the north of the River Colostre (only a few hundred metres from the main square and allées Louis-Gardiol in Riez, and a slight detour off-route: the way to them is signposted). The four Corinthian columns are all that remain of a Roman Temple thought to be dedicated to Apollo.

2. The Baptistery and ruins of the cathedral (on the southern side of the river, off the D952). These date from the fifth century and are some of the earliest surviving Christian buildings in France. Riez was made a bishopric in the fifth century, being thus one of the oldest dioceses in Gaul.

3. The Maison de l'Abeille (bee or honey museum). A visit here can be thoroughly recommended. It is about 0.5km from the main square in Riez, off the road to Digne (follow the signs from the town centre). Admission is free, and opening hours are usually 9am to 6pm. The staff in this visitor's centre are friendly and enthusiastic and you will probably get a short guided tour. Most aspects of bee physiology are demonstrated, with emphasis on honey production. There are hives with transparent sides, so that the bees and their queen can be identified and seen at work. Finally there is an opportunity to taste all the many different varieties of honey produced in the region (the taste depends to a large extent on the main flowers visited by the bees). Small scale

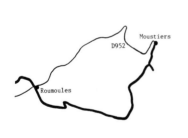

honey production is an important rural industry in much of southern France, and you have no doubt seen several hives already whilst on your travels. Honey is often for sale at many of the farmsteads passed en route: it is highly nutritious, easily digested and therefore ideal for sustaining the long distance walker.

4.   Musée Nature en Provence. A small natural history museum (closed on Tuesdays) near to the Hôtel de Ville. This is worth a short visit.

ROUTE

If leaving from the *gîte d'étape*, simply retrace the 500 metres back to the point at which the GR 4 was left yesterday. Turn right on the dirt track opposite a small bridge. If leaving from the centre of Moustiers, turn right off the N592 just after the Hôtel Belvédère onto a lane. This leads down to the small bridge over the stream, at the footpath junction 500 metres south of the *gîte d'étape*. Cross over to rejoin the GR 4.

The GR 4 heads south-west towards the wooded hill seen ahead. Where the track forks, take the left-hand track. Remain on the main track which climbs gradually to reach a minor road on a plateau. Turn left for 80 metres before turning left off the road onto a poorly surfaced track with woodland to the left and a lavender field to the right. Remain on this track which later becomes unsurfaced and which provides views down through the trees to the Lac de Saint Croix (yesterday's route on the ridge can be traced from this point). After about a couple of kilometres the route reaches a pylon. Leave the track here by turning right onto another track heading towards the west. This leads to a road at a farmstead, Chaudon, where turn right. Leave the road after 80 metres where the road bends to the right; here turn left along a track (ignore the track ahead) to pass to the left of a metal barn. The track follows a line of electricity cables soon meeting a surfaced lane to pass under high tension cables near a pylon. Where the road branches take the left fork straight ahead. Continue on this lane along the plateau for over 2 miles (3.2km). Where the road swings to the right and begins to descend, take an acute-angled left turn onto a track. This is easy to miss: there was no waymarking at this junction in 1991 (if this junction is not found then all is not lost: simply remain on the lane, which also leads to Roumoules). After about 450 metres reach a cross-tracks at a slight rise. Here turn right on another track, resuming a westerly direction. This track swings sharply to the right in just under a mile, and 150 metres later turns to the left to descend towards Roumoules. Before reaching the village the track meets another at a T-junction where turn left. On reaching the road go straight ahead for a visit to the village (café, *épicerie*) or alternatively turn right to continue along the GR 4.

One hundred metres after the right turn the GR 4 forks left downhill, passing the houses on the outskirts of the village. On reaching the main road turn right, but in 5 metres left on the road signposted to La Garenne. Where the road bends to the right at an electricity pylon, turn left on a gravel track uphill. The track levels out in an area of lavender fields, and reaches a T-junction, where turn left. This pleasant track crosses lavender fields to reach a road at a hairpin bend. The GR 4 takes the right branch of this road, downhill (choose the left branch for a visit to the chapel of Riez). The road zig-zags down to the town of Riez, soon seen below. Pass the cemetery, descending the Montée du Cimetière to reach the High Street, where turn left to the Place des Ormeaux at the public washing area and fountain.

DAY 11
RIEZ TO GREOUX-LES-BAINS

DISTANCE:				13.9 MILES (22.4km)				
TOTAL ASCENT:				1708ft (521m)				
TOTAL DESCENT:				2128ft (649m)				
TOTAL ESTIMATED TIME:				5 HOURS 25 MINUTES				

| | Height Above Sea Level | | Distance | | | | Est. Time | |
| | Sea | Level | Sect. | | Cum. | | Sect. | Cum. |
	ft	m	mile	km	mile	km	hr m	hr m
RIEZ	1731	528						
CHATEAU DE PONTFRAC	1606	490	2.2	3.5	2.2	3.5	0.50	0.50
ROAD (D15)	1901	580	3.0	4.9	5.2	8.4	1.15	2.05
SAINT MARTIN-DE-BROMES	1213	370	4.4	7.0	9.5	15.4	1.40	3.45
RIVER VERDON	1049	320	3.2	5.0	12.7	20.4	1.15	5.00
GREOUX-LES-BAINS	1311	400	1.2	2.0	13.9	22.4	0.25	5.25

FACILITIES
Accommodation
The small, pleasant village of Saint Martin-de-Brômes boasts two hôtels, Le Chaudron and La Fontaine. A stay here might be preferred to an overnight stop in Gréoux-les-Bains, as the latter has little of the character associated with old Provence. On the way out of Saint Martin-de-Brômes on the GR 4 "La Maison de Pays" will be passed. This establishment offers accommodation in individual rooms and in group dormitories.

There are at least 15 hôtels (1- to 3-star categories) in thriving and ever expanding Gréoux-les-Bains. Note that some of these are "Hôtels Residences" catering only for those staying for a period of time to "take the cure". The 2-star Les Alpes (avenue des Alpes, tel. 92.74.24.24) is comfortable. Try also the 2-star Grand Jardin (avenue des Thermes, tel. 92.74.24.74) or the 1-star La Tanière (avenue des Alpes, tel. 92.74.23.46).

Backpackers have the choice of a small campsite just outside Saint Martin-de-Brômes (passed en route) and the Terrain de Camping Municipal in Gréoux-les-Bains (tel. 92.78.00.62 - near to the River Verdon, south-east of the town centre).

Restaurants/Cafés/Bars
There is a buvette and a hôtel-restaurant at the Château de Pontfrac, about 2.2 miles (3.5km) west of Riez. Saint Martin-de-Brômes has a restaurant, ideal for

a long, leisurely lunch. There is also a café here. There are many restaurants, cafés and bars in Gréoux-les-Bains.

Shops
There is an *épicerie* and a *boulangerie* in Saint Martin-de-Brômes. Gréoux-les-Bains has a large selection of shops of all types.

Water
There is a water fountain in Saint Martin-de-Brômes beneath the village chestnut tree.

Public Transport
A bus service from Gréoux-les-Bains to Manosque and on to Avignon operates twice daily in low season and thrice daily in high season (journey time approximately 25 minutes to Manosque and 2½ hours to Avignon). Another service runs three times per day to Marseille (journey time about 1½ hours) and each time connects with the TGV train to Paris (tel. Autocars Sumian 42.67.60.34).

Miscellaneous
Those wishing to "take the waters" at Gréoux-les-Bains, to sooth the aches and pains no doubt accumulated over the last 10 days, should enquire at the modern thermal baths complex or the Office du Tourisme (5, avenue des Marronniers, tel. 92.78.01.08). It is possible to use the numerous facilities on an hourly or "session" basis. The town abounds in medical practitioners of all specialities. If your feet are in bad shape the *podologie* at the Cabinet de Pied Curie may be just what you need!

Every Sunday from April to October there is a concert of music in the Parc Morelon in Gréoux-les-Bains. Every morning at the large, modern hall of the Thermes Troglodytes Celtes Gallo Romains the resident artist can be seen at work. There is even a cinema in town. Tennis and swimming are popular activities for a rest day in Gréoux-les-Bains.

SUMMARY
The day has a rather unpleasant start with a long and tedious trudge along a fairly busy road to the Château de Pontfrac, but once this is over the walking is all on good, undulating tracks through woodland to Saint Martin-de-Brômes. Here, in this typical Provençal village, the ancient and modern world live contentedly side-by-side: note the sea of television aerials projected from roofs slated with traditional "lauzes". Lauzes are calcareous roof tiles which rather resemble fish scales, and will be seen on many other occasions on old houses and barns as the wayfarer proceeds further west through Provence and into the Massif Central. The village is worthy of a short stop to see the Romanesque church, the thirteenth-century Templars' tower, and the small museum devoted

to the local Roman remains.

Be sure to look back when at the top of the climb out of Saint Martin-de-Brômes. From here it is possible to trace the route that you have taken over the last few days, and the mountains ahead on the far bank of the Durance are now much in evidence. There are more lavender fields and woods before a descent to the River Verdon. When on the hill above Gréoux-les-Bains note the castle of the Knight Templars on the hill above the town. The stroll along the river bank into Gréoux-les-Bains is very pleasant: the wide, slow flowing River Verdon is now very different in character from the mountain watercourse last encountered in the Grand Canyon. The River Verdon, which started its journey high up in the mountains above Allos in the north, has now careered through the Grand Canyon and is soon to pour its waters out into the River Durance which flows south towards the Mediterranean. This will be the last occasion to see the Verdon; there are usually several anglers lining its banks on this stretch into Gréoux-les-Bains, hoping to hook one of its many trout.

The Knights Templar had an important influence on this area in medieval times (witness the Templars' tower in Saint Martin-de-Brômes) and it is they who built the town of Gréoux-les-Bains, on the remains of an original Roman site. Both the Romans and the Templars were no doubt attracted by the natural sulphurous waters of the region, a feature which has formed the basis of a modern health industry. The thermal baths at Gréoux-les-Bains attract thousands of patients from all over France and abroad who come for extended visits to "take the cure". The resort specialises in treatments for rheumatism, arthritis and chest complaints. The modern town, which is considerably larger than the original old village, consists predominately of large modern hôtels and luxury residences to house the visitors undergoing treatment in the large thermal baths complex in the town.

Strong walkers may wish to combine Days 11 and 12 to reach the Durance valley in one day, although it would constitute a very long day, with little time to spare for exploring Saint Martin-de-Brômes or Gréoux-les-Bains en route for Manosque. Those not wishing to spend the night in Gréoux-les-Bains might like to take a bus from here to Manosque, thereby omitting the only poor section of the entire route from Grasse to Langogne (see "Summary" - Day 12).

ROUTE

From the square in Riez containing the water fountain and washing area, take the road signposted to Valensole. This crosses a bridge within a couple of hundred metres. Turn left on the D6 and remain on this road for almost 2 miles (3.2km). Shortly after passing a farm selling lavender and honey, and where the road bends to the right and uphill, continue ahead on a surfaced track downhill. Continue on this as it becomes a dirt track and later bends and climbs gently to the right to the Château de Pontfrac (Hôtel-Restaurant). The track bends to the left at the château. Continue on the main track, later ignoring a track down to the left (Gîte de France - Domaine de Bertrandy). At a cross track continue ahead to begin an ascent. At the top of the climb on reaching a field, turn left. Follow the left-hand edge of the field for about 300 metres (direction is changed several times) and then turn sharp right across a field to an isolated stone barn in the centre of a field. The route continues ahead between fields, but 80 metres past the barn, turn left onto a grassy track (it is important not to miss this change of direction). Continue on this new track, passing an isolated tree on the left, to reach a road (D15) at a hairpin bend.

Turn right on the road for about 0.5km, before leaving it by taking a track on the left. Remain on this main undulating track, along the crête through forest, for at least 3 miles (4.8km). On approaching Saint Martin-de-Brômes look out for a right turn off the main track onto a narrower track. After nearly another kilometre locate a footpath on the left descending to the old church of Saint Martin-de-Brômes. Pass between the church and adjacent tower and descend to the houses of the village. Descend through the old narrow streets passing an *épicerie* to the Carriera dei Templiers. Turn left for the village: restaurant, café, hôtels, water fountain.

The GR 4 to Gréoux-les-Bains turns right at the T-junction at the Carriera dei Templiers. Cross over a bridge and 80 metres later take the right fork. Ascend this poorly surfaced road passing a campsite on the right and soon, when the route becomes a wide unsurfaced track, pass to the right of La Maison de Pays (accommodation). Near the top of the climb ignore paths off to the left and right and continue ahead. After a few hundred metres along the field edge, turn left at right angles onto another track. Continue on this main road (red/white waymarks are now accompanied by single blue flashes) until the track divides. The blue waymarked route goes to the right, but the GR 4 takes the left-hand fork. Ascend to a tree where there is another track junction: go right again. At the next T-junction turn left downhill, rejoining the "blue" route. Gréoux-les-Bains is now visible spread out in the valley below (note the castle of the Knights Templar on the hill overlooking the town). After a few hundred metres ignore a track to the right. At a clearing above the town take a track down to the left (ie. do not go straight on at this point) aiming for a pylon somewhat to the left of a ruined building. Turn left on reaching this pylon on a path across a field (note the vegetated cliffs on the other side of the River Verdon). When the path descends through woodland take care to locate a right fork down to a road (D952). Cross the road and turn left on a poorly surfaced lane that runs parallel with the road for a while before swinging to the right to head towards the Verdon. Turn right at a T-junction, with the River Verdon now to the left. Walk along the bank of the river until a narrow lane is reached on the right, by a house before the road bridge spanning the river. Emerging from the rue des Eaux-Chaudes the GR 4 turns right on the avenue du Verdon to enter the spa town of Gréoux-les-Bains.

DAY 12
GREOUX-LES-BAINS TO MANOSQUE
(THE DURANCE VALLEY)

DISTANCE:	8.2 MILES (13.2km)
TOTAL ASCENT:	515ft (157m)
TOTAL DESCENT:	679ft (207m)
TOTAL ESTIMATED TIME:	3 HOURS 15 MINUTES

	Height Above Sea Level		Distance				Est. Time	
			Sect.		Cum.		Sect.	Cum.
	ft	m	mile	km	mile	km	hr m	hr m
GREOUX-LES-BAINS	1311	400						
LES QUATRE CHEMINS	964	294	4.6	7.4	4.6	7.4	1.50	1.50
RIVER DURANCE	957	292	0.6	1.0	5.2	8.4	0.15	2.05
MANOSQUE	1147	350	3.0	4.8	8.2	13.2	1.10	3.15

ALTERNATIVE
There is a bus service operating betwen Gréoux-les-Bains and Manosque.

FACILITIES
Manosque is the largest town encountered on the GR 4 since leaving Grasse.
Only Pont-Saint-Esprit in the Rhône Valley and Langogne at the end of the Trail,
approach it in size. Consequently it has every facility likely to be needed by the
foot traveller.

Accommodation
There are at least 14 hôtels in Manosque (categories 1 to 4). The first to be
encountered on the walk into town is the Hôtel-Restaurant Le Provence (2-star,
tel. 92.72.39.38) on the route de la Durance. The 2-star Hôtel Peyrache (37, rue
Guilhempierre, tel. 92.72.07.43) can be recommended. Another good possibility
is the nearby Hôtel Francois 1èr (18, rue Guilhempierre, tel. 92.72.07.99). The
youth hostel (Auberge de Jeunesse) is some way from the town centre (see
Appendix 1).
    Camping is available at Manosque in the Camping Municipal on the avenue
de la Repasse (tel. 92.72.28.08).

Restaurants/Cafés/Bars/Shops
The walker is spoilt for choice in Manosque. The food in Le Mont d'Or Hôtel-
Restaurant (tel. 92.72.13.94), in the place de la Mairie in the centre of the old

town, is excellent. There is a large supermarket for the restocking of provisions: no comparable shops will be encountered for many days.

Public Transport

Manosque is on the main railway line between Marseille and Gap. The railway station (gare SNCF) lies to the south of the town centre and is but a short detour from the direct walking route into Manosque (see "Route"). For the mainline to Paris change at Marseille. Train tickets can be purchased in some of the travel agents in town, avoiding the necessity of walking to the station until the train is to be taken.

There are a number of bus services that operate from the Gare Routière on the boulevard Charles de Gaulle. Principal services run north and south along the Durance valley (but the train is generally better) and east to Gréoux-les-Bains and Castellane, and west to Les Granons, Cavaillon and Avignon (telephone 90.74.36.10 or 92.72.40.58 for more information, or enquire at the Gare Routière or Tourist Office).

Miscellaneous

The Tourist Office (tel. 92.72.16.00) is in the place du Dr Joubert, a little outside the old town to the east. There are several banks and post offices.

SUMMARY

Today's short stage has little to offer, and its latter stages along busy roads into Manosque are quite unpleasant. Those not intent on covering the entire distance on foot between Grasse and Langogne would be well advised to take a bus between Gréoux-les-Bains and Manosque. This is the only section on the entire 26-day journey that the author would not unreservedly recommend.

The Château of Gréoux-les-Bains, passed en route is of little interest, although the view of Gréoux and the surrounding countryside is worth a short rest here. The first half of the route along tracks through woodland is pleasant enough (although even here there is a short section of road walking) but once past the crossroads of Les Quatre Chemins, a fast pace is recommended to reach the old town centre of Manosque as quickly as possible. The noise and fumes of heavy traffic make this an unpleasant journey. The original route of the GR 4 followed tracks to the north of the D907 after crossing the road bridge over the River Durance. However at the time of writing, the route described along the D907 is the only viable one, as the whole area has been greatly disturbed with the building of the new motorway, the A51, which connects the town with Aix-en-Provence and Marseille. However, once the motorway development is complete, the area will probably be re-landscaped and a new route to the centre of Manosque may be waymarked. Even so the area will never be a quiet and attractive one. Care should be taken when following the route described as the traffic, which includes many heavy lorries, will probably be fairly heavy.

Manosque

A sprawling, industrial centre in the Durance valley, Manosque is a major town in the département of the Alpes-de-Haute-Provence. The small and compact old town at its heart is nevertheless quite charming and worth a short stay. The town was made famous by the writings of the twentieth-century novelist, Jean Giono, and the walker will approach the old

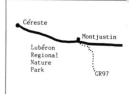

town along the avenue named after him. Vieux Manosque is entered by the fourteenth-century Porte Saunerie, a tall gate with crenellated towers. A network of pedestrianised streets then leads through the heart of the medieval town to exit at the Porte Soubeyran which has an interesting bell tower. Two churches of note are found within the old town walls, the Eglise de Saint-Sauveur and the Eglise de Notre-Dame-de-Romigier, the former housing one of the famed Black Virgins of southern France to which is attributed a number of miracles (it is said to be the oldest Black Virgin in France). But the main attraction of the old town is simply to wander through its old, narrow streets and window shop at the many boutiques. A busy market is held here on several weekdays

The presence of a mainline railway down the Durance valley to Marseille (good connections for a fast train service to Paris) and the position of Manosque, 12 days walking from Grasse, make this destination an excellent one for those with only two weeks available for their holiday. The second half of the walk from here to Langogne also fits into a fortnight's holiday.

If a rest day is sought here, it is convenient to take a day trip from Manosque by train or coach to Aix-en-Provence, the "capital" of the region. The train journey takes only about 40 minutes and it is thus possible to spend a full day in Aix, before returning to a hôtel in Manosque, to continue the GR 4 on the following day. For those returning to Britain, a morning train from Manosque would allow a full day in Aix, before continuing the journey to Marseille, for the night train to Paris (or a train to Nice for a flight home). Aix is an elegant, sophisticated and chic city, famous as the birthplace of the painter Paul Cézanne. There are many museums and art galleries to visit and numerous fine buildings to admire.

ROUTE

The avenue du Verdon leads to a small roundabout. From here take the narrow road climbing past a large crucifix and the Jardin Public on the right-hand side. At the chemin de Sainte Annette turn left to reach a cross-roads where proceed ahead uphill towards the château. At the chemin des Seigneuers turn left to inspect the castle and to admire the view of Gréoux-les-Bains and the surrounding countryside.

From the chemin des Seigneuers take the narrow lane signposted with an arrow (C.P.2.3.) which climbs gradually (signpost "La Garenne", a house). The lane soon becomes a rough, stony track which climbs the hillside ahead. Remain

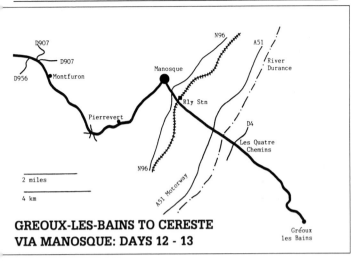

D907

D907

Montfuron

D956

N96

A51

Manosque

River
Durance

Rly Stn

D4

Pierrevert

Les Quatre
Chemins

N96

A51 Motorway

2 miles

4 km

**GREOUX-LES-BAINS TO CERESTE
VIA MANOSQUE: DAYS 12 - 13**

Gréoux
les Bains

on this main track, ignoring any side tracks, until reaching the main road (D82) where turn left. Walk along the road for almost a kilometre, ignoring tracks off to the left and right. Where the D82 swings to the right and Manosque comes into view, take a track heading downhill towards Manosque (the waymarking is unclear in this area). Remain on this track until it finally descends to a road (D82 again). Turn right for 20 metres and then left on another track; in another 20 metres turn left again on a track and in a further 50 metres take the right fork. This track soon ascends to buildings: keep to the track between the buildings and head downhill towards the sprawl of Manosque now seen clearly ahead. Descend to a road (D6) where turn left. A major crossroads is reached in 500 metres, ie. that of the D4, D6 and D907, named as "Les Quatre Chemins" on the map.

Cross over the D4 heading along the straight and busy D907 over the floor of the Durance valley towards Manosque. In just under a kilometre the road passes over the River Durance (fortunately there is a footpath on the road bridge). Continue straight on at the roundabout ahead and pass over the new motorway, the A51 (note that this Autoroute does not appear on maps produced prior to the late 1980s). Proceed ahead at the next roundabout signposted to Manosque. Continue ahead at the next crossroads, pass Le Provence, a hôtel-restaurant, and maintain direction over the bridge above the canal, heading into the heart of Manosque. The railway station is only a short detour (about 200 metres to the right) from the direct line of approach into the town (it is signposted as "Gare-SNCF"). The route leads eventually along the avenue Jean Giono and enters the old town through the Porte Saunerie.

121

DAY 13
MANOSQUE TO CERESTE (THE LUBERON)

DISTANCE: 12.8 MILES (20.5km)
TOTAL ASCENT: 1921ft (586m)
TOTAL DESCENT: 1705ft (520m)
TOTAL ESTIMATED TIME: 6 HOURS

	Height Above		Distance				Est. Time	
	Sea	Level	Sect.		Cum.		Sect.	Cum.
	ft	m	mile	km	mile	km	hr m	hr m
MANOSQUE	1147	350						
CHAPELLE SAINT-PANCRASSE	1459	445	1.1	1.7	1.1	1.7	0.30	0.30
PIERREVERT	1403	428	1.4	2.2	2.5	3.9	1.00	1.30
MONTFURON	2187	667	4.3	6.9	6.8	10.8	2.00	3.30
MONTJUSTIN	1803	550	3.5	5.6	10.3	16.4	1.30	5.00
CERESTE	1364	416	2.5	4.1	12.8	20.5	1.00	6.00

FACILITIES
Accommodation
Céreste:
1.   Hôtel l'Aiguebelle. A 2-star hôtel-restaurant. It is situated in the place de la République, set back from the main road.
2.   *Gîte d'étape*. This is in the rue du Bicentenaire, off the place de la Républic. If locked the key can be obtained from the reception at the Village de Vacances (see below and Appendix 1).There are the usual kitchen facilities, or meals may be taken at the l'Aiguebelle or at the Village de Vacances.
3.   Village de Vacances - Le Grand Lubéron. This complex is situated in the avenue des Plantiers, about 400 metres from the main road (follow the signs from the village centre). It may be possible to obtain a bed for the night here, although it is primarily intended for longer periods of stay. If permission is not given to stay, it may nevertheless be possible to take meals here whilst staying at the *gîte d'étape*.
Note that there is no possibility of accommodation between Manosque and Céreste.

Restaurants/Cafés/Bars
There is a bar and restaurant in Pierrevert. The food at the l'Aiguebelle in the place de la République in Céreste can be recommended.

Shops

There is a small *alimentation* in Pierrevert. There is an *épicerie, boulangerie, pâtisserie* and greengrocers in Céreste.

Public Transport

There is a bus service between Manosque and Avignon which stops in Céreste. The route to the west stops after Céreste at Apt, Bonnieux, Robion, Cavaillon and Avignon. The service, which operates twice a day, connects with the mainline train (SNCF) at both Cavaillon and Avignon. The journey time from Céreste to Avignon is approximately 1 hour 35 minutes. In the other direction the service continues past Manosque to Gréoux-les-Bains and on to Digne. There is also a bus service to picturesque Folcalquier, north of Manosque, the ancient capital of upper Provence. For further details contact Autocars Jauffred, avenue du Moulin-Neuf in Manosque (tel 92.72.40.58) or Autocars Villardo Bernard in Apt (tel. 90.74.36.10).

The bus stop in Céreste is located on the main road through the village. Note that an irregular bus service also stops in Montfuron.

Water

There is a water fountain in Pierrevert, which should be used to fill water bottles, as there is no further water available until reaching Céreste, where another fountain will be found in the high street.

Miscellaneous

Céreste has a bank (Crédit Agricole - open am and pm but closed on Mondays) and a post office (PTT). There is a small Office de Tourisme in the high street of Céreste (tel. 92.79.04.66).

SUMMARY

The Trail now pulls away from the Durance Valley and climbs into the celebrated Lubéron Regional Park, a land of wooded, sun-drenched hills and ridges, and ancient hill-top towns dating back to Roman times and beyond. It is ideal walkers' country which attracts ramblers from all over the world.

The walk out of Manosque is pleasant, in total contrast to the march along congested roads on the approach from the River Durance. The town is soon left behind for leafy lanes and tracks up to the Chapelle-de-Toutes-Aures dedicated to Saint Pancrasse, the patron saint of Manosque. The chapel is the site of an annual pilgrimage at Easter, during the local festival of "La Saucissonade". There are good views from up here of Manosque sprawling in the wide plain of the Durance valley, and of the approaching Lubéron hills.

The Trail continues towards the south-west, eventually climbing to the picturesque hill-top town of Pierrevert, where the restored church is well worth a quick visit: note the thirteenth-century portals. Pierrevert is now a small

Mechanical harvesting of grapes near Pierrevert

dormitory village of Manosque, and the home of a number of local artisans. The town is famous for its wines (the Pierrevert label will no doubt have been seen frequently in Manosque's restaurants) and the Trail passes through several of its vineyards before beginning a climb to the north-west through pine and oak woodland to skirt another hill-top town, that of Montfuron. On the ascent into these hills of the Lubéron there are extensive distant views back over the Durance valleys to the plains and mountains traversed a few days ago.

After Montfuron, where there is an interesting restored windmill, the Trail follows a long, moderately level ridge for several miles, heading westward to meet the Tour of the Lubéron, the GR 97, at Montjustin, yet another attractive hill-top village. The views to the south-west from this ridge are first-rate, over to the higher and longer crête of the Grand Lubéron, whose highest point, the Sommet de Mourre Nègre (3688ft; 1125m) which bears an enormous TV mast, should be discernible.

Céreste, on the N100, is a town of antiquarian interest. It was originally a Roman settlement called Cataiuca, the only remains of which, a small Roman bridge, is crossed on the GR 4 on the lane to Carluc (see Day 14). The town was of economic and strategic importance in that it lay on the Domitian Way, a major thoroughfare between Italy and Spain. Later it functioned as a staging post for pilgrims making their way into Spain to visit the shrine of Saint James at Compostella. Today the sad ruins of its chateau, the ancient fortified ramparts, and the narrow streets and tiny squares of its old quarter, make a picturesque scene. A stroll around the old town is recommended, perhaps following an itinerary suggested on a wall chart that should be found in the Village de Vacances. Include a visit to the tranquil Place de Verdun, in the very heart of the old town.

Céreste lies on the eastern shoulder of the Lubéron and is an ideal centre from which to explore the Lubéron Regional Park, particularly the high ridge of the Grand Lubéron, to the south-west.

ROUTE

Descend from the place du Terreau in the centre of Manosque to the boulevard Elemir Bourges. From here take the rue Leon Mure down to the place Doctor Caire. Cross the main road and ascend the Monté de Toutes-Aures, heading in a south-westerly direction. The first red/white waymarks since before Manosque will be encountered along this road. Follow the signs to the Chapelle-de-Toutes-Aures. Remain on this road ignoring any side turnings: it climbs and eventually becomes the chemin de Sant Brancaï which leads to the large chapel (also known as the Chapelle Saint-Pancrasse).

Take the track to the right of the chapel (note that there is a multitude of paths in this area, some waymarked with yellow paint stripes - it is important to take care, only following the route waymarked with red/white flashes - the waymarking is rather unclear hereabouts). Soon the village of Pierrevert is seen on the hill ahead. The route passes to the left of a large electricity pylon and under high tension cables. The path eventually crosses a water-chute to reach a poorly surfaced track where turn right. Follow the track downhill, turn right at a road and continue ahead at a crosstracks uphill on the Monté de la Calade to the picturesque village of Pierrevert.

Walk past the church to locate rue Osco Manosco. At the bottom of this road turn right on the rue du Quair which leads to the avenue Marius Grassi where turn right. Later turn right on the Traverse de la Croix Verte, but after 60 metres turn right downhill on the Montée de Camp Maurin. Remain on this lane to a T-junction with another minor road where turn left. This leads to the D6 road where turn left. After about 0.5km cross a bridge over a stream and 100 metres later turn right on a surfaced track, climbing steadily uphill towards the north-west. The famous Pierrevert vineyards are hereabouts and there are pleasant views of the tree covered hills ahead. After about a kilometre ignore a track off to the right (leading to La Blaque), but stay on the narrow gravel track ahead which begins to climb. Navigation is a little tricky in this region as there are many side tracks, tree felling is common and the waymarking is very poor. Endeavour to remain on the principal track heading generally to the north-west, and all should be well. The track climbs up through vineyards and pine and oak woods. The homestead of La Blaque should be seen over to the right whilst on this ascent. The stony track eventually becomes surfaced and at this point the village of Montfuron comes into view. The lane climbs to reach the church of this settlement, the second hill-top village of the day.

Do not enter the village but remain on the lane which skirts to the right of it, aiming towards the restored windmill. Continue past the windmill to a point where a road joins from the right. Ignore both roads here, but take a track between the two which descends gently downhill following a line of telegraph poles. This track becomes grassy after a while and leads to the road at the junction of the D907 and the D956. Turn left on the latter in the direction signposted to La Tour d'Aigues and Pertuis. Climb on this road for about 0.5km to a point at which the road swings to the left: here continue ahead on a dirt track. The route now follows a splendid ridge for about 3 miles (4.8km) with views of the distant wooded hills of the Lubéron and the fertile valley down to the left. Eventually the hill-top village of Montjustin comes into view on the right of the track. Nearing the village the GR 4 is joined by the GR 97 (Tour du Lubéron) which climbs up to the ridge from a lane on the left. The Trail does not enter Montjustin, but continues ahead on the track. Blue stripe waymarking accompanies the route in this region. The track eventually reaches a narrow lane. Here turn left and continue to an electrical transformer, where turn right down a track. Shortly leave this for a footpath to the left which skirts a house and reaches a main road, the N100, at the Chapelle Notre Dame-de-Pitié-de-Céreste. The GR 4 turns right at this point, but for Céreste and its facilities, turn left along the main road. This forms the High Street of the town, the centre of which is reached in about 400 metres.

Restored windmill at Montfuron

DAY 14
CERESTE TO VIENS, VIA THE OPPEDETTE GORGE

	DISTANCE:	11.4 MILES (18.3 km)
	TOTAL ASCENT:	2170ft (662m)
	TOTAL DESCENT:	1541ft (470m)
	TOTAL ESTIMATED TIME:	5 HOURS 10 MINUTES

	Height Above Sea Level		Distance				Est. Time	
			Sect.		Cum.		Sect.	Cum.
	ft	m	mile	km	mile	km	hr m	hr m
CERESTE	1364	416						
GRAND CARLUC	1511	461	2.0	3.2	2.0	3.2	0.50	0.50
SAINTE-CROIX-A-LAUZE	2026	618	2.9	4.6	4.9	7.8	1.20	2.10
OPPEDETTE	1639	500	2.8	4.5	7.7	12.3	1.10	3.20
(COURNILLE)	1442	440	2.0	3.2	9.7	15.5	1.00	4.20
VIENS	1993	608	1.7	2.8	11.4	18.3	0.50	5.10

OPTIONAL EXCURSIONS
A waymarked path along the western rim of the Oppedette Gorge can be followed, whilst the more adventurous can explore the bed of the gorge (see text for details).

ALTERNATIVE ROUTE FROM OPPEDETTE TO SAULT
A more direct, but less interesting route follows the GR 4 north-west from Oppedette to Sault. The route is as follows: Oppedette - Ferme de Chaloux - Simiane-la-Rotonde - Ferme du Château du Bois - Lagarde d'Apt - Berre - Croix de la Lavande (possible link with described route) - junction with GR 9 (where the route described in this book is rejoined) - Signal de la Peine - Sault.

The route (from Oppedette to the point where it rejoins the described footpath south of the Signal de la Peine) is approximately 19 miles (30.6km) in length (about 9 hours walking) and involves around 2500ft (763m) of ascent. However, this shorter route covers less ground in the Lubéron Regional Park, and in particular omits two of the most attractive features in the area, the Oppedette Gorges and the Provençal Colorado. Walkers with sufficient time available are strongly advised to take the described route.

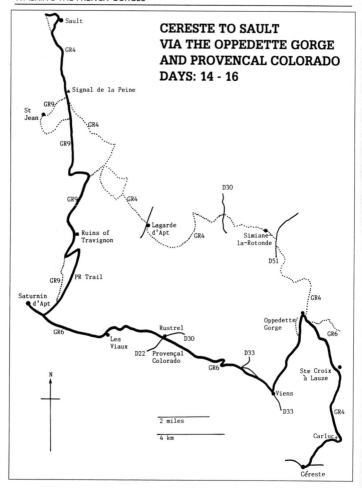

**CERESTE TO SAULT
VIA THE OPPEDETTE GORGE
AND PROVENCAL COLORADO
DAYS: 14 - 16**

FACILITIES
Accommodation

There are two possibilities:

1.   Le Petit Jardin, the café-restaurant opposite the Portail in Viens offers rooms for the night. Ask here also for the possibility of a *chambre d'hôte* in the village.

2.   The *gîte d'étape* in the hamlet of Cournille. This is a slight detour off-route, but is very convenient for those wishing to make further explorations into the

The tranquil River Verdon at Gréoux-les-Bains (Day 11)
The Oppedette Gorge (Day 14)

Rock formations in the Provençal Colorado (Day 15)
On the ridge leading to the summit of Mont Ventoux (Day 17)

Oppedette Gorge. The accommodation here is very pleasant, somewhat more luxurious than is normally expected in a *gîte d'étape*. There is an excellent view from the *gîte* over to the hill-top town of Viens.

There are two *Gîtes de France* in Oppedette, but it is unlikly that these can be used for a stay of only one night. For those continuing on the GR 4 from Oppedette (ie. not following the route described in this book - see alternative route above) there is a *gîte d'étape* at Chaloux (2 miles; 3.2km) north of Oppedette.

Restaurants/Cafés/Bars
The café in Oppedette, next to the church, usually also provides snack meals on request. Meals are not always available at the *gîte d'étape* at Cournille, in which case those staying overnight will either have to make use of the kitchen facilities at the *gîte*, or else make a long excursion to Viens for the Petit Jardin restaurant.

Shops
There is a small shop and post office in Viens. Oppedette also has a post office.

Public Transport
An irregular local bus service stops in Viens (enquire at Le Petit Jardin).

SUMMARY
A relatively short stage today, allowing plenty of time for the two highlights of the walk, the ruins of the priory of Carluc, north-east of Céreste, and the gorges of Oppedette to the south of the village of the same name.

The ruins of Carluc Priory occupy a romantic setting in a wood beside a running stream. The Priory was founded in the eleventh century, and by 1116 came under the jurisdiction of the abbot of Montmajour, a large abbey near Arles. Following the religious wars of the sixteenth century the Priory was abandoned and the buildings soon fell to ruins. It has been partly restored by a largely voluntary organisation, the Friends of the Priory of Carluc. The society cares for the historical monument, but has considerable problems in preventing the surrounding woods and undergrowth from invading the site. The Priory complex must have been very extensive when the community was at its height, but the only section which remains standing today is the apse of the main church: note the capitals carved with animal and vegetable motifs. The charnel house contained the bones of venerable martyrs *(Ossuaire de Carluc)* and the stone tombs on the floor are rather strange. The scallop shells of the pilgrims of Santiago de Compostella have been discovered here carved into the rock.

Easy walking along tracks and minor lanes in pleasant wooded country leads to the outskirts of the village known as Sainte-Croix-à-Lauze, the name relating to the calcareous roof tiles (Lauzes) which adorn the old houses. The lavender fields scattered about the hillside below the village create an attractive rural setting. The GR 4 does not enter Sainte-Croix-à-Lauze, but it is only a short detour to visit its Romanesque church and see the eighteenth-century iron gates guarding the entrance to the manor house.

The GR 4 continues to the north to meet and join another long distance trail, the GR 6, just before the village of Oppedette. Up until now the Trail from Grasse has followed, with a few minor diversions, the GR 4. This trail continues to the north-west to Simiane-la-Rotonde and Lagarde d'Apt, eventually following a long ridge over the Signal de la Peine to reach Sault. In so doing it moves north of the Lubéron and avoids two of the most scenic and interesting features in the whole area, the Oppedette Gorges and the Provençal or Rustrel Colorado. In order to include an exploration of these areas, the route described in this book leaves the GR 4 at Oppedette and instead takes the GR 6 south along the eastern rim of the Oppedette Gorges and on to the hill-top town of Viens. Here it changes direction to head west through the Colorado region to Rustrel and then to Saint Saturnin d'Apt on the River Calavon. This is a suitable town to spend the night before leaving the GR 6 to climb out of the valley of the Calavon over the mountains to the north, making use of both local trails and yet another GR route, the GR 9. The GR 4 is finally rejoined near the Signal de la Peine. By following this GR 6/GR 9 route, the walker is, as it were, following two sides of a triangle, rather than the one side of the GR 4.

Several viewpoints for peering down into the deep, steep-sided, canyon are passed during the well waymarked walk along the eastern rim of the Oppedette Gorges on the GR 6. These most impressive limestone gorges would perhaps be far better known if it were not for big brother Verdon to the east. In a land so rich in spectacular gorges, those of Oppedette have been somewhat overlooked by the general tourist. There should be ample time available to explore both rims of the gorge, if desired, and even delve, with care, into the bottom of the Gorge. Brief details of the various possibilities for exploring the gorges are given at the end of the route description.

On leaving the rim of the Oppedette Gorges and walking south on the D155, the walker will cross, at the farmstead of Grosse Blaque, the boundary between the département of the Alpes-de-Haute Provence and that of the Vaucluse. From this point until the Rhône Valley the walk traverses the hill country of the Vaucluse.

Viens is another attractive hill-top Provençal village. The church is larger than that at Oppedette and is worth a short visit.

ROUTE

Return along the N100 to the Chapelle Notre Dame-de-Pitié-de-Céreste. Just before reaching the chapel turn left at a GR 4 signpost to the Prieuré de Carluc. Follow this lane, the avenue du Pont Romain, and look over the left shoulder for a fine view back to old Céreste. After crossing the small but well preserved Roman bridge, turn left on a poorly surfaced track signposted to Carluc. Turn

Walkers relaxing at the café in Oppedette

right at a T-junction and follow the surfaced lane to the ruins of the Priory.

Just after the Priory turn left on the dirt track that passes behind the small car park. Ignore a track on the right in a few hundred metres, continuing ahead on the track until a lane is reached. Here turn right, pass the drive up to La Pourraque and continue ahead on a gravel track that follows a line of telegraph wires, descending to cross a small bridge over the Grand Vallat (usually dry). About 40 metres after the bridge, where the lane swings sharply to the left, continue ahead uphill on a dirt track. This leads to a lane to the right of a building. Turn right but in 30 metres turn left to climb on another track for over a mile to the outskirts of Sainte-Croix-à-Lauze.

The GR 4 does not enter the village, but on reaching the road at the roadsign Sainte-Croix-à-Lauze, take the higher of the two roads to the left, passing to the right of the madonna. Climb on this track as it bends to the right, ignoring the path ahead at this point. Continue the climb, later ignoring a track off to the left, and remaining on the main track ahead passing through lavender fields. The track eventually begins to descend towards the village of Oppedette and the eponymous gorges which, together with the Lubéron mountains, form the view ahead and to the left. The track becomes a surfaced lane near the buildings of the Grand Blanc. Continue downhill on this snaking road. Farther down, where the road bends to the right, walk ahead on a rough dirt/grass track heading for a concrete pylon. This track continues to a small shrine and a transformer and pylon, where turn left. The picturesque village of Oppedette now soon comes into view. The path runs parallel with the road, eventually joining it just above Oppedette. Turn left to descend into the village.

Leave Oppedette from the communal washing area following the GR 6 sign to climb above the village. Keep to the right of the cemetery, soon reaching the edge of the gorge. Here keep to the path going towards the left. The gorges can be observed from several viewpoints along this rim. The path meanders through woodland to emerge on a road. Cross this to continue on the GR 6 (good waymarking in this area). When the path reaches the road a second time turn left but after a few hundred metres leave the road on the right (GR 6 sign on a tree) onto a narrow footpath which keeps to the rim of the gorge before emerging for the last time at the road (D155) by a small bridge. Turn right along the road. In about 700 metres a narrow lane on the right is passed. This leads up in 200 metres to the *gîte d'étape* at the hamlet of Cournille. This is a convenient place to stay whilst exploring the Oppedette Gorges further. However, the Trail continues along the road to the village of Viens seen on the hilltop ahead.

Continue on the D155 until a large, ruined chapel is reached on the left-hand side. A few metres farther, when the road crosses a bridge, immediately turn right on the road climbing the hill towards Viens. When directly below the village, and where the road swings to the left, take a footpath on the right which climbs through trees up to Viens. Turn left on meeting a track at a T-junction, and continue to the road by the church, where turn right to enter the village.

The Oppedette Gorge

There are a number of possibilities for exploring the gorges further. The *gîte d'étape* at Cournille is a good base from which to make these excursions.

1.   Western Rim. At the small bridge on the D155 about 700 metres north of the lane leading to Cournille (referred to in the text above) a footpath, waymarked with blue single paint stripes, leads north along the western rim of the gorge. Like the GR 6 on the opposite rim, this provides excellent views of the gorges.

2.   Valley floor of the Gorge from the south. Also from the bridge on the D155 at a point where cars are often parked, a track leads down to the bed of the Gorge. Pass under the bridge and follow a path along the bottom of the Gorge. This trail is waymarked, rather infrequently, with red arrows. However, this route is difficult to traverse in places and should certainly not to be attempted in wet conditions, or by the inexperienced.

3.   Valley floor of the Gorge from the north. There is a very steep path down into the Gorge from one of the viewpoints on the GR 6, just to the south of Oppedette. Note that the author has not attempted this route: it is very steep and probably has a loose surface, so great care would be necessary. Again it should not be attempted by the inexperienced or by anyone in poor weather conditions.

DAY 15
VIENS TO SAINT SATURNIN D'APT
VIA THE PROVENCAL COLORADO

DISTANCE:	12.5 MILES (20km)
TOTAL ASCENT:	426ft (130m)
TOTAL DESCENT:	1206ft (368m)
TOTAL ESTIMATED TIME:	5 HOURS 5 MINUTES

| | Height Above Sea Level | | Distance | | | | Est. Time | |
	Sea ft	Level m	Sect. mile	km	Cum. mile	km	Sect. hr m	Cum. hr m
VIENS	1993	608						
PROVENCAL COLORADO	1475	450	3.1	5.0	3.1	5.0	1.15	1.15
RUSTREL	1344	410	3.1	5.0	6.2	10.0	1.15	2.30
LES VIAUX	1049	320	2.5	4.0	8.7	14.0	1.00	3.30
GR 6 / GR 9 JUNCTION	1082	330	2.4	3.8	11.1	17.8	1.00	4.30
SAINT SATURNIN D'APT	1213	370	1.4	2.2	12.5	20.0	0.35	5.05

ALTERNATIVE ROUTE
See note under Day 14.

FACILITIES
Accommodation
Rustrel: Auberge de Rustreou: 3, place de la Fête (tel. 90.74.24.120). A Logis de France. There were tentative plans for a *gîte d'étape* in or near Rustrel, which might have materialised by the time of your visit.
Saint Saturnin d'Apt: There are two hôtels: 1) The Hôtel des Voyageurs (tel. 90.75.42.08). The owner is a keen walker. 2). Auberge Saint Hubert (tel. 90.75.42.02).

There is a campsite about 1.2 miles (2km) to the south-west of Rustrel, on the south side of the road to Apt (D22). The GR 6 (after the point at which it is left on this itinerary) passes by a campsite, about 1km south of the centre of Saint Saturnin d'Apt, near to the small lake, the Etang de la Bruyère.

Restaurants/Cafés/Bars
The Auberge de Rustreou in Rustrel is a hôtel-restaurant serving meals to non-residents. There are also two cafés/bars in Rustrel. There are cafés and a restaurant in Saint Saturnin d'Apt.

Shops
Rustrel has an *épicerie,* but the author was unable to buy bread in the town (it is baked here, but there is a reluctance to sell it to outsiders - this fact has been noted by others). Saint Saturnin d'Apt has an *épicerie* and a *boulangerie.* There are post offices in both Rustrel and Saint Saturnin d'Apt.

Public Transport
There is an irregular bus service to Avignon which stops in the towns of Rustrel and Saint Saturnin d'Apt.

Water
There is a water fountain in Rustrel and another good source of water, drawn by an interesting handpump, in the hamlet of Les Viaux.

SUMMARY
The day's walk is not a particularly long or arduous one, thus allowing plenty of time to explore the Rustrel Colorado, a unique area of France. Some care in navigation will be required in the Colorado area, although straying from the actual line of the route would have few consequences as a route to Rustrel should be found after a little more wandering, which would in any case provide a greater intimacy with this bizarre area. Apart from this highlight, there should also be time to relax in a café or restaurant in Rustrel before continuing along the GR 6 along tracks and minor lanes to the town of Saint Saturnin d'Apt at the northern end of a wide valley, immediately beneath the high wooded hills of the Vaucluse to the north. The town is overlooked by the ruins of its old castle. Both the Romanesque chapel and the fifteenth-century upper gate of the old town walls are worth a quick visit. There is a good view of the surrounding Apt countryside and the Lubéron range from the chapel.

If time is available, transport should be sought to the larger town of Apt, about 9km (5.6miles) to the south, where there are Roman remains and a cathedral to visit, as well as the possibility of a guided tour of the confectionery factory: Apt is renowned for its glacé fruits (orchards of cherry, pear and plum trees, which provide the basic material, will have been passed on today's walk to Saint Saturnin d'Apt).

Rustrel
The street names in Rustrel are interesting in that they are given in both French and Langue d'Oc, the ancient Provençal language. This tongue was derived from the vulgar Latin introduced by the Romans and is distinguished from classical or northern French by the richness of its vowel sounds. This Romance language has had something of a revival in the last hundred years, following its promotion by intellectuals and poets such as Frédéric Mistral. It is seen as a symbol of the pride and independence of the Provençal people.

Rustrel Colorado

The area to the south and east of Rustrel on the southern side of the Dôa valley is known as the Provençal Colorado, a reference to the coloured rock formations that are such a prominent feature of the landscape. The name Rustrel is derived from the word for red, the predominant hue in the multiple layers of rock that make up the formations. The area was once mined extensively for ochre dyes. There is evidence of ochre mining in prehistoric times, but the operation was at its height during the latter half of the nineteenth and the early part of the twentieth centuries. The business ran out of commercial markets with the introduction of modern synthetic dyes, with the result that production rapidly declined until the mines, together with those near Roussillon to the west of Apt, finally closed in the late 1950s. The mining activities have exposed many of the rock faces to good effect, and the walker can enjoy them in peace since they are some way from the nearest road and consequently, unlike the ochre mines near Roussillon, are not the focus of much tourist attention. The colours of the multiple strata range from white or very pale yellow, through numerous shades of orange and brown to deep red. The dyes were popular because they did not fade with sunlight and gave a large range of colours: up to seventeen ochre tints were quarried in the region. Take care not to get the ochre dust on your clothing as it is very difficult to remove, even with persistent washing.

ROUTE

From the little square in Viens take the road signposted to Simiane, Banon and Apt. Opposite the Portail (gate) follow the road to Banon, the D33. Remain on this balcony road, with excellent views to the right, for a about a kilometre, after which bear left on a grassy track (blue waymarks in addition to the red/white). This rejoins the road at a bend in the latter after another kilometre. Turn left, ignore the first road on the left after 20 metres, but after 40 metres turn left on a gravel track. Descend on this track, ignoring a right fork in a couple of hundred metres. After about another kilometre it is important to locate a narrow path on the right - this is easily missed. It descends through trees, but soon reaches a road at a rather awkward rock step. Do not take the track opposite, but turn right downhill on the road.

Shortly after passing a house and vineyard on the left, turn sharp left on a track. The Trail is now entering the Provençal Colorado region. Note the ochre rock formations on the right. Remain on the main track which later swings sharply to the right to provide a balcony path with first-rate views down to the Colorado formations. Keep to the right-hand edge of a vineyard on a sandy path until at the far corner locate a thin, sandy path descending through the trees. This narrow path emerges at a junction of tracks by a field edge. Here turn right to follow the left-hand edge of a field. Note that in this area, which traverses private land including vineyards, there are several waymarked paths forming a number of local walks (purple and yellow waymarking). Care is required to follow the correct line of the GR trail. Twenty metres after entering trees leave the main track by taking a path on the left. This narrow path descends to a track: cross over this to continue ahead on a track which soon becomes a narrow path which descends between rock formations. The route winds through this rather bizarre area of different coloured sandstones on narrow sandy paths. It is essential to follow the red/white waymarkings very carefully. The route eventually leads to a track where turn right. Remain on this sandy track passing melon fields and heading for the small town of Rustrel now seen ahead, until a lane is reached opposite a house on a bend. Turn left along the minor road for 550 metres before turning right on another lane which continues to the main road, the D22. Cross over to follow the surfaced track ahead to the D30A, where turn left to enter Rustrel

Walk west out of the village passing the château and *mairie,* and onto a wide gravel track. Where this forks take the left-hand branch downhill. Continue on this balcony track, with fine views over to the left (note the château on the plain below) to a junction of three paths. Take the centre path and climb over rough ground to reach a track where turn left. On reaching a road (signpost "La Gavotte") turn right uphill. Where this road (D34) bends to the right, follow a track off to the left and continue to another road (D179) where cross over to head for the buildings of Les Viaux. Pass through the hamlet to reach the D214 where turn right. Remain on this road, heading to the west towards Saint Saturnin d'Apt, for over 2 kilometres (1.2 miles). Continue ahead at a crossroads (Villars to the left and Les Grands Cléments to the right). Soon reach another road where turn right, but in 20 metres turn left on a dirt track. Turn left on the D179. In 400 metres reach the road junction with the D111A (left to Apt). The GR 9 and our Trail turns to the right here to head north over the mountains, but if seeking accommodation in Saint Saturnin d'Apt, continue ahead for just over a mile to enter the town.

DAY 16
SAINT SATURNIN D'APT TO SAULT
(TRAVERSE OF THE VAUCLUSE MOUNTAINS)

DISTANCE:	15.8 MILES (25.5km)
TOTAL ASCENT:	2764ft (843m)
TOTAL DESCENT:	1419ft (433m)
TOTAL ESTIMATED TIME:	7 HOURS 25 MINUTES

	Height Above Sea Level		Distance				Est. Time	
	Sea ft	Level m	Sect. mile	km	Cum. mile	km	Sect. hr m	Cum. hr m
SAINT SATURNIN D'APT	1213	370						
GR 6 / GR9 JUNCTION	1082	330	1.4	2.2	1.4	2.2	0.30	0.30
TRAVIGNON (RUINS)	3055	932	4.5	7.2	5.9	9.4	3.00	3.30
GR 9 / GR 4 JUNCTION	3367	1027	6.1	9.9	12.0	19.3	2.30	6.00
SIGNAL DE LA PEINE	3472	1059	0.7	1.2	12.7	20.5	0.20	6.20
SAULT	2557	780	3.1	5.0	15.8	25.5	1.10	7.25

ALTERNATIVE ROUTES
1. A more direct route to Travignon to that described below (which makes use of a PR trail) is to follow the GR 9 all the way from its junction with the D179, east of Saint Saturnin d'Apt. This would save about 1.2 miles (2km) of trail (about 30 minutes) but is somewhat less interesting than the route described.
2. The route of the GR 9 from Travignon, described here, passes to within 800m of the GR 4 at the Croix de la Lavande. The GR 4 can be reached at the "croix" by climbing on a link path from Savouillon, heading north-east. The GR 4 descends to the north-east from the Croix de la Lavande, before turning north-west to pass the building of Ballegros and attain the ridge leading to the Signal de la Peine. This is a very fine ridge walk. The distance is approximately the same as that on the GR 9 described below.

OPTIONAL DETOUR
Those wanting *gîte d'étape* accommodation rather than a hôtel in Sault may wish to descend to the village of Saint Jean-de-Sault in the valley to the west of the ridge leading to the Signal de la Peine. This can be achieved either by taking the minor road descending first to the hamlet of Les Molières, or by turning left on the GR 9 a few hundred metres before reaching La Peine. However, the *gîte d'étape* in Saint Jean, the old schoolhouse, is very basic. After a night in the *gîte* the route can be regained by reascending on the GR 9 the 777ft (237m) to the GR 4, south of La Peine. The total detour takes 1¹/₂ to 2 hours.

PROFILE 4 - SAINT SATURNIN D'APT TO MALAUCENE (MONT VENTOUX): DAYS 16 - 18

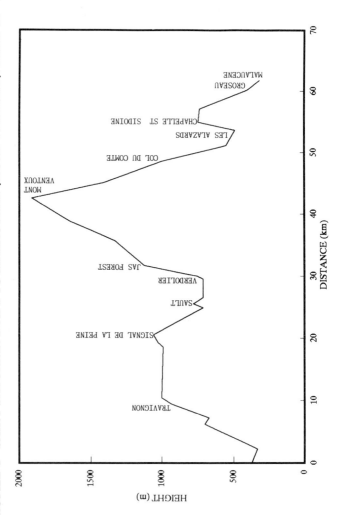

FACILITIES

Accommodation

The stage finishes at Sault where there are several hôtels. The 2-star Hôtel du Louvre in the main square is convenient. Try also the Hôtel du Deffends (route Saint Trinité, tel. 90.64.01.41) or the Hôtel Signoret (tel. 90.64.00.45). There is a Camping Municipal (tel. 90.64.02.30).

Those preferring *gîte d'étape* accommodation will find it in Saint Jean-de-Sault, which is reached by a considerable detour (and descent and reascent) from the ridge above the Sault valley. It has the distinction of being the poorest *gîte d'étape* that the author has ever spent the night at (it is very "atmospheric": considerable courage is required to sleep there alone on a dark and stormy night, when the wind is howling through the broken windows!).

A simple and very dirty refuge will be found amongst the ruins of Travignon. It would be most welcome in bad weather, but otherwise would certainly not be a comfortable or pleasant place to spend the night (unless it is considerably restored). There is a table and two benches inside the building. There is a good level area at Travignon suitable for wild camping, although water could well be a problem (see below).

There are *gîtes ruraux* in the hamlet of Savouillon, between Travignon and the Signal de la Peine, but it is unlikely that permission would be given to spend just one night there.

Finally, the Restaurant Les Lavandes at Monieux, on the D942 south-west of Sault, has a *dortoir;* this can be reached on foot along the GR 9, and is convenient for those wishing to visit the Nesque Gorges.

Restaurants/Cafés/Bars

Sault has several cafés and restaurants (eg. the Café de la Promenade). Choose a balcony café looking out towards Mont Ventoux; the mountain seems but a stone's throw away, but considerable toil will be expended to reach its summit. There is a small café/bar in Saint Jean-de-Sault (from where the key to the *gîte d'étape* can be obtained).

Shops

Sault has food shops of all types, including two small supermarkets. There is a bank, post office and small tourist office here also. Note that no shop or place of refreshment will be found on the route described between Saint Saturnin d'Apt and Sault, unless the detour to Saint Jean-de-Sault is taken.

Public Transport

A bus service operates between Sault, Villes-sur-Auzon, Mormoiron, Mazan, Sarrians, Pernes-les-Fountaines and Carpentras (connection to Avignon for the mainline train service). For further details contact Les Cars Comtadins, tel. 90.67.20.25.

Water

This is a long stage, involving a considerable amount of ascent in fairly remote country, so plenty of water should be carried at the outset. Note that the large water supply at Travignon is stagnant and probably undrinkable. There are water fountains in Sault.

SUMMARY

The day starts with a long climb up into the mountains of the Vaucluse to the north. It is an area of lonely but beautiful, steep wooded hillsides. An early start is recommended to avoid climbing in the heat of the midday sun. The route described below makes use of a PR trail in the early stages of the ascent, but those wanting a slightly shorter alternative can take the GR 9 all the way from Saint Saturnin d'Apt.

By taking the described PR route a *borie* will be passed. These drystone huts are a feature of this part of France, particularly in the Lubéron hills and on the Vaucluse Plateau. One or two stories high, the *bories* were homes for shepherds and the like from the Iron Age until the eighteenth century, but now are mainly used as sheep pens or to store equipment. They are circular, oval or rectangular in shape, generally having just one entrance and a domed roof. There are reckoned to be over 3000 of these buildings in the Vaucluse, several of them built together in "villages". They were built from stone found on the spot, and maintained a fairly constant temperature inside during both summer and winter. Similar buildings are found in the Ardèche where they are known as *capitelles,* in the Velay *(chibottes)*, Quercy *(cayrons)* and in the Bourgogne *(cadoles).*

On nearing the top of the Vaucluse Plâteau the Trail passes the picturesque, but sad ruins of Travignon, a hamlet high up on the hillside overlooking the Apt valley way below. The encroaching vegetation is slowly engulfing the ruins, which have now almost reached the stage where they are almost part of the natural landscape. Travignon is a place for rest and reflection. This settlement has encountered the same fate as so many of the mountain communities in southern Europe in the twentieth century, following depopulation, the loss of traditional skills and occupations, and with a large exodus to the towns and cities for employment. Another abandoned hamlet will be passed later in the Ardèche (see Day 23).

Once on the Vaucluse Plâteau the first sighting will be made of Mont Ventoux with its large summit tower, the highest peak in Provence, and a mountain that will dominate the landscape and the walk for the next few days. The route continues towards the north, eventually rejoining the GR 4 for a final ridge walk into Sault. The route described below follows the GR 9 over the Collet de Travignon, past the hamlet of Savouillon and the farmstead of Castelet with its lavender fields, to climb to meet the GR 4 just to the south of the rounded summit of the Signal de la Peine. From here there is a fine view of the ever beckoning Mont Ventoux to the north-west, and over the treeless, undulating
140

Plâteau d'Albion to the east. It would be equally feasible to join the GR 4 a few miles earlier at the Croix de la Lavande, another fine viewpoint (for details see "alternative route 2" above, and the "route" section below). Wherever the GR 4 is rejoined it is to be followed from now on until the end of the journey at Langogne, with the possible exception of taking the GR 9 once again to avoid the summit of Mont Ventoux (see Day 17).

Sault and the Nesque Gorges

Sault stands high on a rock on the edge of the Vaucluse Plâteau. A pleasant market town, it is well situated for views of Mont Ventoux. The peak looks deceptively close from here, but it is in fact 16.2 miles (26km) from Sault to the summit by road. Furthermore the peak lies over 3700ft (1129m) above the height of the town. Sault has a reputation for its fine *saucisson* which can be bought in its several *charcutéries*. The fairly tranquil town comes to life on its market days, especially at the times of its principal market fairs, held once every three months. Many of Sault's inhabitants work in the lavender processing industry: one of the main factories is passed on leaving the town on the approach to Mont Ventoux. The scent that often pervades the town as a result of the activities of these lavender mills is extremely pleasant. The twelfth-century Romanesque church and a small museum (Roman and Celtic remains) are the main places of interest for the visitor.

Unfortunately the Trail does not visit the Nesque Gorges, which are a few miles to the south-west of Sault. However, those with a day to spare are recommended to make the excursion to visit them - a convenient place to stay is the dortoir at Monieux near the entrance to the Gorge (see "Facilities"). The River Nesque, a tributary of the River Sorgue, is dry for much of the summer, but nevertheless over the eons has carved a most impressive gorge. The D942 between Sault and Carpentas runs along the entire length of the gorge, a considerable feat of engineering. The main viewpoint is at the highest point of the road, about 7 miles (11.3km) from Sault. From here there is a view of the 1300ft (397m) high Rocher du Cire, an immense crag whose sheer face plunges straight down to the river. The rock, which inspired the poet Frédéric Mistral to verse, is the home of many colonies of bees: in bygone days the men of Monieux were said to climb the rock to retrieve honey.

ROUTE

Return to the GR 9 at the junction of the D179 and D111A, 1.4 miles (2.2km) to the east-south-east of Saint Saturnin d'Apt. Turn left (north) on the GR 9. Follow the track past a house and continue to a crosstracks (telegraph and electricity cables and pylons) where turn right, heading a little east of north following a line of electricity cables. The GR 4 red/white waymarking is poor in this area. When the track divides, take the right fork, well waymarked with green paint "dots" and blue stripes. You have now left the GR route but are instead following a PR trail. Climb, keeping to the right of a field (cherry trees) to reach an enclosed footpath. Continue the climb, eventually reaching a track. Follow the green dots and blue stripes which are quite numerous. The Trail, although obvious, is rather narrow and overgrown with bushes in a few places. The path passes just to the right of an interesting shepherd's shelter *(borie)* with a conical, domed roof. Where the track divides take the left fork downhill (no waymarking at this point) to cross over to the other ridge of the mountain. The path turns left at the bottom to cross the ravine and then follows a more or less contouring route (still waymarked in green and blue) heading generally in a south-westerly direction, until it eventually meets the GR 9 (at the letter "n" of the word "Mon" on the 1:50000 map). At this point turn right uphill, now following the red/white markings of the GR, as well as the blue stripes and green dots.

Climb steeply on the GR 9, heading a little to the east of north along the ridge. The Trail eventually reaches a T-junction of paths: here turn right continuing uphill. The path zig-zags up to the ruins of Travignon, a small hamlet built high up on the hillside. Climb past the buildings to reach the water source once so vital for this community. Follow the GR waymarks still climbing, but soon continuing along a track enclosed by pine trees. At a clearing the route bends to the right to enter trees again. Emerge at a track T-junction at another clearing. Turn right and keep ahead at another clearing where there are slanting crosstracks. Pass a small memorial to a French Resistance fighter who was killed at this point in 1944. Continue on this track through the forest until, a few hundred metres after the hamlet of Savouillon comes into view on the left, a surfaced lane is reached. From this point it is possible to climb to the north-east to regain the GR 4 in 0.8km, at the Croix de la Lavande (see "alternative route No. 2" above).

However, the GR 9 turns left along the lane, passing the access road to Savouillon. Mont Ventoux with its summit tower is now visible in the distance ahead. After almost a mile (1.6km) along this lane look for a track through pine trees leaving the road on the right. Keep on this track ignoring turns to the left and right. When the track emerges into an open area continue ahead until reaching the edge of a lavender field. Turn right heading towards the buildings of the farm of Le Castelet. Swing to the left about 250 metres before the farmhouse, heading north, aiming for the peak of Mont Ventoux in the distance. On reaching the edge of a field turn right, continuing to a surfaced lane where turn left heading north again. This lane eventually reaches a crossroads, with a track to the right and a lane on the left. Continue ahead. The GR 9 leaves this lane when it bends to the left. Those wishing to visit Saint Jean-de-Sault in the valley below to the west, or spend the night in the *gîte d'étape* should leave the Trail here (see below for a description of the route down to Saint Jean-de-Sault and for an alternative trail back onto the ridge to rejoin the GR 4 south of La Peine).

Turn right off the lane up a gravel track near to an electricity pylon (near "point 992" on the 1:50000 IGN map). This rejoins the GR 4 on the ridge in 600 metres. Turn left heading north to resume the GR 4. After 900 metres the path passes the GR 9 ascending on the left from Saint Jean-de-Sault (Saint Jean-de-

Lavender field near Le Castelet on the GR9

Durfort). Here is a comprehensive GR signpost. Climb to the summit of La Peine (3472ft; 1059m). Note the surveying point here. Pass to the left of the buildings on the summit and continue on the track heading for the wide Sault valley seen below. The track enters trees and descends gradually. Remain on this main track ignoring a track to the right when much lower down. Lower still be sure to take a right fork and continue the descent. The track finally ends at the D943, less than a kilometre south of Sault. If continuing on the GR 4/9 then take the lane opposite heading north-west (this connects with the route described at La Loge - see Day 17). However, for Sault turn right along the main road (this is in fact part of a GR route, the GR 91C). The road crosses the river, La Croc, to reach a T-junction with the D942. Cross and take the road signposted "l'Hôpital" (hospital). After a short distance turn sharp right on a cobbled, partly stepped track which climbs to the old town of Sault. Walk along the rue Porte Sainte Anne to enter the town.

Detour to Saint Jean-de-Sault

Where the GR 9 ascends a gravel track at "point 992" (see above) remain on the lane as it descends to the valley. At the T-junction with the D230 turn right. Mont Ventoux now seems deceptively close. The road first enters Les Courtois. The GR 9 soon comes in from the left: follow this to meet the D943. Cross this main road to follow the red/white markings along an old lane. The lane soon becomes an unsurfaced track which leads in 300 metres to the buildings of Saint Jean-de-Sault.

From the village cross the main road and follow the track (GR 9) signposted to La Peine (1 hour) and Sault (2 hours). Just before the first house (Les Nouveaux) turn left to climb steeply on a narrow footpath to regain the ridge. The path levels out to pass to the right of farm buildings (La Tour) to pick up a track which leads to the top of the ridge at 3400ft (1037m) where there is a GR 9/GR 4 signpost. Turn left to resume the GR 4 to Sault.

DAY 17
SAULT TO THE STATION DE SKI DU MONT SEREIN
(ASCENT OF MONT VENTOUX)

DISTANCE: 12.8 MILES (20.6km)
TOTAL ASCENT: 4072ft (1242m)
TOTAL DESCENT: 2072ft (632m)
TOTAL ESTIMATED TIME: 6 HOURS 5 MINUTES

| | Height Above | | Distance | | | | Est. Time | |
| | Sea | Level | Sect. | | Cum. | | Sect. | Cum. |
	ft	m	mile	km	mile	km	hr m	hr m
SAULT	2557	780						
VERDOLIER	2472	754	2.8	4.5	2.8	4.5	1.10	1.10
JAS FOREST	3691	1126	1.1	1.7	3.9	6.2	0.50	2.00
TETE DE LA GRAVE	5396	1646	4.4	7.1	8.3	13.3	1.40	3.40
MONT VENTOUX SUMMIT	6268	1912	2.4	3.8	10.7	17.1	1.10	4.50
ABRI DU CONTRAT	4632	1413	1.5	2.5	12.2	19.6	1.00	5.50
STATION DE SKI								
DU MONT SEREIN	4557	1390	0.6	1.0	12.8	20.6	0.15	6.05

ALTERNATIVE ROUTE

For those who cannot face the long climb to the summit of Mont Ventoux there is an alternative path, the GR 9 again, which contours in the woodland to the north of the long summit ridge of the mountain, eventually rejoining the route described, at the foot of the zig-zags, to the east of the Abri du Contrat. However, it is only to be recommended in poor weather conditions when the outstanding summit view would not be on display and when an attempt on the summit could be dangerous. When the mistral is blowing the summit route should certainly be avoided.

FACILITIES
Accommodation

The stage ends at the ski station of Mont Serein, on the northern slopes of Mont Ventoux. Although this is predominantly a winter resort, accommodation should be found here during the summer months as well. Some of the hôtels only open during the winter, but the Chalet Hôtel Liotard (tel. 90.63.08.01) is generally open all year. There are also *chambres d'hôte* in Mont Serein. Accommodation is likely to be most scarce during the periods between the skiing season and the main summer season, ie. during the late spring and

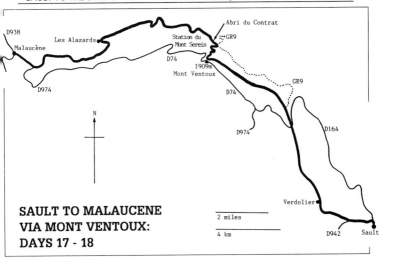

**SAULT TO MALAUCENE
VIA MONT VENTOUX:
DAYS 17 - 18**

autumn. During the main holiday season the hôtels in Mont Serein should be open, but even then there is the possibility of finding these fully occupied. If in doubt check first by telephone or at the *Office du Tourisme* in Sault.

The Abri du Contrat beneath the summit of Mont Ventoux and near to the road leading to Mont Serein, would be most welcome in bad weather, but is unsuitable for an overnight stop. It is a fairly modern building, but quite small. There is a concrete seating area (room for 2 to 3 seated) and a fireplace. When the author visited the refuge the building was home to a family of mice!

Those who are not carrying a tent and who fail to gain accommodation at Mont Serein are in quite a predicament, as the nearest place for an overnight stop from here is probably Malaucène (see day 18). Only the very fittest and experienced long distance mountain walker could expect to traverse the mountain from Sault to Malaucène in one day, and even then it would require a very early start and a late finish, with little time to spare at the summit. Omitting the summit by taking the GR 9 to the Abri du Contrat would save a lot of time and effort, but it would still be a very long day to continue on to Malaucène. There is just a possibility of getting a bed for the night at or near Brantes, north-east of Mont Ventoux on the GR 9, but this is a very considerable detour (approximately 3 hours 15 minutes from the Abri du Contrat, and at an altitude of 1967ft; 600m, ie. 2665ft (813m) lower than the Abri). Full consideration to the overnight stop should be given to this stage of the walk before setting out from Sault.

There is a campsite at Mont Serein (on the right-hand side of the road about

350 metres from the Abri du Contrat). This is mainly for caravans, although permission to pitch a tent would probably be given (tel. 90.63.42.02).

Note that there is a *gîte rural* in Verdolier, just over an hour's walking from Sault. As is usual with this type of establishment, it is unlikely that a bed would be available here for one night only.

Restaurants/Cafés/Bars

The bar-restaurant on the summit of Mont Ventoux is open most of the year. This is quite expensive and caters for the thousands of tourists who arrive here by car or coach; during the winter months skiers are the main customers.

There are several restaurants (eg. Au Feu de Boi and Le Chalet-Reynard) and cafés in Mont Serein. These are all open during the winter skiing season, and many are open during the main summer holiday. Outside these periods several of them are closed. Most of the hôtels are bar-hôtel-restaurants, serving drinks and meals to non-residents. There are snack bars, crêperies and self-service restaurants open during the main seasons.

Shops

The summit of Mont Ventoux is graced with a souvenir shop, of little use to the walker.

There is a shop in Mont Serein, but this is closed out of the main seasons. To be confident it is better to carry sufficient food for two days from Sault.

Water

There is a water tap on the cemetery wall in Verdolier. Note that there is no possibility of obtaining water between Verdolier and the summit of Mont Ventoux. As the climb to the top is such a long one, it is inevitable that part of the ascent will have to be accomplished during the heat of the day, and so it is imperative that sufficient water is carried from the outset. There is a source of water at the Abri du Contrat, but this sometimes dries up. In this case water could be obtained from the ski station of Mont Serein.

SUMMARY

With the exception of the short descent to Mont Serein at the end of the day, the whole of today's effort is devoted to a long approach march and an ascent of the highest peak in mainland France outside the Alps and Pyrenees: Mont Ventoux. This climb of 3700ft (1129m) is the longest single ascent on the entire route and should not be underestimated, particularly when the weather is very hot, as it often is in summer, or when the mistral is blowing. The latter stages of the climb, along the barren ridge to the summit, is totally exposed to the elements. Wear a sunhat and protective sun-screen when the fierce southern sun is blazing down, and do not attempt the ridge if the wind speed is gale force or above. Sunglasses are recommended to ease the considerable glare from the bright exposed limestone on the upper slopes which carry little vegetation. In poor or dangerous weather conditions the GR 9, contouring the lower slopes of the mountain, is a good alternative. Ensure that sufficient water is carried and make an early start from Sault, in order to minimise the time spent climbing in the heat of the day.

The first part of the walk through La Loge and up to the attractive hamlet of Verdolier is gentle enough, but from here on the climb begins in earnest. The ascent from Verdolier can be thought of in two parts, both quite different in character. First there is a long section through the huge forest which covers the lower slopes of the mountain. Here navigation can be a little tricky, and care is required in order not to become frustrated and exhausted, before the second part of the climb is reached, an interminable crawl along the dry, rock strewn ridge leading to the summit. Once out of the trees and onto the ridge the top may seem but a short stroll away, but Mont Ventoux is a highly deceptive mountain and it will almost surely take much longer than expected to reach the meteorological tower on the summit. No doubt the bar on the summit will be most welcome, despite the hordes of tourists for whom it is intended.

The ascent by car from Sault to the summit of Mont Ventoux, uses the D 164 which meets the D 974 for the long, twisting climb to the very top. Both these roads are crossed on the ascent by foot, the latter at the Chalet Reynard, where information on the possibilities for skiing on the mountain can be obtained by those who wish to return in the winter months (tel. 90.61.84.55). Unfortunately, even on weekdays out of season, the summit is often bustling with tourists, but this should not detract from the achievement of reaching the highest point on the entire walk between the Côte d'Azur and the Cévennes. Plenty of time should be allocated to rest and admire the landscape spread out below. The view from this perch at 6268ft (1912m) above sea level is really outstanding, although it is quite often spoiled by heat haze, particularly during the summer months. This is another reason to attempt the walk during the spring or autumn, aiming to arrive at the summit as early as possible in the day to reduce the chance of afternoon haze obscuring the view.

The view is probably the most celebrated in all France. The Panorama is certainly most extensive. The peaks of the Préalpes, the Vercors and the French Alps stretch away to the north-east. In the far distance Mont Blanc may be visible and the giants of the Dauphiné Alps in the Ecrins (Mont Pelvoux, La Meije,) and in the Queyras are also on display; the distinctive shape of Monte Viso just over the border in Italy can also be distinguished. Nearer to hand are the Lubéron and the Plains of Vaucluse, and the starting point of today's expedition, Sault, will be easily identified. The huge cleft of the Durance valley between Manosque and Gap is distinguishable, and to the south-west lies the wide valley of the Rhône, the next major objective on the walk. Further west rises the great bulk of the Massif Central wherein lies journey's end: the principal ranges and summits of the Cévennes and Vivarais (Mont Lozère, Gerbier de Jonc, Mont

Mézenc) are identifiable. On very clear days it is said that Canigou in the eastern Pyrenees is visible. To the south lies Marseille and the Mediterranean coast.

Mont Ventoux is such a grand viewpoint because its huge bulk rises directly from the broad Provençal Plains forming a summit which is considerably higher than any of the neighbouring ranges and which is completely isolated. It dominates this whole area of Provence: its distinctively shaped peak crowned with the tall observatory tower can be seen for many miles around in every direction. It has been on view since crossing the hills north of Saint Saturnin d'Apt and will be seen for several more days to come as the walk proceeds westwards. Even without the summit tower the peak would be instantly recognisable with its topping of white limestone; many summer tourists mistake this for a covering of snow when seen from a distance. Trees at one time covered more of the higher slopes, but over the centuries the deforestation started by the Romans continued unabated. It was only in the last century that much of the oak, beech and pine forest that the Trail passes through today, was planted.

The mountain, a considerable landmark in the region, features widely in the mythology and culture of Provence. It has the distinction of being probably the first peak to have had an account written of its first recorded ascent. The poet Petrarch climbed to the summit as early as 1327 and left a detailed account in Latin of the ascent.

In modern times its mountain road often forms one of the more gruelling stages on the Tour de France cycle race (a roadside monument marks where the British racing cyclist, Tommy Simpson, collapsed and died in the 1967 race).

The assorted paraphernalia which adorns the summit includes an air force radar station and a television mast. The red and white "chimney" on top of the white observatory building is an eyesore visible for many miles around. Meteorological observations are also made from here: the extremes of weather recorded here make interesting reading. The mountain experiences heavy snow falls and extremely low temperatures during the winter, whilst the mistral, blowing from the north-west, can reach speeds greater than 150 miles per hour (240km per hour).

As can be judged from the size of the Mont Serein ski complex and the number of ski lifts in the area, Mont Ventoux attracts a considerable number of skiers every year. The climb to the summit from either Mont Serein on the north side or from Le Chalet Reynard on the south, and the descent on skis is a popular winter pastime.

On the steep descent from Mont Ventoux to the north on a well constructed footpath, there is an opportunity to admire the immense crags and scree slopes of the northern face of the mountain. On regaining the tree line and meeting the GR 9 for the last time, the small shelter of Contrat is soon reached, and from here it is only a short detour from the GR trail to Mont Serein and hopefully a bed for the night.

The observatory tower on the summit of Mont Ventoux

ROUTE

Leave Sault by reversing the inward route down the cobbled track to the road below. Cross the road to take the lane opposite going downhill. Within 200 metres turn left down an unsurfaced track (single red stripe waymark) to reach a lane where turn left. On reaching the D942 turn right, pass a lavender factory and walk through the village of La Loge. About 250 metres after the roadsign at the exit of La Loge take a footpath off to the right (at a "Réserve du Chasse" sign). This enclosed footpath leads to a track where turn right, but leave it after about 80 metres on a footpath on the right. Turn right on reaching a poorly surfaced lane. In another 100 metres do *not* enter the garden of the house ahead, but instead turn left on a track. Before reaching the next house leave this track, which bends to the right, by proceeding ahead on a footpath. This becomes a track which leads to a road where turn right to continue into the village of Verdolier seen ahead.

Pass around the back of the church and continue climbing on a lane until, at the far end of the cemetery, turn left on a track. The long climb of the day now begins in earnest. On reaching a point where the track divides into three, take the left-hand track uphill. The climb is a steep one. Immediately after the track levels out turn left on a footpath still climbing steeply. The climb mercifully ends at an open area where turn left for 80 metres to reach a building at the Jas Forest. Here the GR 4 meets the GR 9 coming up from Monieux in the south.

The two trails combine on a gradual ascent of a forest track heading north-west. Turn right, at cross tracks, heading north. The waymarking along the next section is particularly poor. This is mainly due to the forestry operations in the area: trees once carrying waymarks have been felled. Continue along the wide forest track, passing a track on the left, after just over a mile (1.6km), to Le Rat. This is the GR 91B and leads west in just over a mile to a *maison forestière*. Ignore this but continue ahead, still climbing towards the north, to reach the D164 road. Cross and continue on the track opposite near a sign that indicates the summit of Mont Ventoux to be 2 hours 30 minutes walking time from here (the Abri du Contrat is 2 hours 45 minutes from here, but note that this is on the GR 9, not the GR 4, ie. by contouring around the mountain rather than over its summit).

The next section can be very confusing on account of logging activities in the area. Continue climbing on the track until a cross tracks is reached. Here the GR 9 goes to the right on a track, leaving this for a path to the left through trees after a few hundred metres. However, take the GR 4 which continues ahead at this point, climbing for about another 500 metres to a sharp left turn into the wood. Follow some faded *ski de fond* signs on a path climbing through trees towards the Col de la Frache. When the author was last here there were very few red/white markings until the latter stages of this section, where waymarks appeared on several sawn-off tree stumps. About 150 metres into the forest turn right up another path. The waymarking should be satisfactory from here on as the path climbs, levels out and reaches a road by a signpost indicating a *terrain militaire* (military installation), just to the right of the Trail. Take the path opposite, climbing to emerge from trees with the summit of Mont Ventoux now clearly visible. The route along the ridge all the way to the summit is now obvious (in conditions of clear visibility). Pass to the right of some ski lifts and continue along the undulating ridge, passing the Tête de la Grave and the Col des Tempêtes, to reach the summit of Mont Ventoux. The way should be obvious even in hill fog, as it follows lines of red and blue, 2-metre high poles, which lead all the way to the top. The latter stages are fairly steep. Nearing the top pass to the right of a fenced-off area (another *terrain militaire*) and continue to cross the road, making the final climb between red and blue poles to the summit. Pass to the left of the lower car park and viewpoint and climb to the upper car park where there is a souvenir shop. The bar-restaurant is 100 metres from here, below the observatory.

When the time has come to leave the summit, first return to the main or northern viewpoint. Walk down the road from here, heading west. At a yellow/black striped pole, about 100 metres from the viewpoint, turn right down a steep footpath. The path descends the mountain by a series of zig-zags. Do not attempt to descend this very steep scree slope until the correct footpath has been located. This expertly engineered path zig-zags down towards the buildings of the Station du Mont Serein seen below. The path meets the road at a hairpin bend. Do not take the road, but immediately turn off sharply to the right to continue on a zig-zagging, descending, stony path which cuts across more scree. The path enters trees and continues on a well graded descent. Eventually the GR 9, which has contoured around the mountain massif to the north, joins from the right. Continue downhill on the joint GR 4/GR 9 track, taking care not to miss a footpath off to the right in about 500 metres. This path leads to the Abri du Contrat, a small shelter. At this point the GR 9, which descends gently to the right, leaves the GR 4. For the latter take the footpath up to the left which leads in 60 metres to a surfaced lane, where turn left ascending gently. After about 200 metres the GR 4 turns right off this lane onto a track, but continue ahead on the road for the Station du Mont Serein. Fifteen minutes' walking along this road leads to a number of hôtels, rooms and restaurants.

DAY 18
STATION DE SKI DU MONT SEREIN TO MALAUCENE

DISTANCE: 11.3 MILES (18.2km)
TOTAL ASCENT: 1079ft (329m)
TOTAL DESCENT: 4596ft (1402m)
TOTAL ESTIMATED TIME: 4 HOURS 40 MINUTES

	Height Above Sea Level		Distance				Est. Time	
			Sect.		Cum.		Sect.	Cum.
	ft	m	mile	km	mile	km	hr m	hr m
STATION DE SKI DU MONT SEREIN	4557	1390						
COL DU COMTE	3268	997	3.2	5.1	3.2	5.1	1.30	1.30
LES ALAZARDS	1606	490	3.1	5.0	6.3	10.1	1.00	2.30
LA CHAPELLE SAINTE-SIDOINE	2446	746	0.8	1.3	7.1	11.4	0.30	3.00
GROSEAU	1311	400	3.3	5.3	10.4	16.7	1.20	4.20
MALAUCENE	1039	317	0.9	1.5	11.3	18.2	0.20	4.40

FACILITIES
Accommodation
There are at least three hôtels to chose from in Malaucène, all in the 2-star category (eg. "Le Venaissin" in the centre of town, and the Hôtel l'Origan, tel. 90.65.27.08).

The *gîte d'étape* "Les Ecuries du Ventoux" one mile to the north-east of Malaucène on the GR 91 can be recommended (see Appendix 1). This is a centre for horse riding (*écuries* is French for stables). Horses can be hired from here on an hourly or daily basis, or longer. There are also guided treks on horseback (*promenades et randonnées à cheval*)

Signs for a campsite "Aire Naturelle" will be seen on the D974 between Groseau and Malaucène. However, this is situated at Le Crestet, many miles away in the direction of Vaison la Romaine, and is consequently of no use to the walker.

Restaurants/Cafés/Bars
A large bar-restaurant (called Le Grozeau) is passed on the Trail at the Source du Groseau, a mile before Malaucène. There are picnic tables on the opposite side of the road from here, by a small lake.

Malaucène has several cafés and restaurants.

Shops
Malaucène has a variety of shops of all types, including supermarkets. However there are no shops passed en route until Malaucène is reached.

Public Transport
There are local buses from Malaucène to Vaison-la-Romaine in the north-west and Carpentras to the south-west. Bus services operate from both these towns to Avignon.

Water
There is a water fountain in the hamlet of Les Alazards (no other facilities here).

Miscellaneous
There are banks, a post office (PTT), an *Office du Tourisme* and several souvenir shops in Malaucène. It is also the place to hire horses to go hacking in the surrounding countryside (see Les Ecuries du Ventoux above).

SUMMARY
The GR 9, which has been followed in part since it was first encountered in Saint Saturnin d'Apt and which has been co-incident with the GR 4 for some of the way since the Signal de la Peine, is left behind for the last time at the Abri du Contrat. The GR 9 descends to the north-east to the village of Brantes, whereas the GR 4 makes a long descent into the valley to the west aiming for the town of Malaucène.

In contrast to yesterday's walk, which was mainly all ascent, today for the most part is a relatively easy stroll down the long western slopes of the Mont Ventoux massif. The high slopes are slowly replaced by the cherry and apricot orchards and the vineyards in the valley on the approach to the hamlet of Les Alazards. The destination of the day, the town of Malaucène, should be have been spotted from high up the mountainside, but once again the deceptiveness of this landscape may convince you that it can be reached in an hour or so. It is still a long walk to the town, and furthermore, a further ascent of some 850ft (256m) over foothills is required before the day is done.

The short ascent from Les Alazards provides time to admire the crags of the escarpment of Trempe above. After passing the high point of the climb at the tiny chapel dedicated to Sainte-Sidoine, the balcony path traverses the Plateau du Sueil, before dropping down to the road and valley at the Source de Groseau and following the road into Malaucène.

Groseau
The small pond and grotto here makes an attractive spot for a picnic. The spring which pours from fissures in the large 328ft (100m) high crags, was an important source of water for the Romans, who built an aqueduct to carry the

water to Vaison-la-Romain. Such a small place has a great deal of history, for it was here that Clement V (the first of the Avignon Popes) built a summer residency where he stayed from 1309 to 1314. This and a Benedictine abbey are both gone from the site, but there remains a small chapel (Chapelle Notre-Dame-de-Groseau) which houses a fourteenth-century fresco bearing the arms of the French Pope.

Malaucène

It was from Malaucène that Petrarch set off on his famous ascent of Mont Ventoux in 1327. The main street of this attractive town is shaded by large plane trees. The huge church, built by Pope Clement V in the fourteenth century, was once part of the fortified town walls. It is reached by turning left when reaching the high street on the walk from Groseau. The old town is a rather fascinating jumble of narrow, winding alleyways, old houses, street fountains and public washing places. Follow the signs through its narrow streets to the *site panoramique* on the citadel (bring along a camera). The surrounding countryside is seen to good effect from here, with once again Mont Ventoux (now conquered!) dominating the scene: the size of the massif can now be fully appreciated, as it has taken two long days of walking to make a complete traverse of the mountain from Sault.

If a spare day is available a trip by bus or taxi to the town of Vaison-la-Romain (the "Pompeii of France") can be recommended. There are numerous Roman ruins, including several mansions and a Roman theatre, spread over two large sites. Mont Ventoux is once again clearly visible from the town.

ROUTE

Return east along the road to the point at which the GR 4 takes a track on the left. This soon becomes a path descending through woodland. Turn right at a T-junction, descend, and remain on this wide forest track until a sign indicates a path to the left. This path descends through woodland and then crosses scree on a well constructed path over Le Grand Vallet, the head of a steep mountain valley. After the scree the descent continues on a good forest path which soon crosses a forest track. On reaching another track bear to the left, but in 20 metres take the path on the right still descending. After a while the route takes a path on the right which ascends. The climb is only a short one, the path soon levelling out to contour on a slope of the mountainside meeting a road (D153) at the Col du Comte.

Cross over the road to pick up another descending path through more woodland. The hamlet of Les Alazards below and even the day's destination, Malaucène, in the distance, come into view. The path soon crosses the head of the wide valley and descends on the other slope of the mountain before bending tortuously back again continuing the descent. At long last the path emerges at a track near a small building, where turn right. The track descends

Malaucène seen from the Site Panoramique

down the valley, soon becoming a surfaced lane (D153) which passes between cultivated fields (apricot and cherry trees) and later through a vineyard. Do not miss the left turn into the hamlet of Les Alazards.

The next section involves a climb of over 800ft (244m) to the chapel of Sainte-Sidoine. Pass through the hamlet of Les Alazards, taking a track which leads up from the water fountain. Pass a second fountain 50 metres later and 10 metres after this turn left on a path which climbs steeply through the trees. When the path levels out bear to the right to pass behind a small simple chapel (Sainte-Sidoine). Continue on a balcony track (superb views over to the right). After a little under a kilometre along this track take great care not to miss a thin footpath leaving the track on the right through trees. This soon emerges at another track where turn left uphill. Continue to a T-junction, turn right and after a while look for a track off to the right (clearly marked). This soon becomes a narrow stony path which descends through woodland. The path emerges from the trees onto a track - continue ahead but after a few hundred metres, where this track swings to the right, turn left onto another track (this left turn is easily missed). Climb gradually to meet a T-junction where turn left to descend. Bear to the left at a cross track to zig-zag down, passing a derelict building and bridge to reach the D974 at the Source du Groseau, opposite a bar-restaurant.

Turn right on the D974 following this road as it gradually descends all the way to Malaucène. The GR 4 joins the GR 91 at Groseau and the two trails are co-incident along this road into the town of Malaucène. On reaching the high street turn right for the town centre. Those walkers wanting the *gîte d'étape* should continue north-east out of Malaucène on the GR 91 for about 1.6km (1 mile): follow the signs from the centre of Malaucène to Les Ecuries du Ventoux.

DAY 19
MALAUCENE TO RASTEAU

DISTANCE:	15.2 MILES (24.5km)
TOTAL ASCENT:	1328ft (405m)
TOTAL DESCENT:	1711ft (522m)
TOTAL ESTIMATED TIME:	6 HOURS 40 MINUTES

	Height Above Sea Level		Distance				Est. Time	
			Sect.		Cum.		Sect.	Cum.
	ft	m	mile	km	mile	km	hr m	hr m
MALAUCENE	1039	317						
COL DE LA CHAINE	1547	472	3.2	5.2	3.2	5.2	1.30	1.30
PASSAGE DES LOUPS	1928	588	1.3	2.1	4.5	7.3	0.50	2.20
SEGURET	1177	359	4.3	7.0	8.8	14.3	1.50	4.10
ROAIX	554	169	4.3	6.9	13.1	21.2	1.45	5.55
RASTEAU	656	200	2.1	3.3	15.2	24.5	0.45	6.40

OPTIONAL WALKS

1. The Tour des Dentelles de Montmirail is a circular walk waymarked with red/yellow paint flashes. It encircles the entire range, providing views of the jagged pinnacles and ridges from all angles. In a clockwise direction from Vaison-la-Romaine the Tour visits Crestet, the Cirque de Saint Amand, Le Barroux, Beaumes-de-Venise, Vacqueyras (near), Gigondas (near) and Séguret. A short section of the trail is co-incident with the GR 4.

2. Those wishing to stay a while in Rasteau will find details of several local footpaths in the Centre Départemental d'Animation. Leaflets are available on several short local walks; some have a special botanical or geological interest.

FACILITIES

Accommodation

The walk is now entering a rather trendy area, a haunt of artists and wine connoisseurs. Consequently, accommodation tends to be rather expensive. However, the *gîte d'étape* at Rasteau at the end of the stage can be recommended.

Séguret: There is a very expensive 3-star hôtel at the upper end of this chic village. For those on a tight budget, the youth hostel (Auberge de Jeunesse) on the route de Sablet will be more suitable.

St Just: A little before the D977 road between Séguret and Roaix there are *chambres d'hôte* (Gîte de France).

Rasteau: The *gîte d'étape* is located within the Centre Départemental d'Animation, a large modern building a short walk from the village centre, adjacent to the Stade des Deux Julien (see Appendix 1). The *gîte* is excellent value for money: the *dortoir* consists of two-bed cubicles, each with a curtain for privacy. There are large, modern wash rooms, with showers and facilities for washing clothes. The Centre stages a number of exhibitions throughout the year, and there will usually be a number of paintings and sculptures on display in the building. From the *gîte* there is a good view of Mont Ventoux and the *mamelons* (rounded hillocks) that the route skirted north of Séguret. Look your last on the graceful shape of Mont Ventoux.

For those wanting more comfort there are a few *chambres d'hôte* in Rasteau, as well as the Hôtel-Restaurant Bellerive (tel.90.46.10.20). The latter is a modern Logis de France hôtel, but is some distance out of town on the D69.

Restaurants/Cafés/Bars
Séguret has the Café des Poternes, a salon de thé and the restaurant Le Nesclun. Note that the 3-star hôtel in Séguret serves meals to non-residents, but that the cheapest set menu costs around 280FF! The restaurant A Qui Sian Ben will be found by turning left on the D975 on approaching Roaix. The route also passes a bar on the D975. There are three cafés in Rasteau, one of which is in the main village square. For a restaurant in Rasteau try the Bellerive (see above).

Shops
There is a small *épicerie* in Séguret (bread can be bought from the Café des Poternes). There is an *alimentation* on the D975 in Roaix, opposite the point where the GR 4 emerges. Rasteau has an *épicerie*, *boucherie-charcuterie*, *boulangerie* and a greengrocers. Most are situated in the village square.

Public Transport
There is a bus service that operates between Avignon and Gap stopping at Séguret, Cairanne, Rasteau, Roaix and Vaison-la-Romaine. Not all of the services (usually two or more a day) stop at Cairanne or Rasteau (tel 90.36.05.22 or 75.26.35.58 for information).

Water
Take plenty of water for the walk from Malaucène to Séguret, which traverses dry and wild terrain. Séguret has two water fountains. Plenty of cafés will be encountered from there on.

Miscellaneous
Séguret has few small wine cellars and a number of art and craft shops. Rasteau

boasts a bank and a post office, whilst tourist information is available from the Centre Départemantal d'Animation. There are many large wine *caves* in and around Rasteau which can be visited (free samples!).

SUMMARY

Now that Mont Ventoux is over do not assume that all the best mountain country has been left behind. Today's walk, traversing the wild, rocky and windswept landscape just to the north of the Dentelles de Montmirail, is far from an anticlimax after Mont Ventoux. Although the Dentelles are much lower in altitude than Mont Ventoux (the highest summit is Saint Amand, 2406ft; 734m), the jagged limestone ridges and pinnacles rise steeply from the surrounding plateau providing a favourite subject for the landscape painters of nearby Séguret. The name "Dentelles" does not refer to "teeth", but rather equates the sharp, needle-like pinnacles on the crêtes with the pins on a lace-makers board (*dentelle* means lace). The range is a result of the folding of the earth's crust, thrusting up the upper strata of Jurassic limestone, which has then been weathered into a series of serrated ridges. There are good views of the Dentelles on the walk, particularly at the Col de la Châine and from the balcony at Séguret. Several paths lead to the jagged crags, a favourite playground with local climbers, for those with more time and curiosity. A closer inspection of the Crête and Cirque de Saint Amand can be recommended.

The walk from Malaucène to Séguret is through an area of wild and austere beauty, a landscape dotted with numerous limestone outcrops, boulders and ridges weathered into a variety of shapes and sizes. Our Trail threads a tortuous

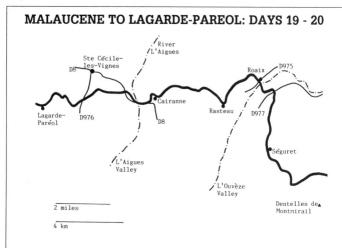

MALAUCENE TO LAGARDE-PAREOL: DAYS 19 - 20

route through this country until the way appears to be blocked by the crags of a long rocky ridge. However, the secret to further progression lies in locating a gap in the rock, known only at one time to the shepherds who guarded these remote hills: the Passage des Loups (or Le Pas du Loup as it is shown on some maps). *Loup* is the French word for wolf, but these animals have not roamed this region now for over a century. The popularity of the area with walkers is borne out by the several local walks that have been waymarked using a variety of symbols (eg. red dots and blue triangles). The Tour des Dentelles de Montmirail is a popular excursion, part of which is co-incident with the GR 4. The latter leaves this GR de Pays north of Séguret, but walkers wishing to visit the Roman remains at Vaison-la-Romain (see "Summary - Day 18") could remain on the Tour des Dentelles, following it to the north-east to reach the town.

Séguret

This attractive artist's enclave is built on the side of a steep hill overlooking the wide valley of the River l'Ouvèze. The twelfth-century church of Saint Denis, the fourteenth-century belfry with its one handed clock, and the fifteenth-century ramparts and Mascarons Fountain are all worth a quick visit, but the main pleasure is merely to wander up the steep narrow streets, admiring the much restored medieval houses, to the little square where there is a viewing platform. There is an extensive view from here out over the fertile plains that lead to the valley of the Rhône. Stretched out before you are the world famous vineyards of the Côtes de Rhône, the scene of tomorrow's walk. The hills seen in the distance are those of the Cévennes in the Massif Central, the ultimate goal of this trek across southern France. For much of the summer the village is the venue for an outdoor painting course organised by local artists. The students and their work will be much in evidence. Also during August a drama and folklore festival is held, when the narrow streets will be jammed with tourists.

The route from Séguret scribes a large arc, crossing the River l'Ouvèze and the Route des Vins (D975) at Roaix and then entering vine growing country. From here to the Lagarde-Paréol the route traverses some of the most renowned vineyards in all France.

Rasteau

The stage ends at the village of Rasteau, which like Séguret and several of the neighbouring wine-producing villages, has the distinction of having its own *appelation contrôlé* within the Côtes du Rhône area. The church and ramparts date from the twelfth century. The ruins of the small château (only one wall is intact) on top of hill in Rasteau is worth a visit for the glorious view over the plain to the mountains beyond.

But the main places of interest in Rasteau all involve one item: wine! The Musée du Vigneron (on the D975 between Rasteau and Roaix - follow the signs) explains the whole process of wine production. All aspects are covered, from growing the grapes to bottling the final product. A *Vinothéque* is included with a half-hour video on the whole of the Côtes du Rhône region. There is *dégustation* or wine tasting on offer, but with no obligation to buy. Several wine-cellars or *caves* are within strolling distance of Rasteau. The Domaine des Coteaux des Travers is in the village itself whilst the Domaine des Nymphes is only 100 metres outside the boundary of the village on the D69. These offer guided tours with the possibility of tasting and, of course, buying wine at the end of the visit. Ask at the reception desk of the Centre Départemental d'Animation for details of other *domaines* (wineries) in the vicinity.

ROUTE

From the church in Malaucène take the D938, the avenue de la Libération, signposted to Carpentras. About 150 metres after the church, at a major green road sign, turn right along a narrow lane. Proceed ahead at a cross track. Where the track bends to the right walk ahead up a grassy bank to the left of a house. Turn right on reaching the D938, but in 50 metres take the left of the two lanes on the right, ie. the lane going downhill. Ignore a dirt track ahead as this roughly surfaced lane bends to the right. Walk ahead at a crossroad. After the houses the lane becomes a gravel track which zig-zags up to a house, after which a footpath is taken which soon resumes the climb. Where the path splits take the right-hand fork. The route soon levels out forming a very pleasant balcony path with excellent views to the left and ahead. Later ignore a path off to the right, remaining on the balcony path ahead. Later still, ensure that a right turn is taken at the point where the GR de Pays route (waymarked with red/yellow stripes) meets the GR 4 - do not continue ahead on the GR de Pays. The GR 4 and GR de Pays are co-incident for the next few miles to the Passage des Loups. The path later climbs to reach a narrow track where turn left, but turn left again on a narrow path after only 25 metres. This soon joins another track where turn right uphill. Remain on this to the road at the Col de la Chaîne.

Turn left on the D90 until about 100 metres after the track leading to the farm, where turn right to climb on a stony footpath. The path winds its way through a rough, rocky landscape, eventually crossing over the ridge ahead by a gap in the rock (the *Passage des Loups*). Now enter trees on a narrow path and descend to an area where there are several crossing tracks. Continue ahead, ignoring these and another path off to the left (blue dots) in 50 metres. In a further few hundred metres, where the tracks divide, take the right-hand fork. Shortly, where the track divides again, turn 90 degrees left. Continue, ignoring the track off to the right to La Verrière farm. Note the prominent

Parascending from the summit of Mont Ventoux (Day 17)
At the Passage des Loups (Day 19)

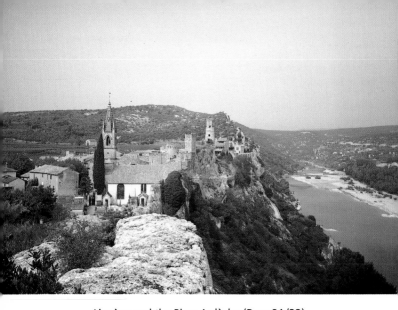

Aiguèze and the River Ardèche (Days 21/22)
The Chassezac Gorge (Day 23)

The distant Dentelles de Montmirail from the Col de la Châine

white/red/white horizontal stripes on the trees in this area. These refer to forestry activities and are not GR trail markings. Remain on the main track for over a mile (1.6km) after which it is imperative to locate and take a very sharp left-hand turn off the main track onto a narrower track. This climbs very gently for a short distance before beginning a descent to the valley seen below. Turn left at a T-junction of tracks continuing downhill. After a further 400 metres of descent, turn right on another track at a point where there is a tree which has a yellow paint stripe or band encircling it. The route now climbs somewhat, continuing up a poorly surfaced drive. At a cross tracks at the top of the climb, continue ahead, commencing the descent. Follow the lane steeply down as it zig-zags, but leave it for a while at one point, on a thin path off to the right - this cuts off a hairpin bend on the lane. Meet the road again and turn right continuing down the lane. The attractive hill-top village of Séguret comes into view. Remain on the road to reach Séguret.

After a visit to the village walk along the main (lower) street past the *mairie* to exit from the old town by the north gate. The Trail now turns to head north for a few miles to Roaix, before resuming its westerly journey to the Rhône. Turn right on the road, but in 60 metres turn left down a slope with a wall on the right. This leads to a road, where turn left, but in 100 metres, by a small chapel, turn right up a lane. Where the lane forks in a further 100 metres take the right fork uphill. This soon becomes a stony, gravel track. Just after a gate down to a house, turn left off this track onto a narrow path. At a T-junction of paths near a track, turn right uphill on another footpath. Follow this charming path

The picturesque village of Séguret

contouring the lower slopes of two rounded hillocks or *mamelons*. The red/white markings of the GR 4 are accompanied by the yellow stripes of a local trail for a while, before these lead off to the right: continue ahead for the Trail to Roaix. Soon after the PR trail departs, the GR 4 begins to descend, eventually reaching a poorly surfaced drive, where turn right. After about 500 metres look for a path leading off to the right at a telegraph pole. This soon leads to a gravel track where turn left for about 250 metres, after which turn right on a path. On reaching a track turn left downhill. At a vineyard locate a narrow path on the right between woodland to the right and a thin band of trees on the left: note that this path is easily missed. This eventually emerges at a track (GR de Pays route marked in yellow/red): turn left ignoring the GR de Pays which turns off to the right within 5 metres of joining it. About 200 metres later turn left at a T-junction. This lane descends through vineyards to reach the main road, the D977.

Turn left along this road (there is a grassy verge) for 250 metres to turn right on a narrow lane which leads to the D7 - here turn right and walk along this road, crossing the River l'Ouvèze to reach a T-junction at the D975 (the Routes des Vins). Turn left for 80 metres and then right opposite a bar on the Montée du Moulin. Climb on this lane to reach the old village of Roaix, where turn left.

Follow the chemin des Hautes Granges alongside the cemetery. Remain on this lane as it bends round to the left in front of farm buildings. Later ignore a right turn, continuing on the main, poorly surfaced track as it climbs above a large building (corrugated metal roof). There is a good distant view of Mont Ventoux over to the left. Ignore a turn to the right at the top of the climb and remain on the stony track. This soon becomes surfaced again and descends. Take a muddy cart track which leads to an asphalt lane, where turn left to continue the descent. Soon Rasteau comes into view on the hill ahead. Remain on this lane all the way to the village. On entering Rasteau note the point at which the GR 4 continues on its journey westward. Continue to the main square of Rasteau. The *gîte d'étape* is housed in the Centre d'Départemental d'Animation, a large modern building on the outskirts of Rasteau. To get there leave the village on the road C1, signposted to the Stade, heading in a south-westerly direction.

DAY 20
RASTEAU TO MONDRAGON

DISTANCE: 18.3 MILES (29.5km)
TOTAL ASCENT: 295ft (90m)
TOTAL DESCENT: 754ft (230m)
TOTAL ESTIMATED TIME: 6 HOURS 15 MINUTES

| | Height Above Sea Level | | Distance | | | | Est. Time | |
| | Sea | Level | Sect. | | Cum. | | Sect. | Cum. |
	ft	m	mile	km	mile	km	hr m	hr m
RASTEAU	656	200						
CAIRANNE	459	140	3.8	6.1	3.8	6.1	1.30	1.30
SOUTH OF								
STE CECILE-LES-VIGNES	328	100	3.5	5.7	7.3	11.8	1.25	2.55
LAGARDE-PAREOL	466	142	2.8	4.5	10.1	16.3	1.05	4.00
LES FARJONS	452	138	2.7	4.3	12.8	20.6	1.00	5.00
MONDRAGON	197	60	5.5	8.9	18.3	29.5	2.15	6.15

FACILITIES
Accommodation
Note that no place of accommodation is passed en route between Rasteau and Mondragon, although there may be a possibility of finding a room by making a detour into Sainte Cécile-les-Vignes (this was not checked by the author).

There are three hôtels in Mondragon. The best is probably Le Sommeil du Roy, a 2-star Logis de France. Another bar-hôtel-restaurant will be found next door.

There is a campsite 1.5km from Mondragon, along the D26 in the direction of Bolléne.

Restaurants/Cafés/Bars
The route passes close to a restaurant (Le Grillade d'Helios). It is 100 metres along the road (sharp right turn) off the D11, south of Les Farjons.

Mondragon has a number of restaurants and cafés. The best is probably the Auberge de la Table Ronde where rooms for the night are also available. The Café de Provence in Mondragon offers cheap meals. A restaurant that could be missed is La Caleche as it is 150 metres off route, near the beginning of tomorrow's walk, to the left along the N7.

Shops
Mondragon has several food shops of all types. There is also a pharmacy.

Public Transport
There is a bus service that operates several times a day between Avignon, Orange and Valréas which stops at Sainte Cécile-les-Vignes (Sociètè des Cars Mèry, tel. 90.34.00.33, or Lieutaud et Fils, tel. 90.36.05.22). Buses also run from Mondragon to Bollène and Montélimar in the north and to Orange and Avignon in the south (Rapides du Sud-Est, tel. 90.82.48.50). Another service operates from Mondragon to Pont-Saint-Esprit and on to Aubenas and Lalevade-d'Ardèche (Voyages Sotra, tel. 75.39.40.22). Note that trains no longer stop in Mondragon. The high speed trains that thunder past are from Lyon, heading for Orange, Avignon and Marseille.

Water
A water tap is passed en route, in the vineyards to the south of Sainte Cécile-les-Vignes.

Miscellaneous
The route passes near to several wineries, where tours and wine tasting are on offer (eg. the *caves* at Cairanne).

There is a bank (Crédit Agricole) in Mondragon.

SUMMARY
Today's route is mainly through vineyards until the wood and scrub covered hills west of the tiny village of Lagarde-Paréol are reached. The importance of viticulture in the region can be appreciated by some of the place names, eg Sainte Cécile-les-Vignes (*vigne* is French for vine). The latter village holds a place in history as being the site of an important Calvinist assembly in 1563. Note that the actual route does not pass through the centre of either Sainte Cécile-les-Vignes, or the earlier village of Cairanne: detours will be necessary if these are to be included for visits to wineries. The wooded ridge between Lagarde-Paréol and Les Farjons (Bois de la Montagne) is a pleasant change from the vineyards; with luck some of the deer that roam these hillsides will be spotted.

Much of the walk is fairly intricate, through a complex series of vineyards, across fields and through scrub and woodland. The waymarking varies in quality and quantity from adequate to poor, and so care will be necessary with map and compass to avoid making errors. A particularly detailed route description has been provided to help in navigation.

A different world from that of rural Provence will quite suddenly come into view as the walker approaches Mondragon. The scene is dominated by rows of ugly tower blocks, and no one will fail to notice the roar of the motorway traffic and the express trains in the Rhône Valley below. Although Mondragon has several hôtels, the town is a rather dour, depressing place, with little to interest the visitor. Some may wish to continue to Pont-Saint-Esprit, although this would make for a very long day's walk. The alternative would be to catch a local bus to Orange, Bollène or Pont-Saint-Esprit. The problems of the section relate only to its length and the intricate navigation required in a few places, as the terrain is flat for the most part, with plenty of easy, fast walking along tracks and lanes. Some may wish to divide Day 20 and the first half of Day 21 to Pont-Saint-Esprit into two full days, stopping before Mondragon on the first night (but note the problems of accommodation; even backpackers will have some difficulty in that permission will be required to camp in much of the country passed en route).

Vineyards and the Wine Industry

Vines were first planted in this region by the Greeks, whose vineyards were extended later by the Romans, although the main concentration was further north, around Valence. Wine production declined after the Romans left, but was revived by the Church from the ninth century onwards, particularly by the Avignon Popes in the fourteenth century. Viticulture forms the basis of a major French industry today. The extent of the wine growing country will be fully appreciated on this walk, which traverses many miles of vineyards, particularly on the section from Rasteau to Lagarde-Paréol. The Rhône vineyards occupy a huge area, estimated at some 424 square miles (110,000 hectares). Most of this is in the plains where vast quantities of *vin ordinaire* are produced, but it is the mountain villages that are responsible for the better, more delicate wines,

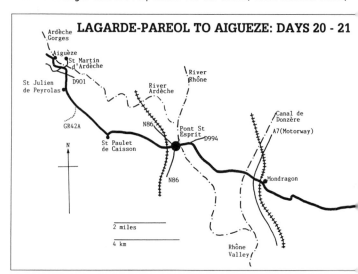

produced from grapes grown on the surrounding hillsides - these wines carry the general name of Côtes du Rhône. Some of the most famous vineyards in France are traversed on the walk, such as those of La Présidente, south-east of Sainte Cécile-les-Vignes. The most celebrated wines however, come from an area a little to the south of the GR 4 trail, on the hillsides around Châteauneuf-du-Pape. It was from this region that the *Appellation Contrôlée* system originated in the 1930s, a guarantee of the origin and quality of French wines. Many of the villages passed en route have their own *Appellation Contrôlée*. The best wines from the region are the red ones, dark and strong.

The autumn is a good time to be here when the grapes are being gathered *(le vendange)*. In some of the smaller vineyards this is still done by hand, but, as with all things, the mechanisation of the twentieth century has taken over this industry to a large extent. Many of the vines grow to only a few feet in height so that they can be picked by machine. The large harvesters which do the job should be seen in the fields in September and October; they drive between the rows of vines, passing over the plants tearing the bunches of grapes free as they do so.

ROUTE

Return to the main square of Rasteau and retrace the route back to the point just above this at which the GR4 was left yesterday. Follow in the direction of the Salle de Dégustation (GR 4 signpost indicating Cairanne) passing a fountain and public washing area.

Soon ignore the sign to the Salle de Dégustation off to the right, but continue ahead up the hill on a narrow lane. Pass a cemetery at the top of the climb and continue on the level road for a while until the point where the lane swings to the right to begin a descent. Here continue ahead on a dirt track (note that the route is waymarked with yellow & white stripes in this area as well as the standard red/white of the GR trail). Ignore a path off to the left, but continue climbing up a slight rise, remaining ahead until a clearly marked left turn is reached. Take this to descend to the end of a tarmac road where turn right on a gravel track. Within 150 metres turn left on a path, reaching a track after 100 metres. Turn left, but take the right fork ahead uphill. Later, be sure to turn right on a descending track. At a stony track, turn left downhill. On

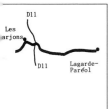

reaching a T-junction of tracks at a vineyard, turn sharply to the right on the track (this is easy to miss - at this point the yellow/white waymarks part company temporarily with the GR route - do not follow a trail towards the north). Climb on the track to a road where turn left (the yellow/white markings will be encountered again along here). Where the lane divides, take the right fork, passing to the left of the house called La Tabourrette. The village of Cairanne now comes into view. Remain on this lane to a T-junction; here turn left on the D51 heading towards Cairanne.

At the first buildings the yellow/white waymarked local trail heads to the left, but for the GR 4 take the right turn. The route circles below the village. Turn left on reaching a T-junction, descend for a few hundred metres to take a sharp left turn uphill. Soon after the lane levels out, head steeply down a bank on the right. Descend to a lane, crossing over this to pass to the right of a large co-operative wine-producing "factory". Turn right on reaching the main road, the D8. Follow this road over the bridge above the River l'Aigues, leaving the D8 about 100 metres later (building on left) by turning right onto a drive through vineyards. This soon becomes a dirt track which heads towards the river on the right. The track leads through the vines back to the D8 road; turn left. Soon leave the road again by turning right onto a dirt track through the vineyards of La Présidente.

The long, straight, gravel drive leads to the principal buildings of the Présidente *domaine*. Turn right here, but in 40 metres turn left along the side of a building. Turn right on reaching a lane. Continue through the vineyards until, on reaching a water tap in about 800 metres, turn sharply left still remaining in the vineyards. In about 500 metres, at a small ruined building, turn right onto another track. Continue on this to a road, where turn right to reach the D976. Turn left, but in about 500 metres turn right on a lane signposted to Lagarde-Pol *(sic)*. After about half a mile, turn right on a dirt track. About 100 metres before meeting a road (D 168) turn left on another gravel track through vineyards. This soon bends to the left. At a small solitary tree in the middle of the vineyard, turn right and continue on a magnetic compass bearing of approximately 295 degrees to reach a road at a junction of three ways. Take the road heading towards the west (signpost on tree indicating Arnaud). Turn left on reaching a crossroads in 80 metres. This lane climbs slightly, but leave it after 200 metres by turning left on a stony track. Cross over a gravel track and continue ahead on the grassy/dirt track to meet the road in Lagarde-Paréol. Turn right.

At the top of a short climb where the road swings to the right, turn left on a gravel track. In 60 metres take the grassy track climbing to the right of a house, and in a further 100 metres turn right at a lamppost, climbing steeply on a footpath with a wall to your left. This meets the road at the church of Lagarde-Paréol. Turn left to walk through the village, passing the new *mairie*. On reaching the D65 turn right, signposted to Valence, but after 200 metres turn left, signposted to Les Planes (among other places). Climb on the lane and where it ends continue ahead on the track, heading towards the west, climbing gently through woodland (note: the waymarking in this area may be poor, probably the result of tree felling). After about 500 metres be sure to take a right turn off the main track onto a narrower track. Join the wide track again and continue uphill. The track narrows: continue ahead passing under high tension electricity cables, soon joining a GR de Pays trail waymarked with yellow and red stripes. Climb to reach a T-junction, where turn left. At a junction of several tracks continue ahead, with a vineyard on your right, still heading towards the west. There are several confusing paths and tracks in this area, but for the correct route always remain on the main track maintaining a westerly direction. After passing a large aerial and generator, the track begins to descend. Follow this down quite steeply to a track T-junction, near to a building; here turn left continuing down to the D11 road, to the south of Les Farjons.

Turn left on the D11, ignoring the right turn on the D12 into Les Farjons in 100 metres, to reach and take a sharp right turn beneath high-tension electricity cables. After passing the gates of the ferme-château Massillan take the lane that ascends immediately to the right of the small roadside cross. In about half a mile, opposite a house on the left, turn right off this road onto a sandy track through woodland. Once amongst the trees there is a maze of paths; follow the red/white waymarks very carefully until a principal track is attained. Remain on this for some distance, maintaining a westerly direction. Keep ahead at a crosstracks to reach a wide stony track at a T-junction. Here turn left, but in 100 metres turn right on a sandy track. This emerges at a crosstracks; continue ahead here, passing immediately to the left of a large pylon carrying a high-tension cable. Continue to a T-junction, where turn right. Ignore an arrow in 20 metres which indicates a left turn off this track onto a narrow path, but remain instead on the track which heads first towards the north, before bearing left towards the west once again. The track soon becomes a surfaced lane which eventually descends to a road, the D152. Turn left. Remain on this road for about half a mile, until directly underneath the high-tension electricity cables, turn right up a gravel drive. This continues as a cart track between houses. Remain on this track until it reaches a road, where continue straight ahead. Pass to the left of the ruined château of Mondragon. The ugly tower blocks of the town will come into view on the left. Descend the lane, passing a primary school on your left and then take a track down to the main road. Turn right on the D26 to enter Mondragon and continue to the Place de la Paix (alternatively turn right before descending past the school and locate some steps near to the château de Mondragon: these lead down to the Place de la Paix). Hôtels and other facilities are close at hand.

DAY 21
MONDRAGON TO AIGUEZE VIA PONT-SAINT-ESPRIT AND THE RHONE VALLEY

DISTANCE: 10.7 MILES (17.2km)
TOTAL ASCENT: 426ft (130m)
TOTAL DESCENT: 331ft (101m)
TOTAL ESTIMATED TIME: 4 HOURS 15 MINUTES

| | Height Above Sea Level | | Distance | | | | Est. Time | |
	ft	m	Sect. mile	km	Cum. mile	km	Sect. hr m	Cum. hr m
MONDRAGON	197	60						
CANAL DE DONZERE	131	40	0.6	1.0	0.6	1.0	0.15	0.15
PONT-SAINT-ESPRIT	164	50	3.2	5.2	3.8	6.2	1.15	1.30
SAINT-PAULET-DE-CAISSON	229	70	3.0	4.8	6.8	11.0	1.15	2.45
SAINT-JULIEN-DE-PEYROLAS	393	120	2.6	4.1	9.4	15.1	1.00	3.45
AIGUEZE	292	89	1.3	2.1	10.7	17.2	0.30	4.15

FACILITIES
Accommodation
There are many hôtels in Pont-Saint-Esprit, mainly in the 2-star category. The Hôtel-Restaurant Le Commerce (tel. 66.39.12.79) is pleasant enough and conveniently situated in the centre of town.

Aiguèze has two hôtels: l'Auberge Sarrasine in the Cadre Medieval and Le Rustic Hôtel. Saint-Martin-d'Ardèche (off-route) has hôtels and a *chambre d'hôte*.

There is a campsite (Les Oliviers) between Saint-Paulet-de-Caisson and Saint-Julien-de-Peyrolas (turn left along the chemin de Tête Grosse, about a kilometre after the Chapelle of Sainte Agnès). Another campsite will be found by turning right at the point where the GR 42A joins the GR 4 from the left. There is a small campsite (Les Cigales, 30 places) about 50 metres from the point where the Trail emerges opposite the suspension bridge leading across the river to Saint-Martin-d'Ardèche. Finally, a farm on the outskirts of Aiguèze offers simple accomodation in a barn (12 places) or *camping à la ferme* (tel. 66.82.15.51).

Restaurants/Cafés/Bars
There is plenty of choice in Pont-Saint-Esprit. Close to the campsite near Saint-Paulet-de-Caisson there is a restaurant, but the next village, Saint-Julien-du-

Peyrolas, has two restaurants and a bar (the better of the two restaurants, La Moliére, is in the place du Donjon). Saint-Martin-d'Ardèche (off-route) has a number of cafés and restaurants. Aiguèze possesses a café, a snack bar and two restaurants. The food at l'Auberge Sarrasine in Aiguèze can be recommended.

Shops

Pont-Saint-Esprit has many shops of all types. There is a busy Saturday market in the town. Pont-Saint-Esprit is a good place in which to stock up for the next stage of the journey; no equal selection of food shops will be encountered until Les Vans, 3 days from here. In the village of Saint-Julien-du-Peyrolas there is an *épicerie* as well as a *boulangerie* and *pâtisserie*. There are food shops in Saint-Martin-d'Ardèche.

Public Transport

Although there is a railway station (Gare SNCF) in Pont-Saint-Esprit, only freight trains operate along this départemental line. Therefore in order to join the fast mainline services that run along the Rhône Valley, it is necessary to take the bus to Avignon. These operate several times a day, with a journey time of just over an hour (Autocars Auran, tel. 66.39.10.40, Rapides du Sud-Est, tel. 90.82.48.50 or Voyages Sotra, tel. 75.39.40.22). There are also buses to Orange and Nîmes. In the other direction a service runs to Aubenas and on to Lalevade-d'Ardèche, and another to Montélimar.

Local buses run from Saint-Martin-d'Ardèche to Pont-Saint-Esprit and other towns in the Rhône Valley.

Miscellaneous

There are several banks (eg. Crédit Agricole, Crédit Lyonaise) and a post office (PTT) in Pont-Saint-Esprit. The Office de Tourisme is on the rue Vauban, near to the point where the GR 4 enters the town ie. on the right just after crossing the bridge over the Rhône. Saint-Julien-du-Peyrolas and Saint-Martin-d'Ardèche also both have post offices. There are a few antique and craft shops in Aiguèze.

SUMMARY

Today's short section is one of considerable significance, for the crossing of the wide, flat valley of the River Rhône marks a final departure from the foothills of the alpine system and an introduction to the gorges and wooded hills of the Ardèche, on the approach walk to the mountains of the Massif Central. The walking is easy and fast, mainly on level terrain along minor lanes, with few navigational problems. If anything the walking is rather tedious, and some may prefer to take a bus from Mondragon to Pont-Saint-Esprit, or even another on to Aiguèze. This would allow more time for sight-seeing and general relaxation in Pont-Saint-Esprit.

However, for those with an interest in twentieth-century engineering and communications, the walk across the valley of the Rhône to Pont-Saint-Esprit will provide much to occupy the mind. Only the first kilometre or so is along busy roads and even these for the most part are provided with pavements. Walkers need have no fear of crossing the busy roads and motorway, the railway, canal and river, as these are all provided with underpasses or bridges to which the pedestrian has access. After the canal is crossed the Trail takes to quiet lanes through a fruit growing area, the route lined with orchards of pear, apple and other fruit crops. Pont-Saint-Esprit soon comes into view, perched on a hill on the far bank of the River Rhône. Trainers would be quite adequate for the walk to Pont-Saint-Esprit, as the route is surfaced throughout.

The River Rhône and the Rhône Valley

The Val de Rhône is one of the principal valleys in France, indeed in western Europe. The motorway, mainline railway, the huge electricity pylons, and of course the mighty River Rhône itself, with its attendant canal, all of which will be observed on the walk across the floor of the valley, form part of the massive communications network that daily passes up and down this valley. From the earliest times the Rhône Valley has formed the only viable route between the uplands of the Massif Central and the even higher mountains to the east, providing a trade route between the Mediterranean and the north - Paris, Germany and Switzerland. However, the river was fast flowing and liable to flood and consequently has witnessed countless disasters since Roman times; many a merchant ship has been wrecked over the centuries, with loss of both life and fortune. For 700 years there were only three bridges across the Rhône, at Lyon, Pont-Saint-Esprit and at Avignon, the latter being frequently washed away by the fury of the river at its lower reaches. From 1825 onwards a programme of bridge construction resulted in the building of a total of eleven bridges across the river by the mid-nineteenth century, with more to follow. The advent of steam boats in the same era considerably increased the commercial importance of the river, but this was soon to fade with the coming of the railways and later road haulage. But the wide, flat valley itself will always retain its importance as the only viable passage between this mountainous country. In recent years the modification of the railway along the Rhône Valley, to enable it to take high speed express trains (TGV) has led to considerable opposition from locals and conservationists; anti-TGV slogans will no doubt still be seen daubed on buildings, road surfaces and elsewhere whilst walking this section.

The Trail soon crosses the Canal de Donzère-Mondragon, a considerable feat of twentieth-century engineering. The continual flooding of the river and the need to harness more of the enormous energy of the Rhône, resulted in the formation, in 1933, of the Compagnie Nationale du Rhône, a company which undertook the development of the river with respect to navigation, irrigation and in particular, its potential for hydroelectricity. The canal and hydroelectric scheme at Donzère-Mondragon is probably the most impressive undertaken by

Pont-Saint-Esprit and the River Rhône

the company. The waters of the Rhône were redirected, on leaving the gorges at Donzère, into the canal, which is 17.4 miles (28km) long, 145 metres wide and 10 metres deep. The hydroelectric power station on the canal at Bollène provides about one-thirtieth of all Frances's electricity. More water is allowed into the canal when the river rises so that flooding is now a problem of the past.

Pont-Saint-Esprit

The town owes its existence entirely to the medieval bridge built here between 1265 and 1309. The construction was given the blessing of the Holy Spirit, hence the name of the settlement that grew up around the bridge. It was one of only three bridges spanning the Rhône until the modern era, so was a place of considerable importance. The passage of boats through the bridge, with its 25 low arches, was fraught with danger and required great skill and daring on the part of the mariners; nevertheless the "shooting of Pont-Saint-Esprit" resulted in many shipwrecks.

The main sights of Pont-Saint-Esprit are as follows:

1. The Bridge itself. It is nearly 1km in length, 19 of its 25 arches being very old. It was at one time fortified with central towers and bastions at either end. There is a superb view of the river and the town from the footpath that crosses the bridge.

2. The Terrace (Terrasse). This provides a good view of the river and bridge. Nearby is the seventeenth century church of St Pierre (large dome) which is no

longer in use, the Penitents' Chapel and the church of Saint Saturnin.

3.   Musée Paul Raymond. Local archeological finds and religious art. Situated in the place de l'Hôtel de Ville.

4.   Rue Saint Jacques. Many old buildings dating from the twelfth to the seventeenth century.

These places and others of interest are visited on a *Circuit Touristique,* a waymarked route around the town for pedestrians (enquire at the Tourist Office for details).

Some walkers may wish to have a very short walk today, finishing at Pont-Saint-Esprit, and spending the rest of the available time on sightseeing. Alternatively, Pont-Saint-Esprit is a good place to terminate the walk or to take a rest day or two before continuing on into the Ardèche. There are a number of major places of interest to the visitor within a bus ride of Pont-Saint-Esprit:

1.   Orange is 14.9 miles (24km) from Pont-Saint-Esprit. The Theatre and the Triumphal Arch are two of the most remarkable Roman monuments in the world.

2.   Avignon is another 18.6 miles (30km) further south from Orange. There is much to interest the tourist here, including the Cathedral and Palace of the Popes, and the famous "Pont".

3.   Walkers with a sweet tooth will no doubt head north for Montélimar (24.2miles; 39km from Pont-Saint-Esprit), the home of the nougat industry. Factory tours are available, with plenty of free samples on offer!

For those who spend the night in Pont-Saint-Esprit, the recomended daily stages would then be: Day 22 - Pont-Saint-Esprit to Labastide-de-Virac; Day 23 - Labastide-de-Virac to Comps; Day 24 Comps to Les Vans (or the very fit could even go on to Thines).

The walk to Aiguèze is of little note except for the final stages as the River Ardèche is approached, where the Trail provides excellent viewpoints of the river, Saint-Martin-d'Ardèche on the opposite bank, the suspension bridge and the picturesque village of Aiguèze itself, perched on high cliffs directly above the river. For details of Aiguèze, see the Summary for Day 22.

ROUTE

From the Place de la Paix in Mondragon, cross the D26 and take the rue des Clastres. Pass under the railway line and take the narrow subway under the main road (N7). Continue ahead on the D44 on the fly-over above the motorway, the Autoroute du Soleil. Remain on the D44 to cross the bridge over the huge Canal de Donzère-Mondragon. 200 metres later turn left on a road signposted to Lamiat, but turn right after a further 60 metres onto a straight, long lane. Remain on this road to pass under high tension electricity cables supported by huge pylons, and continue forward at a crossroads heading towards the buildings. This narrow, quiet lane approaches to within half a mile of the River Rhône before bearing to the right under small electricity pylons. Later ignore a turning off to the right, but continue ahead following the lane as it swings to the right for a final, long straight section to rejoin the main road, the D44, at more large pylons. Turn left along the D44 to reach the D994, a little before Pont-Saint-Esprit. Turn left again and keep to the pavement to cross over the River Rhône and enter Pont-Saint-Esprit.

After a visit to the town, leave Pont-Saint-Esprit by taking the D23 signposted to Saint-Paulet-de-Caisson and to the Chartreuse de Valbonne. Pass under the railway and take the next right turn (the Chemin du Calvaire) after the cemetery. Turn left in 100 metres and continue ahead to reach the Chemin des Sables. The route maintains a direction slightly north of west for a couple of miles after the cemetery. Eventually proceed ahead at a crossroads near Le Pigeonnier and 200 metres later turn left at a T-junction to enter the village of Saint-Paulet-de-Caisson.

Turn right at a large crucifix (signpost to camping site and restaurant). The route joins the GR 42 at this point - the two trails are coincident from here until just before Aiguèze at the end of today's stage). Continue ahead on the Chemin de la Plane, passing to the right of the twelfth-century chapel of Sainte Agnès, and under two series of high-tension electricity cables. When about a mile before Saint-Julien-de-Peyrolas, turn left at a T-junction a few hundred metres after a signpost to a camping site near Tête Grosse. The Trail is eventually joined on the left by the GR 42A (turn left here for Chartreuse de Valbonne, 1hr 30 min, and Bagnols-sur-Cèze, 5hr 30 min). The GR 4 continues ahead at this point, soon following the lane to the right over a very small bridge. About 200 metres after this bridge turn left on a lane signposted to Saint-Julien-de-Peyrolas. The road ascends gently into the village, the first climb since entering the Rhône Valley.

Bear left at the Place du Château and turn right at the T-junction opposite the Place du Barry. Bear right just before leaving the village and just after a metal roadside cross take the left fork descending to a road. Cross over and walk ahead through an orchard to reach the D901. Turn left, but in 70 metres turn right onto a track just before the roadsign indicating the Gorges de l'Ardèche (3km). Where this track divides take the left (lower) branch which soon becomes a thin footpath. Cross a stream by means of a small bridge and continue to meet a road just before the large suspension bridge over the River Ardèche (the village of Saint-Martin-d'Ardèche is visible on the opposite bank). Turn left on the drive immediately before the bridge (ie. do not walk over the river, unless a detour to Saint-Martin is envisaged). Soon the village of Aiguèze, perched on the cliffs above the River Ardèche, comes into view. Leave the lane at a small roadside cross to walk over rough ground to reach a good viewpoint overlooking river and village. Return to the lane which leads into Aiguèze.

DAY 22
AIGUEZE TO SALAVAS (THE ARDECHE GORGES)

DISTANCE:	15.3 MILES (24.6km)
TOTAL ASCENT:	1262ft (385m)
TOTAL DESCENT:	915ft (279m)
TOTAL ESTIMATED TIME:	6 HOURS 15 MINUTES

	Height Above		Distance				Est. Time	
	Sea	Level	Sect.		Cum.		Sect.	Cum.
	ft	m	mile	km	mile	km	hr m	hr m
AIGUEZE	292	89						
GR 4/GR 4B JUNCTION	1282	391	7.2	11.5	7.2	11.5	3.10	3.10
MAS DE SERRET	852	260	1.2	2.0	8.4	13.5	0.25	3.35
LABASTIDE-DE-VIRAC	918	280	3.0	4.9	11.4	18.4	1.10	4.45
SALAVAS	639	195	3.9	6.2	15.3	24.6	1.30	6.15

ALTERNATIVE ROUTES

1.   GR 4B. This is an alternative, waymarked route for the last few miles into Labastide-de-Virac. The trail omits Mas de Serret, but instead heads west to the D217 at La Forestière, before turning north to Labastide. This alternative is particularly useful for those wishing to stay the night at the *gîte d'étape* (Mas des Roches) 1 km south-east of Labastide, as the GR 4B passes close by the *gîte*. Walkers wishing to visit the limestone caves of the Aven d'Orgnac (see "Summary") will also find this variation useful.

2.   There is an alternative but non-waymarked route from Labastide-de-Virac to Salavas for those wishing to see the famous natural arch (Le Pont d'Arc) over the River Ardèche. However, part of the route is through a natural tunnel and over a complex jumble of rocks and boulders; at one point it is necessary to negotiate a *passage dangereux*. A path heads north from the churchyard of Labastide to reach the right bank of the River Ardèche near the Pont d'Arc. This is followed as best as is possible until the Ruisseau de la Fousoubie is crossed and the Camp des Blachas is reached. From here a minor road leads to Salavas. About an hour is required to reach Salavas from Labastide by this "sporting" route.

FACILITIES
Accommodation
Note should be made of the large derelict building of the Maison Forestière du Grand Aven which is passed en route between Aiguèze and Labastide-de-Virac.

The building, which would provide good shelter in an emergency, is clearly marked on the 1:50000 IGN map.

A campsite is passed en route at the Mas de Serret.

The *gîte d'étape* Le Mas des Roches, near Labastide-de-Virac can be recommended. The food is very good. It is situated south-east of the village along the D217 road, close to the point where the alternative GR 4B emerges on the road. If the standard route of the GR 4 is taken, as described in this book, then the *gîte* is reached by turning left on the D217 in Labastide-de-Virac and walking along it for about 1km (it is just off the left-hand side of the road when approached from this direction). It is also possible to arrange pony or horse trekking and guided canoe trips down the River Ardèche from the *gîte d'étape*. Note that there is no hôtel in Labastide.

Salavas has a 1-star hôtel-restaurant called the Hôtel des Sites (Logis de France) and several campsites. Camping Le Casque Roi (2-star) is located 100 metres off the GR 4 on the D579 on the far outskirts of the town. For Camping Le Moulin and the campsite called Le Micocoulier see the beginning of the "Route" section for Day 23. There are several other campsites in the vicinity of the River Ardèche in this area, which, because of the nearby Pont d'Arc, is popular with holidaymakers. There is a *gîte rural* in Salavas but this is unlikely to provide accommodation on a nightly basis. However, if the river is crossed by the road bridge, several hôtels will be found in the larger town of Vallon Pont d'Arc on the north bank of the Ardèche, about 1.2 miles (2km) from Salavas.

Restaurants/Cafés/Bars

Labastide-de-Virac has a restaurant, La Petite Auberge. Good meals are also served at the Mas des Roches *gîte d'étape* (see above).

Salavas has a bar-restaurant, Le Charabanc, as well as the restaurant in the Hôtel des Sites, which is open to non-residents. There are several restaurants and cafés in Vallon Pont d'Arc (off-route).

Shops

There is a small *alimentation* in Labastide, and a larger one, which also sells bread, in Salavas. A small supermarket will be found in Vallon Pont d'Arc, and a wider selection of shops.

Public Transport

There are buses from Salavas and Vallon Pont d'Arc to Aubenas, Vals-les-Bains and Montélimar in the north, and to Orange and Avignon in the south (Voyages Sotra, tel. 75.39.40.22).

Water

Water may be obtained at the campsite at the Mas de Serret.

SUMMARY

Aiguèze is most certainly worth a visit, even for those who are terminating their walk in the Rhône Valley (in the latter case take a bus here if at all possible before leaving for home). It is a much restored medieval village, some might say over-restored, perched on the edge of cliffs above the River Ardèche. A wander around the narrow streets can be recommended, as can the view down to the river from the old ramparts. There are a few art and craft shops in which to browse.

The walk from Aiguèze to Salavas follows the general line of the River Ardèche in the vicinity of the Gorges, but for the most part keeps some way to the west of the river. It would be well worth exploring the gorges further, if time allows, particularly by making a detour to view the Pont d'Arc (see below). Those with a day to spare are especially recommended to take a guided trip by boat or canoe down river from the Pont d'Arc to Saint-Martin-d'Ardèche (these can be arranged in Pont-Saint-Esprit or at Vallon Pont d'Arc). A journey along the river is the only way to appreciate fully the natural rock features of the gorges.

The route soon climbs into woodland after leaving Aiguèze and remains there for much of the walk to Labastide-de-Virac. As has so often been the case in woodland, care is required in navigation in places to remain on the correct

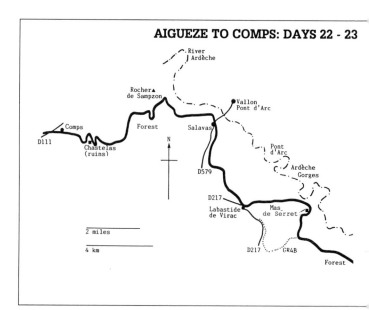

AIGUEZE TO COMPS: DAYS 22 - 23

line of the path. The Trail is coincident with the European Long Distance Path No. 4 (see Appendix 2) from here to Les Vans, and from time to time signposts should indicate this fact.

The château at Labastide-de-Virac is worth a visit. It dates from the fifteenth century and stands on the boundary between the ancient regions of Languedoc and Vivarais, once guarding the passage through the Gorges at Pont d'Arc. During the last century the castle belonged to the sculpture James Pradier who was responsible for some of the statues in the place de la Concorde in Paris. The view from the watchtower down to the river and over to the mountains of the Cévennes is worth the entrance fee to the château (open June to September every weekday, and over the Easter and Whitsun weekends). Note also the sundial in Labastide-de-Virac dating from 1790. Nearby there is an active silkworm farm, an ancient craft and industry in these parts (a display on the silkworm will be found in the château).

On approaching Salavas note the larger town of Vallon Pont d'Arc and the prominent bridge over the River Ardèche. Vallon Pont d'Arc has some fine tapestries in the *mairie* and a large nearby silkworm factory, but its main claim to fame is as a starting point for a trip down the Ardèche Gorges. Slide shows and occasional concerts are held in the town during the main season.

The Ardèche Gorges

The River Ardèche rises in the Mazan Massif in the Massif Central to the north and flows for 74 miles (119km) to join the River Rhône 1km north of Pont-Saint-Esprit. The flow is erratic, from mere trickles during the summer, to huge walls of water travelling at great speed down from Vallon-Pont-d'Arc during the spring. The 18.6 mile (30km) stretch from Vallon-Pont-d'Arc to Saint-Martin-d'Ardèche is through the famed Ardèche Gorges. The gorges twist tortuously and the multi-coloured cliffs are almost 1000ft (305m) high in places. The gorges are popular with tourists as there is a superbly engineered road clinging to the rim of the gorge for much of its length and this is provided with several viewpoints or belvédères. There are many imposing rock features along the Gorge, two of the most well-known being the Cathedral Rock and the Pont

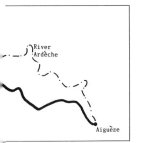

d'Arc. The latter is a huge natural limestone arch, 34 metres high and 59 metres wide at normal water level. This was originally formed as a tunnel by a subterranean river which changed its course eons ago and further enlarged the structure to create the arch seen today. The Pont d'Arc is most easily reached by a footpath leading from the car park on the D290, 3.1 miles (5km) south-east of Vallon Pont d'Arc.

The whole area is riddled with complex limestone cave systems or "Avens". Possibly the most impressive of these potholes is the Aven d'Orgnac, a couple or so miles south of Labastide-de-Virac and very close to the GR 4B variant of the GR 4 (see "Alternative Route No. 1"). A part of this extremely extensive system is open to the public (9 to 12 noon and 2 to 6pm in the summer season only; there is a nearby Museum of Pre-history) The array of stalactites, stalagmites, "organ pipes" and other dramatic natural sculptures, is very spectacular.

ROUTE

Wander through the narrow streets of Aiguèze to locate the Chemin de la Combe des Oiseaux. At the north end of the village follow a concrete track, which after 100 metres divides; take the right fork now on a stony/sandy track. This bends towards the left at a barn and a few hundred metres after this take the right fork. The route alternates between narrow path and stony track, proceeding gently uphill. On meeting a major track at a T-junction, turn right continuing gradually uphill. When this track divides take the left fork. At the next major fork keep to the left again. On reaching a "GR 4-E 4" signpost follow a narrower track to the right and turn left at the next crosstracks (there are many paths and tracks in this area of woodland and it is thus essential to follow the red/white waymarks with care). Climb gradually to a T-junction; turn right here and at the next fork take the right branch (note the many forestry symbols encountered along this section, eg "DFCI K23 Signalisation S. Pompiers et Forestiers" - there is a constant threat of forest fires during the summer months). Continue ahead at the next crosstracks and later take the right, ie. the narrower, of two tracks to reach the Maison Forestière du Grand Aven. This large derelict building could be used as a shelter in an emergency.

Keep right at the next fork and then where the main track swings to the left, continue ahead on a confined track through trees (GR 4 sign). Later, on reaching another fork in the track, ignore the GR 4 sign indicating a track to the left; instead take the track to the right. This leads to a T-junction in about a quarter of a mile where there is another GR 4 sign. Turn right (ie. north) heading in the direction of Serret (the name of this destination with a direction arrow is marked on a nearby rock). Descend on a narrow path through trees, later taking a left fork followed by a right fork on a metre-wide track. At a T-junction turn left uphill and on reaching a large building turn left on the major track, ie not the minor path more to the left through the woods (note the rather strange traffic sign here, ie. the "no parking at any time" sign - in English!). This leads to the campsite at the Mas de Serret.

Take the gravel track heading west from the campsite. This eventually becomes a surfaced road. Remain on this until it swings to the left; here turn right to climb on a narrow path. From here on the route takes a number of tracks and narrow paths through woodland, heading generally in a westerly direction. It would be tedious and unnecessary to describe every minor junction - just follow the ample red/white waymarking. After about 2½ miles (4km) the Trail eventually emerges at the road (D217) in the village of Labastide-de-Virac.

Pass through the narrow streets of the old village, ie. avoid the main road, to pick up the red and white waymarks once again at the north-west end of Labastide. Follow a lane to the crosstracks at Les Claux; walk ahead here until, after about a mile, take a track off to the left. In just over a further mile take a right fork signposted as the GR 4. The route nears a road, the N 579, but does not touch it. Continue to reach a lane, turn left and remain on it until it swings to the right - here walk ahead on a sandy track which eventually becomes a surfaced lane and descends towards Salavas. Finally, leave this road by taking a thin footpath that leads down to the church of Salavas.

DAY 23
SALAVAS TO LES VANS VIA THE CHASSEZAC GORGE

DISTANCE: 18.8 MILES (30.3km)
TOTAL ASCENT: 1439ft (439m)
TOTAL DESCENT: 1492ft (455m)
TOTAL ESTIMATED TIME: 7 HOURS 35 MINUTES

	Height Above		Distance				Est. Time	
	Sea	Level	Sect.		Cum.		Sect.	Cum.
	ft	m	mile	km	mile	km	hr m	hr m
SALAVAS	639	195						
CHASTELAS (RUINS)	905	276	7.4	11.9	7.4	11.9	3.30	3.30
COMPS	426	130	2.4	3.8	9.8	15.7	0.45	4.15
N104 (MAIN ROAD)	397	121	1.5	2.4	11.3	18.1	0.30	4.45
BERRIAS	403	123	2.2	3.6	13.5	21.7	0.45	5.30
CHASSEZAC GORGE	764	233	2.2	3.5	15.7	25.2	1.00	6.30
D901 ROAD NEAR CHASSAGNES	823	251	1.4	2.3	17.1	27.5	0.30	7.00
LES VANS	587	179	1.7	2.8	18.8	30.3	0.35	7.35

FACILITIES
Accommodation
The *gîte d'étape* in Comps has considerable charm, but does not provide meals, although there is the usual equipped kitchen (and see note under "shops"). The *gîte* is located just behind the church.

The village of Grospierres, about 1.5km off-route to the north of the ruins of Chastelas, has a hôtel-restaurant (open summer only) and a small *épicerie*. It may also be possible to camp here.

There is a hôtel and shop in Maison Neuve, about 700 metres north on the N104, from the point where the route emerges on that road, between Comps and Berrias.

Les Vans is a reasonably sized town (the largest between Pont-Saint-Esprit and Langogne), and as such has a number of hôtels, most of which are hôtel-restaurants, serving meals to non-residents. The Hôtel Les Cévennes is reasonable. Walkers looking for a taste of elegance should try the Château Le Scipionnet (tel. 75.37.23.84), a top grade Logis de France; unfortunately this is 1.9 miles (3km) outside Les Vans on the D104a. Those wanting hostel accommodation will find it at the *gîte d'étape* in Chambonas, 1.2 miles (2km) past Les Vans on the GR 4. There are also two campsites close to the River Chassezac, near Chambonas (see Day 24).

Note that wild camping is not allowed in the vicinity of the water source that is encountered a little after the ruins of Chastelas.

Restaurants/Cafés/Bars
Comps has no place of refreshment, Berrias has a bar, but Les Vans has a choice of restaurants and cafés.

Shops
There are no shops in Comps, but it may be possible to purchase certain foodstuffs (eggs, goat's cheese, chickens, rabbits(!) and wine) from nearby houses (these are indicated on a map on the wall in the *gîte d'étape*.

Berrias has an *épicerie, boulangerie, pâtisserie* and a post office.

There is a variety of shops in Les Vans, including a large supermarket. It is the last place for replenishing supplies before Langogne.

Public Transport
A bus service operates from Les Vans several times a day to Aubenas and Lalevade d'Ardèche in the north. A connection can be made from Lalevade d'Ardèche to Montèlimar, for a train connection up the Rhône Valley. Another bus runs from Les Vans southwards to Alès. Both services are operated by Voyages Sotra (tel. 75.39.40.22).

A bus bound for Aubenas stops in the village of Comps at 13.00 on Mondays, Wednesdays and Saturdays. A bus to Alès stops in Comps at 18.00 on the same days. Note that both Montèlimar and Alès have mainline railway stations (SNCF).

Water
It should be noted that no water is available between Salavas and just after the ruins of Chastelas, a distance of about 8 miles.

There is a water fountain in Les Vans.

Miscellaneous
Les Vans has a post office and banks (the last before the end of the walk).

SUMMARY
This is a rather long stage, necessitated by the need to find overnight accommodation at a convenient interval. The walk could, however, easily be divided into two halves by stopping the night at the *gîte d'étape* at Comps. This would make two easy stages of less than ten miles walking each day.

From Salavas the Trail passes close to the attractive homestead of the Mas de Gravier, before climbing on good tracks up into the woods to the west. The route runs parallel and above the River Ardèche for the first couple of miles, approaching another well known feature of the river, the Rocher de Sampzon

(Sampzon Rock). A short detour is necessary to visit this viewpoint; the panorama is extensive over the Orgnac Plateau and the Vallon Basin. Say your goodbyes here to the River Ardèche and its Gorges, as the Trail now pulls away from the river for the last time. However, there is still another set of gorges yet to come, those of the River Chassazac, before the Trail begins its climb up into the Massif Central.

After the Rocher de Sampzon the Trail contours on good tracks through woodland, a favourite haunt of weekend huntsmen (therefore exercise caution). Navigation should be quite straightforward. Eventually, the lonely, ruined hamlet of Chastelas is reached, which will bring back memories of the similar ruined settlement of Travignon on the hills north of Saint-Saturnin-d'Apt. Chastelas was quite a sizeable hamlet, as will be discovered by clambering around its narrow streets and amongst its several dilapidated buildings. The ruins are covered with the tangled roots of trees and in a few places whole trees have grown right out of the walls. Some attempt has been made in the past to restore some of the buildings, but little has been done to halt nature's progress over the last few years. The ruins have taken on a melancholic and mysterious air, which would have been exploited to the full by the Romantic

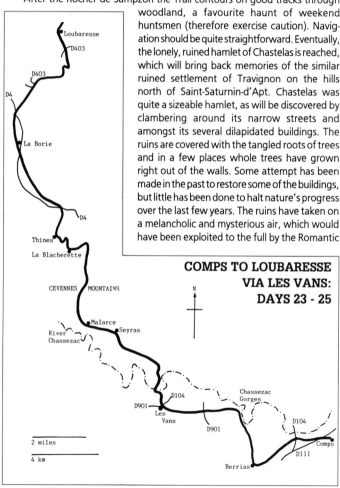

COMPS TO LOUBARESSE VIA LES VANS: DAYS 23 - 25

The ruined hamlet of Chastelas

poets.

The approaching Cévennes mountains are now seen to good effect as the Trail continues towards Les Vans. The tiny village of Comps has little of note other than its old *gîte d'étape*. A new trail, the Sentier des Dolmens, leads from Comps north to Largentière, so linking the GR 4 with the Tour du Tanargue (a large volcanic massif between Aubenas and La Bastide Puylaurent). There are several prehistoric dolmens in the area around Comps and Grospierres (ask locally for directions). There is also a small archeological museum in Grospierres (open July and August, afternoons only).

However, our Trail continues on the GR 4 from Comps to Berrias. This section provides fairly flat walking, across fields, orchards and vineyards, but after Berrias the route crosses rough ground heading north towards the Chassezac Gorges. A weird, but quite beautiful landscape unfolds as the Trail enters the Bois de Païoiive, crosses the D252 and approaches the rim of the Chassezac Gorges. The area is a chaotic tangle of oak and chestnut woods, and limestone outcrops and boulders of all shapes and sizes. The area has many associated legends: it is said that the souls of those who met a violent end wander through the undergrowth. The curving, vertical multi-coloured rock crags of the Chassezac Gorges are perhaps no less impressive than those of the Ardèche. The route reaches a belvédère which offers a good view down to the river far below. Care should be taken when approaching the edge of the cliffs overlooking the gorge, especially when the rock is wet. It would be all too easy to twist an ankle on the limestone pavement.

The Trail eventually leaves this fascinating area and descends to the town of Les Vans, where every opportunity should be taken to stock up with food provisions before entering the Cévennes for the final stage of the walk. Les Vans has several interesting old streets and arcades in a restored old quarter, and a market place with an ancient fountain. It is also a good place to buy souvenirs as many traditional, locally handmade articles are sold in the town. Some of the local crafts, together with archeological finds and geological exhibits, are displayed in the municipal museum (Museum of Archeology, Geology and Local History - closed Sundays, Mondays and Thursday and Saturday mornings).

ROUTE

Head out of Salavas on the D579, but before leaving the town locate a sign on the left indicating the Rocher de Sampzon (2hr) and Comps (5hr) on the GR 4. Turn left here. Head north on this lane, passing apricot trees to reach, in 350 metres, a stone cross. The road divides at this point: the right leads to a campsite, Le Moulin, whereas the GR 4 (and the way to another campsite, Le Micocoulier) follows the lane to the left (note that the red/white waymarks of the GR 4 are accompanied by the yellow paint marks of a PR trail along this section). After a couple of hundred metres ignore the route off to the right to the campsite, but instead continue ahead on the lane signposted to Le Roches. After passing over a river on a bridge, take the "no through road" ahead. Remain on this road for over a kilometre, until it bends to the right heading for a farmhouse; at this point turn left on a dirt track. Soon leave this track on a footpath off to the right heading towards the wooded hills. The path climbs towards the north and the north-west, providing views back to the River Ardèche. The path levels out and continues to a track where the Trail turns left, ie. towards the south. However, it is worth turning right and walking towards the north for five minutes to get a closer view of the impressive "Rocher de Sampzon" and have a last look down to the River Ardèche.

Return to the GR 4 and follow the track towards the south. Remain on this track as it contours around the hillside, changing direction several times, eventually heading back towards the north, when the Rocher de Sampzon will come into view again. The track then swings south-west and then north-west, after which ensure that a turn to the left (south) is taken. After almost a mile the route swings to the south-west for another mile until the "Sentier de Pays" joins from the left. Here the Trail changes direction yet again, this time heading to the north-west to reach the Notre-Dame des Songes. 150 metres after this, where the track swings to the left, take a right turn downhill leading to the ruined hamlet of Chastelas.

Turn left at the ruins, but do not climb ahead. Instead, at the last ruin, turn right descending very steeply on a footpath to reach a stream and water source (the first since leaving Salavas). Turn right. Cross, re-cross and cross again the river (care may be required as this area is often flooded after heavy rain) to reach an open area. Take the obvious dirt track ahead. At a T-junction at the edge of a surfaced road, turn left onto a track (the ruins of Chastelas, over to the left, appear very picturesque from here, on the hillside to the right of a rocky outcrop). After a short climb heading south, turn right onto another track which emerges at a road. Turn right along this road (golf course to the left). At a small traffic roundabout, where the road turns to the right, proceed ahead to reach the village of Comps.

Descend from the village to the main road, the D111, where take the track opposite through fields. Shortly after passing a barn on your right the surfaced track becomes an earthern one; continue ahead. 40 metres after a second barn, this time on the left, turn right on a dirt track, still across fields. In a few hundred metres turn left to cross a stream and continue along an enclosed footpath. The main road (D252) is encountered at the hamlet of Les Lebres. Bear left across the road to take a track which runs parallel with it, on the right-hand side. Pass under the power lines and later, when meeting another track, bear left. Continue on the main track to reach a minor road. Here turn right over a bridge over the river, and take a track heading towards the large house seen ahead. Bear left at the house and continue on the main track with a wall to the right. When the wall ends continue ahead, with orchards to the right and vineyards to the left. Remain on this main track until reaching the lane into the village of Berrias.

Before reaching the church in Berrias, turn right on a road signposted to Casteljau, but turn left after 50 metres to walk up between houses. About 50 metres before reaching a statue turn right down a narrow street, cross a small bridge over the stream and continue to the right of the latter for about 100 metres, before taking the enclosed footpath ahead. The route continues over

The Chassezac Gorge

an area of natural limestone pavement and then on a path between low stone walls. Next follow the Trail over an area of open ground on a stony track still heading north. Later leave this main track by bearing left on a footpath; on meeting another track turn left (in this vicinity the GR is following a PR trail, waymarked with a yellow arrowhead and two yellow circles). Soon bear left onto another track (there are now good views of the gorges of Chassezac to the right).

Turn right on meeting the D252, but after just a few metres turn left off the road to descend on a stony path. Turn left at a small track. The path continues along the rim of the Chassezac Gorges, high above the river. Do not venture too close to the edge, especially if you suffer from vertigo or are otherwise afraid of heights. Take particular care in rain or during damp weather as the rock is limestone and consequently very slippery when wet. The correct route does in fact get fairly close to the edge at times, thus providing dramatic views of the sheer walls of the gorges and the river far below. Eventually pull away from the gorges, following the red and white waymarks very carefully through the wood on a series of narrow paths (note that there are several other routes here waymarked with blue and red paint stripes, and some difficulty may be experienced in keeping to the correct route; follow only the red/white waymarks). The route eventually meets and crosses a main road, the D901, and 100 metres later meets a tarmac lane at a bend - continue ahead. Where this lane bends very sharply to the left, descend on a track to the right; Les Vans now comes into view ahead. Meet and cross a road and take a narrow path skirting the hillside. Turn right downhill on reaching another path at a T-junction (left at this point is the GR 44A - see Appendix 2 for details). The path emerges at the main road at the cemetery (GR 4 and GR 44A signs here). Turn left to a roundabout, where turn right to enter Les Vans.

PROFILE 5 - LES VANS TO LANGOGNE (CEVENNES): DAYS 24 - 26

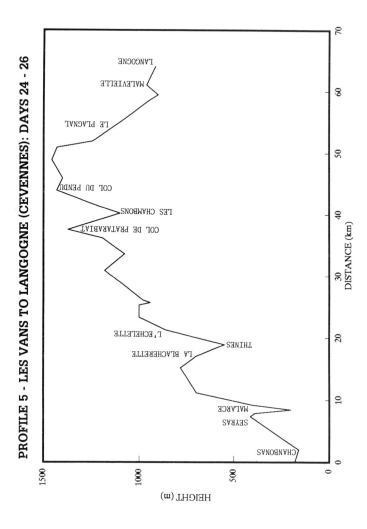

DAY 24
LES VANS TO THINES (INTO THE CEVENNES)

DISTANCE:	11.7 MILES (18.9km)
TOTAL ASCENT:	2862ft (873m)
TOTAL DESCENT:	1646ft (502m)
TOTAL ESTIMATED TIME:	5 HOURS 25 MINUTES

	Height Above		Distance				Est. Time	
	Sea	Level	Sect.		Cum.		Sect.	Cum.
	ft	m	mile	km	mile	km	hr m	hr m
LES VANS	587	179						
CHAMBONAS	518	158	1.2	2.0	1.2	2.0	0.25	0.25
SEYRAS	1351	412	3.3	5.3	4.5	7.3	1.45	2.10
MALARCE	1311	400	1.2	1.9	5.7	9.2	0.30	2.40
LA BLACHERETTE	2295	700	4.8	7.8	10.5	17.0	2.15	4.55
THINES	1803	550	1.2	1.9	11.7	18.9	0.30	5.25

FACILITIES
Accommodation
On the southern side of the bridge over the River Chassezac there is an auberge and a campsite (Camping Les Chataigniers). On the Chambonas side of the bridge there is another campsite, Le Meliet, 400 metres to the left, immediately after crossing the bridge.

There is a *gîte d'étape* in Chambonas.

It may be possible to obtain accommodation for the night in the hamlet of Seyras, but this should not be relied upon. Similarly there may be the chance of an overnight stay in the hamlets of Chastanet or Serret, to the north of Malarce.

Thines: There is a choice of two *gîtes d'étape,* the *Gîte Communal* and the Ferme Auberge (see Appendix 1 for details). M. Fournet, the guardian of the *Gîte Communal,* is very hospitable. The view out of the dining-room window of the *gîte,* over the wooded hillsides of the Cévennes, is first-rate. Note that there is no public telephone in Thines.

Restaurants/Cafés/Bars
There is a restaurant on the northern side of the bridge over the River Chassezac. After this there is no possibility for refreshment until Thines. Here the Ferme Auberge doubles as a restaurant, serving meals to non-residents. The food can be recommended, but note that the establishment is closed on Tuesdays, and out of the main summer season is open only at weekends and during school

holidays, or for groups of ten or more who book in advance. Meals are also served at the café in Thines.

Shops

The guardian of the *Gîte Communal* in Thines usually keeps a small, basic store of food, which can be purchased from him for self-cooking in the *gîte*. Otherwise it is essential to stock up before leaving Les Vans.

Public Transport

None is available. The nearest train station from Malarce is at Villefort, a walk of over 16km (10 miles) along the D113 and D51 roads. Thines is even further from public transport, the nearest railway stations being at Villefort to the south-west or La Bastide Puylaurent to the north-west. The two stations are on the same railway line, that between Paris and Nîmes.

Water

Water should be carried from Les Vans.

SUMMARY

Les Vans lies in a low plain beneath the southern slopes of the Cévennes mountains. The walk has so far crossed the Low or "Bas" Ardèche or Vivarais; the High or "Haut" Ardèche (Vivarais) awaits. It follows that today's walk involves a long climb up into the mountains of the Massif Central, the first ascent of any significance since the Ventoux region.

The first part of the walk, the descent to the River Chassezac, is straightforward and easy. The bridge is an unusual old structure and leads across to Chambonas where there is a twelfth-century church and an impressive four-towered château within a formal French park (marked on the IGN 1:50000 map). After the village the climb into the Cévennes mountains begins in earnest. The hardest section is that between the hamlet of Luminière and Malarce; although they are only a kilometre apart a deep wooded valley separates them, requiring a long steep descent, a river crossing and an equally steep and exhausting climb out of the gorge. But the footpath used is a good one, and in further compensation the scenery, now that the route is in amongst these sylvan hills, has greatly improved.

A number of stone and metal roadside crosses are passed on the walk. Some of these are centuries old and have various types of ornamentation. These ancient wayside markers, protecting travellers from the evils of the road, are particularly common in the Massif Central. They often mark important crossroads.

The climbing continues after Malarce, the route penetrating into the heart of the Cévennes. The woods of oak, beech, chestnuts and conifers hereabout are very old. In the right seasons the woodland floor is a mass of colour from various wildflowers, violets, pansies, orchids, heather and broom. Eventually the gradient eases as the trail takes to forest tracks following a wooded ridge heading north. There are some very old GR 4 signs in this area dating back to 1966 when the long distance path was originated.

Superb views of the Cévennes mountains open out whilst on the descent towards La Blacherette. On approaching this remote hamlet, the tiny village of Thines comes into view below, in an stupendous setting perched on a rock overlooking a steep, complex valley system. Be sure to look back whilst on the descent to Thines to see the three large wooden crosses placed dramatically on the edge of the hillside near La Blacherette. The route taken by the GR 4 is that of the old trail linking Thines with Les Vans and the outside world. It is a well constructed path, the stones that were laid centuries ago remaining in a very good condition. The modern road, which follows the River de Thines down to Malarce, was not constructed until the 1950s and is itself a considerable feat of engineering. Until that surfaced road was built the route of the GR 4 was the only practical way out of the village. On the final part of the climb note the neat and extensive vegetable gardens built into the old terraces on the hillside; even today this small community is largely self-sufficient.

Thines is the gem of this part of the Cévennes. Its atmosphere of tranquility, the result of its isolated and dramatic location in the mountains, and the beauty and veneration of its church attract many discerning visitors from all over the world. But thankfully it is not on the familiar tourist trail, and large coaches would find it difficult to negotiate the narrow road to the village. During the long, harsh winter months the village is virtually cut-off from the outside world. Heavy snowfalls are common in the area, rendering the steep road into the village impassable for weeks at a time. Summer visitors often do not realise how severe the weather can be in these mountains: the never ending mistral can be intolerable and the horrendous thunderstorms are legendary.

ROUTE
From the centre of Les Vans take the D10 (or first follow the sign indicating the D104a) heading north, signposted to Chambonas. Leave Les Vans on this road, which eventually bends sharply to the left to descend to cross the large bridge over the river Chassezac. Once over the bridge the D10 immediately turns sharply to the right. However, the GR 4 takes the D250 road ahead, signposted to Saint Pierre.

Walk through the village of Chambonas on the D250. Descend from the village on the road, but about 200 metres after passing the sign indicating the limit of Chambonas, turn left up a narrow lane signposted to Fontgarnier (Font Granier). Soon take a path to the left, climbing up to the left of a building. The route emerges on a poorly surfaced drive where you continue ahead uphill. At a sign "Les Sielvettes Haut", turn very sharply to the right onto a dirt track. At the house ahead turn sharply to the left onto a stony path, which leads to Les Sielves. Walk through this hamlet to reach a road, the D10. Turn right and continue uphill on this road.

Immediately before the houses of Seyras, turn left at a roadside cross and a signpost indicating the "Pont de Gravières" and "Luminière". 400 metres later ignore the path to the left leading to the Pont de Gravières and to Thines, but keep ahead on the lane to pass through the hamlet of Luminière. Where the road bends to the left, continue straight ahead (very old GR 4 sign here indicating Malarce [40 minutes] and Thines [3hours 20 minutes]). A very well constructed zig-zagging path now drops all the way down to the river far below. Cross the river by an earthen bridge and climb out of the deep wooded ravine on an equally fine zig-zagging path. This eventually emerges at a road in the hamlet of Malarce by a small elaborate crucifix and a GR 4 sign indicating the way to Thines (3 hours).

Turn right and remain on the lane for about 300 metres before leaving it by climbing on a path to the left. The path climbs steeply in woodland as the route now penetrates into the heart of the Cévennes. Reach and continue along a main forest track for some distance, following a principal ridge heading north. On meeting a surfaced lane turn left. This lane soon loses its surface to become another forest track; follow this to the D10 road. Do not walk along this, but turn immediately to the left on another forest track (very old GR4 sign indicating the way to Thines). Descend, but after about 500 metres leave the track by turning left on a descending path which leads to a concrete track where you turn left continuing downhill. This excellently engineered track descends to La Blacherette, a tiny hamlet clinging to the hillside. However, the route to Thines leaves the track a little before La Blacherette, by taking a narrow path to the right (at this point Thines comes into view down below).

This path leads in 50 metres to a calvary, three wooden crosses perched dramatically on the hillside, overlooking a deep valley. The path descends and then skirts the mountainside; on turning a corner Thines comes into view again. The superbly constructed path, the stones of which were laid centuries ago, finally climbs up to the village of Thines, an ideal resting place for the night.

DAY 25
THINES TO LOUBARESSE

DISTANCE:	10.8 MILES (17.3km)
TOTAL ASCENT:	2587ft (789m)
TOTAL DESCENT:	485ft (148m)
TOTAL ESTIMATED TIME:	4 HOURS 50 MINUTES

	Height Above Sea Level		Distance				Est. Time	
	Sea	Level	Sect.		Cum.		Sect.	Cum.
	ft	m	mile	km	mile	km	hr m	hr m
THINES	1803	550						
L'ECHELETTE	2819	860	1.5	2.4	1.5	2.4	0.50	0.50
LA BORIE	3213	980	3.0	4.8	4.5	7.2	1.30	2.20
LOUBARESSE	3904	1191	6.3	10.1	10.8	17.3	2.30	4.50

FACILITIES
Accommodation
Accommodation is not abundant on the last section of the walk to Langogne. The day stage suggested here is to Loubaresse, where there is a *dortoir* at the Relais Ferme-Auberge (see Appendix 1). Some may wish to walk further today, in which case there are only two options for those not carrying a tent, viz. the barn at Le Bez or a *chambre d'hôte* at Le Plagnal (see Day 26). The latter will only be reached in one day from Thines by the very strongest of walkers.

Restaurants/Cafés/Bars
The Bar-Restaurant "Le Pegan" (tel. 75.88.96.48) in Loubaresse serves good food. Note that there are no facilities at either l'Echelette or La Borie.

Shops and Public Transport
Neither will be encountered. The nearest mainline railway station is at La Bastide-Puylaurent, many miles to the west of Loubaresse. Water is best carried from Thines although will no doubt be obtainable at the farms passed en route.

SUMMARY
Be sure to take in the atmosphere of lovely Thines before pressing on along the Trail. The tiny village perched on the hillside is a jumble of old houses clustered around the ancient church. The latter is a magnificent Romanesque building, approached by a wide stairway. A doorway on the left leads into the small courtyard of the Communal *gîte d'étape,* where vines drape trellis work. The church and its attendant large metal cross in front of the steps look out over the

steep surrounding wooded hillsides from their remote hideaway. The building itself enjoys international fame for the quality and delicacy of its stonework, both inside and out. The atmosphere inside the church is an almost uncanny one of serenity and holiness. The statue of the Notre-Dame-de-Thines is no longer housed in the church, for fear of theft or vandalism (it has been removed to a city museum for safe keeping), so that the photograph of it in the church will have to suffice. The war memorial in the church lists the names of 21 men from the village who died in the First World War, more than double the number of people who still live permanently in Thines. M. Fournet, the guardian of the *gîte d'étape* in Thines, will supply more information on the history of the church and village.

Behind the church is a rather interesting large stone monument. The numerous figures (man with a donkey, the descent into hell, etc) have been carved with great skill.

The Trail climbs the ridge behind Thines to reach the road at l'Echelette, and then continues in a north-westerly direction, following part of a Roman road, roughly parallel with the modern D4 road over to the left. Some care in navigation is required as the route follows a series of paths and tracks through the Forêt de Prataubérat. Several hamlets and farmsteads are passed on the way north to the small village of Loubaresse on the D24 road, the largest community passed in this remote area on the journey to Langogne. The high quality of the scenery in this north-eastern corner of the Cévennes is maintained throughout.

ROUTE

Follow the waymarked trail that starts just past the monument in Thines (if merely passing through Thines the monument will be found by turning right when reaching the village on the GR 4 from La Blacherette). The path starts its climb between two tracks. Climb by a zig-zagging path to reach a road (D4) near to l'Echelette.

Cross the road and continue climbing the hillside ahead on a path (GR 4 sign to La Borie, Loubaresse, and Les Bes). A superb panoramic view of the Cévennes soon opens out as the path climbs above the treeline up to a ridge. The Trail soon reaches and follows a Roman Road (Voie Romaine) which provides easy walking as it heads towards La Bombine, Loubaresse and La Fouette. A little under a kilometre after La Bombine farm the track becomes surfaced and descends. Soon after passing a sad, derelict barn, turn left off the track onto a footpath (orange horseshoe sign) which descends to cross a road and continues to the hamlet of La Borie.

Leave the road in the centre of the hamlet to climb up towards the left following red and white waymarks past buildings. After passing the last buildings of Cheminas, above La Borie, continue climbing towards the north to attain the ridge ahead. Pass immediately to the right of the buildings of Les

The carved stone monument at Thines

Caynes and continue ahead on a track. Soon, at a cross tracks to the right of a stone cross, turn right and follow the track to a road (D4 again). Turn left, but in 150 metres turn right off the road onto a footpath at an orange hoofprint sign indicating a long distance bridleway to Le Puy. Continue to cross a stream, before reaching a path junction at the meeting of two ways. To the right lies a yellow/white waymarked trail, the Sentier de Fourches, leading to Sablières (about 3.5 miles; 5.6km to the south-east), but the GR 4 continues straight ahead. Take the latter to climb a little to enter pine woodland. Follow the red and white GR 4 signs carefully through the Forêt de Prataubérat to emerge on the D403 at a bend in this road (diligence is required in navigation here as there are many other paths and tracks in the vicinity; do not be misled by the white-green-white paint marks on trees - they are forestry signs and not an indication of a walking trail).

Walk ahead on the road for about 80 metres to leave it for a track on the right (there is no red/white waymark here, but the track is signposted to the Massif de Prataubérat). After about a mile (1.6km), at a sign indicating the Série Domaniale de Sablières, turn left off this main track onto another, but narrower, track. On reaching a T-junction, turn left on a track heading downhill. Leave this track after about 400 metres, by taking a footpath down to the right. Descend to the road, turn right and in 50 metres, immediately before the road bridge, take the track down to the right to walk over the concrete bridge above the river and then bear to the left to pick up a footpath. Climb and later descend on this path to cross the road and continue the descent. The path meets and crosses the road again before continuing to meet the road yet again at Loubaresse. Turn right on the road and walk up to the church in the centre of the village of Loubaresse.

DAY 26
LOUBARESSE TO LANGOGNE (ALLIER VALLEY)

		DISTANCE:		17.3 MILES (27.8km)
		TOTAL ASCENT:		2282ft (696m)
		TOTAL DESCENT:		3186ft (972m)
		TOTAL ESTIMATED TIME:		7 HOURS 10 MINUTES

	Height Above		Distance				Est. Time	
	Sea	Level	Sect.		Cum.		Sect.	Cum.
	ft	m	mile	km	mile	km	hr m	hr m
LOUBARESSE	3904	1191						
COL DE PRATARABIAT	4491	1370	0.8	1.3	0.8	1.3	0.25	0.25
LES CHAMBONS	3606	1100	1.7	2.7	2.5	4.0	0.45	1.10
LE BEZ	4029	1229	0.8	1.3	3.3	5.3	0.25	1.35
COL DU PENDU	4688	1430	1.5	2.4	4.8	7.7	0.40	2.15
GR 4/GR 7 JUNCTION	4590	1400	1.2	2.0	6.0	9.7	0.25	2.40
LE PLAGNAL	3672	1120	5.4	8.7	11.4	18.4	2.10	4.50
LE VILLARET	3114	950	2.4	3.8	13.8	22.2	0.55	5.45
MALEVIELLE	3147	960	1.6	2.6	15.4	24.8	0.40	6.25
LANGOGNE	3000	915	1.9	3.0	17.3	27.8	0.45	7.10

FACILITIES
Accommodation
Le Bez: The Auberge du Bez has neither rooms nor a *dortoir,* but walkers are usually welcome to sleep overnight in the owner's adjacent barn, provided that meals are taken in the restaurant. There is a public telephone at Le Bez, but no other facilities.

Le Plagnal: There are *chambres d'hôte* in this small village, and also the Auberge de Chapelas. Accommodation in a barn may also be available in Le Plagnal.

There is a *gîte d'étape* at Lespéron, 30 minutes off-route from the GR 4, north of Le Villaret, between Le Plagnal and Langogne.

Langogne: Several hôtels will be found in the town. The food and service at the Hôtel Bel Air (a Logis de France) can be recommended.

Langogne has two campsites: the more basic is on the eastern edge of the town between the railway line and the river, on the route of the GR 4. The larger and more expensive is the Camping de Naussac site, near the reservoir.

There are many hôtels, as well as a youth hostel in Le Puy en Velay (see Appendix 1).

Restaurants/Cafés/Bars
The Auberge de Chapelas and a café in Le Plagnal provide refreshment for the weary foot traveller. After this the walker must wait until Langogne, where there is plenty of choice of both cafés and restaurants.

Shops
There is a simple *épicerie* in La Plagnal. Shops of all types will be found in Langogne. If looking for souvenirs or presents at the end of the holiday, then a journey to Le Puy can be recommended (see Public Transport) as a much better selection of gifts will be found there than in Langogne.

Public Transport
Train: Langogne is on the mainline railway between Paris and Nîmes. There are several trains a day to Clermont-Ferrand, Saint Germain des Fossés and Paris (Gare de Lyon) and also to La Bastide Puylaurent, Villefort, Alès and Nîmes (for connections to Avignon, Marseille, Nice, Montpellier, Toulouse and Bordeaux). *Bus:* A service, operated by Hugon Autocars (tel. 66.65.06.52) to Mende and to Pradelles, Landos, Costaros and Le Puy runs several times a day. A timetable can be obtained free from the *Syndicat d'Initiative.* Journey time from Langogne to Le Puy is approximately one hour. The bus stops outside the Café du Midi in the centre of Langogne and also at the railway station (SNCF).

Miscellaneous
The Tourist Office in Langogne is situated a little way uphill from the old covered market. There are banks and a post office in Langogne.

SUMMARY
The Trail crosses the Tanargue massif via the Col de Pratarabiat. A fairly steep descent from the col leads to the hamlet of Les Chambons where the GR 4 meets another *Grand Randonnée,* the GR 72. A climb on a track leads to the tiny community of Le Bez on the D19. Here there is a small chapel and the large and welcoming Auberge du Bez, but little else. The route follows the direction of the D239 road until a little after the Col du Pendu, which at 4688ft (1430m) is the highest point reached on this walk through the Massif Central. Near to the farmstead of Pra Bargès, the GR 4 pulls away from the road and the GR 7, with which it has been coincident since Le Bez, and follows a long track over the Cham de Cham Longe. A succession of hamlets and villages follows as the Trail heads towards the north-west through the ancient country of Gévaudan, finally to cross the River Allier and enter the town of Langogne, journey's end. Gévaudan was an area terrorised in the eighteenth century by the notorious "Bête" (Beast) which attacked and killed over a hundred victims. Books telling the full story of the Bête de Gévaudan can be purchased in Langogne.

Those walkers with time and energy still to spare are spoilt for choice on

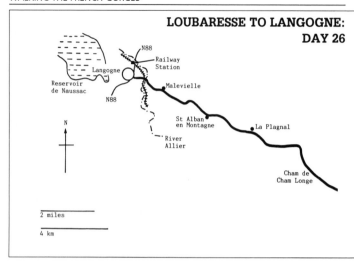

LOUBARESSE TO LANGOGNE: DAY 26

arrival in Langogne as there are a number of other long distance trails that can be taken from here. Firstly, the GR 4 continues in a north-westerly direction over the Margeride to Saint Flour and on to traverse the high peaks of the Auvergne (see *Walks in Volcano Country*, see Bibliography). The Scottish author Robert Louis Stevenson stayed the night in Langogne in September, 1878, on his way south through the Cévennes on his Travels with a Donkey. Walkers may join the modern RLS Trail here, continuing a further 100 miles (161km) over Mont Lozère to Pont de Montvert, Florac and Saint Jean du Gard (see *The Robert Louis Stevenson Trail,* see Bibliography). A third option is to take the RLS Trail north to Goudet on the River Loire, a distance of 31 miles (50km). From here the GR 3 can be followed into Le Puy (see below), or alternatively the circular Tour of the Velay, which passes through Goudet, makes a fine week's walk via Mont Mézenc, through another ancient volcanic landscape (see *Walks in Volcano Country*, see Bibliography).

Langogne
Langogne was much smaller when Stevenson visited it in the late nineteenth century than it is today. Much of the town is modern and semi-industrial, although the old bridge across the Allier and the nineteenth-century covered market are of interest, as is the eleventh-century church. The town is attracting more tourists these days since the flooding of the wide, fertile Naussac Plain after the completion of a dam in the early 1980s. The landscape here, which had

remained largely unchanged for centuries, has now been completely transformed with the formation of this artificial lake. The Reservoir de Naussac on the western side of Langogne, covers an area of about 1100 hectares and provides a shoreline some 25 miles (40km) in length.

Anyone staying for a day or more in Langogne may wish to explore further. There is now a waymarked trail around the reservoir, the Tour du Lac (blue and white waymarks), which is tortuous and slow in places as it negotiates the many ups and downs through the woods around the lakeside; in wet weather some areas become very marshy. There are beaches for sun bathing, whilst the more active can swim, windsurf, fish or hire pedalos.

Le Puy en Velay

Before returning home walkers are strongly advised, if time is available, to visit the town of Le Puy, the capital of the Velay. It can be reached either by bus or on foot (see above). Situated on the River Loire, Le Puy is distinguished by a number of *puys* or pinnacles of rock, volcanic in origin, on which are perched some of the town's best known monuments. The main places of interest are the tenth-century chapel of Saint Michel de l'Aiguille on the 80m high Rocher Saint Michel, and the Rocher Corneille on which stands the huge red statue of Notre-Dame-de-France and the twelfth-century cathedral which contains one of the rare "Black Madonnas of the Auvergne". The town is famous for its lace, which makes good holiday presents for walkers, being both light and easy to carry. Those who want even more walking in France can set out from Le Puy on the Sentier de Santiago de Compostela, the GR 65, the ancient pilgrim's route to the shrine in north-west Spain.

ROUTE

Take the path to the right of Le Pegan Bar-Restaurant in the centre of Loubaresse. Walk up through the village to reach the road again, crossing straight over to follow the footpath climbing the hill ahead. At the top of the climb, at the Col de Pratarabiat, the GR de Pays (yellow/red waymarks) heads towards the right, but ignore this and instead take the GR 4 ahead and downhill. Turn left into a wide track on meeting it at a hairpin bend. After about 300 metres leave this for another track on the right. Head downhill, crossing over another track and continuing the descent to cross a river by a bridge. Remain on the track ahead to reach the hamlet of Les Chambons.

Care is required here to avoid heading off on the wrong GR trail (the GR 72 meets the GR 4 in Chambons). Ignore the red/white waymarks to the left (the GR 72 to the west), but keep ahead (north) on the GR 4. At the far end of the hamlet take the track which descends to cross a small bridge over the river and then follow the path ahead. Take the track which passes to the left of a house and climb to reach a grassy plateau, where bear to the right to reach the tiny settlement of Le Bez (restaurant). The GR 4 joins the GR 7 here and the two paths are coincident for the next few miles to the farmstead of Pra Bargès.

Cross the D19 road and follow the path which starts to the right of the chapel. This joins the D239 where you turn left. After a while leave this for a footpath on the left of the road. On rejoining the road turn left and continue to reach the Col du Pendu. Remain on the road for a while before seeking out a path which runs just a short distance to the left of the D239. Stay on this to the point where the GR 7 leaves the GR 4 just to the south of the farm of Pra Bargès. The GR 7 turns right to head north, but leave this to follow the GR 4 straight ahead. The Trail climbs onto the ridge ahead on a *draille* or drove road, a wide and obvious track. This provides fast and easy walking along the Cham de Cham Longe, at an altitude of about 4800ft (1464m). Much of the route is over open ground, but it eventually enters trees. Remain on the *draille* for a little over three miles, before leaving it on a narrow path descending to the west. Descend to a clearing and continue to a road. Soon turn left off the road, but in 50 metres take a track, which later becomes a footpath which leads back eventually to the road (an alternative is simply to remain on the road). Follow the road past the village of Le Plagnal.

The GR 4 does not enter Le Plagnal, but remains on the D392 road. A short distance past the village locate a track that runs at first parallel with the road. Later follow tracks westward to rejoin the D392 to pass through the village of Saint-Alban-en-Montagne.

Continue along the road, but look out for a short-cut to miss out a bend in it between Saint-Alban and the next hamlet, Le Villaret. At the latter take a footpath down to the left, to rejoin the road once again and follow it over the bridge above the River l'Espezonnette. Climb on the road to reach and take a footpath on the right. Climb and continue to the hamlet of l'Hermet Chabalier and then on to Malevielle.

After Malevielle turn right at the road junction and descend on the road to cross the River Allier. Turn left under the railway bridge just before a campsite which is on the right. Continue ahead at a roundabout, but turn left on reaching a T-junction. Turn right in 80 metres over an old bridge and walk forward to reach the high street of Langogne. For the railway station (Gare SNCF) turn right here; it is about 0.6km to the north, on the left-hand side of the road.

APPENDIX 1
GITES D'ETAPE AND SIMILAR ACCOMMODATION IN PROVENCE AND THE ARDECHE, ON OR NEAR THE TRAIL

Establishments listed in brackets do not lie directly on the route of the Trail. Accommodation is available all year round unless otherwise stated. Where "meals available" is stated, these may not always be available outside the main summer holiday season.

(Le Trayas-Theoule-sur-Mer)
Auberge de Jeunesse (Youth Hostel). 12 miles (19.3km) by bus from Cannes. 100 places. Breakfast only provided (ie. no dinner available). Closed most of January. Tel. 93.75.40.23.

Grasse
M.J.C. de Grasse. Situated on the northern outskirts of the town at the Stade Nautique, near to the start of the GR 4 (see route description for Day 1). Bus No. 8-G (Circulaire de la Piscine) from the Gare Routière stops at the Stade Nautique. 35 places in dormitories. Meals available. Open main season only. Tel. 93.36.35.64.

(Greolières-les-Neiges)
1.   "L'Etrier d'Or". 10 places in dormitories. Meals available. Tel. 93.59.71.77.
2.   Centre des Vacances de Gréolières-les-Neiges. "Les 4 Saisons". 250 places. Meals available. Open main summer and winter seasons only. Tel. 93.59.70.23.

Aiglun
Auberge Le Calendal. 23 places in dormitories. Meals available. Open main seasons only. Tel. 93.05.82.32.

Collongues
A relais d'étape here was closed several years ago.

Amirat
Gîte d'étape d'Amirat (GTA). L'Estelle. At Les Agots. 15 places. Meals sometimes provided by the mayoress who lives nearby. Tel. 93.05.80.53. or 93.05.81.74.

Entrevaux
Gîte d'étape communal. Behind the public washing area near the bridge (aquaduct). 18 places. No meals provided, but several restaurants nearby. Tel. 93.05.42.45. If closed enquire for the key at the mairie in the central square in the old town. Note that a new gîte d'étape may be opened in Entrevaux by 1993 (enquire at the mairie for details).

Ubraye
Note that the gîte d'étape here was closed in 1988.

Le Touyet
There is no *gîte d'étape* here, but a barn for sleeping will usually be provided on request.

La Garde
Gîte d'étape de La Garde. On the Route Napoléon, N85. 24 places. Restaurant in La Garde. Open March to November. Tel. 92.83.62.26. Note that this establishment could be closed in the future.

(Blieux)
Association Blieuxoise, *gîte d'étape*. 20 places. Open March to November. Tel. 92.34.22.53.

La Baume)
Au Soleil Levant. Near the Lac de Castillon. 22 places. Tel. 92.83.70.82.

Castellane
Gîte d'étape La Galoche. 30 places. Tel. 92.83.63.20. If closed the key can be obtained from a building near to the church (there should be a map on the *gîte* door showing where the key may be located).

Villars
Gîte d'étape Le Villars. 20 places. Meals available. Guardian from April to November, but otherwise open all year. Tel. 92.83.61.82. or 92.31.07.01.

Rougon
Relais d'étape La Vigne. A few yards off the GR 4 between Rougon and Point Sublime. A small "tent village" consisting of large pre-erected tents equipped with bunk camp beds. There is a water source and toilet. The tents are taken down between October and April. Tel. 92.83.70.09.

La Mâline
Refuge de la Mâline. Chalet C.A.F. 82 places (42 in one large dormitory, the rest in dorms of 6-12 beds). Meals available. Open from mid-March to mid-November. 50% reduction for Alpine Club members or holders of a Reciprocal Rights Card. Tel. 92.77.38.05.

La Palud-sur-Verdon
1. Auberge de Jeunesse (Youth Hostel). La Trait d'Union. The Trail passes the hostel before entering the town of La Palud. 66 places. Meals available. Open from early March to late November. Tel. 92.77.38.72.
2. La Valdenay. *Gîte d'étape*. 60 places. Tel. 92.77.33.57.
3. Le Vignal. *Gîte d'étape*. M. et Mme Maquigny. Tel. 92.77.30.94.

(Les Subis)
Buvette du Ribasson. *Gîte d'étape*. 5 miles (8km) from La Palud. Tel. 92.83.65.34.

Moustiers-Sainte-Marie
Gîte d'étape La Cavalier. 1km south-west of Moustiers-Sainte-Marie (signposted from the GR 4). Stabling for horses available. Meals available in the adjacent restaurant.

Riez
A *gîte d'étape* here was closed several years ago.

Saint-Martin-de-Brômes
This village also no longer offers *gîte d'étape* accommodation.

Manosque
Auberge de Jeunesse (Youth Hostel). Parc de la Rochette. 60 places. Tel. 92.87.57.44. 750 metres north of the old town, along the boulevard Martin-Bret and the Avenue de l'Argile, near a covered swimming pool.

(Aix-en-Provence)
Auberge de Jeunesse (Youth Hostel). 3, avenue Marcel Pagnol. 100 places. Meals available. No cooking facilities. Tel. 42.20.15.99. Bus No. 8 or 12 in the direction of the Jas de Bouffan - alight at the Estienne d'Orves Vasarely.

Céreste
Gîte d'étape communal. The *gîte* is in the rue du Bicentenaire, off the place de la Republic, but if closed the key can be obtained from the Village de Vacances (Le Grand Lubéron) which is about 400 metres from the centre of the village (follow the signs). Alternatively enquire at the Tourist Office in the High Street. 18 places in 3 bedrooms. Meals available at the Village de Vacances. Tel. 92.79.03.99. or 92.79.04.66 (Office de Tourisme) or 92.79.00.15 (Mairie).

Cournille
Gîte d'étape de Cournille. In the hamlet of Cournille, 2 miles (3.2km) south of the village of Oppedette. 15 places. No meals available. Tel. 90.75.22.80.

(Chaloux)
Gîte d'étape de Chaloux. On the GR 4, 2 miles (3.2km) to the north of Oppedette. 30 places. Meals available. Closed in winter. Tel. 92.75.99.13.

(Saint-Jean-de-Sault)
Gîte d'étape de Jean-de-Sault. In the old village schoolhouse. Very basic. When closed the key can be obtained from the village café. 12 places. No meals available. Tel. 90.64.00.56.

(Monieux)
On the GR 9/92, convenient for the Nesque Gorges. The Restaurant Les Lavandes has a *dortoir*. 8 places. Tel. 90.64.05.08.

Abri du Contrat

This is a small shelter, not suitable for an overnight stay. It is situated below and to the north of Mont Ventoux, near the point where the GR 4 and GR 9 part company.

Malaucène

Gîte d'étape "Les Écuries du Ventoux", 1 mile (1.6km) north-east of Malaucène on the GR 91. 20 places (two dorms of 8 beds and one of 4 beds). Meals available. There is a buvette and swimming pool, but no kitchen is available. Te. 90.65.29.20.

Séguret

Auberge de Jeunesse (Youth Hostel). Route de Sablet. 52 places. Meals available. Open mid-March to end of December. Tel. 90.46.93.31.

Rasteau

Gîte d'étape de Rasteau. 700 metres south-west of the centre of the village, along the C1 road. Situated in the Centre Départemental d'Animation. 32 places. Meals available. Tel. 90.46.15.48. or 90.46.11.06.

Labastide-de-Virac

Gîte d'étape "Le Mas des Roches". 1 km south of Labastide-de-Virac on the D217, and on the GR 4B. 22 places. Meals provided. No kitchen available. Tel. 75.38.63.12.

Comps

Gîte d'étape de Comps. A Chamina *gîte*. 25 places. No meals provided. Tel. 75.39.00.19.

Les Vans

The small *gîte d'étape* in Les Vans is now closed. (tel. 75.37.22.83. for further information).

Chambonas

Gîte d'étape de Chambonas. Near Les Vans. 15 places. No meals provided. Tel. 75.37.24.99.

Thines

1. *Gîte d'étape Communal.* On the left-hand side of the steps, immediately below the church. If closed ask for M. Fournet on arrival in the hamlet. 24 places. No meals provided. Open March to November. The guardian keeps a small food store. Tel. 75.36.94.30.
2. Ferme Auberge. 16 places. Meals provided. Closed on Tuesdays. Tel. 75.36.94.47.

(Montselgues)

Relais La Fage. 1.5 miles (2.4km) south-west of La Borie. 18 places. Meals provided. Tel. 75.36.94.60.

Loubaresse
Relais Ferme-Auberge. 15 places. Meals provided. Open early April to the end of September. Tel. 75.88.99.38.

Le Bez
Auberge du Bez. Walkers are usually permitted to sleep in the barn at the rear of the restaurant, on the understanding that meals will be taken in the latter.

Le Plagnal
There are *chambres d'hôte* in the village.

(Le Puy-en-Velay)
Auberge de Jeunesse de Le Puy (Youth Hostel). Centre Pierre Cardinal. rue Jules Vallès. Near the Cathedral. 62 places. Tel. 71.05.52.40.

APPENDIX 2
OTHER GR TRAILS IN PROVENCE AND THE ARDECHE

Several other GR trails will be encountered when walking the route described in this guidebook. It can sometimes be frustrating to come across a signpost indicating a trail when no further details are given: how long is the route, where does it lead and what are its special features? The following list should be of some assistance in this respect. The GR trails are listed in the order in which they are met when walking from Grasse to Langogne. Details of the complete GR 4, GR 6 and GR 9 trails, which form the basis of the walk described herein, are also included.

GR 4 - Mediterranean to the Ocean
A very long east to west route from Grasse, above the Côte d'Azur, to Royan on the Atlantic coast. The LDP passes through the following regions: Provence, Vallée du Rhône, Cévennes, Margeride, Auvergne, Limousin, Saintonge and Océan. A guidebook to the Auvergne section from Volvic to Langogne has also been published (see Bibliography).

GR 51
This trail leaves the Côte d'Azur near La Napoule and heads north to Grasse (Day 1). It then continues eastwards, parallel with the coast, passing above Nice to finish at Menton near the Italian border.

GR 49
A relatively new GR route leaving the GR 4 at Rougon (Day 7) near the entrance

to the Verdon Gorges, and running south to Mons (from where the GR 49A leads east to rejoin the GR 4 at Caussols, Day 1, north of Grasse). After Mons the GR 49 passes to the west of the Lac Saint Cassein and then continues south heading for the Mediterranean coast.

GR 99
The GR 99 starts in the Verdon Gorges, below La Mâline (Day 8). From here it leads to Aiguines and then south-west along the southern shore of the Lac de Sainte-Croix to Bauduen. The route then heads generally in a southerly direction to Baudinard, La Verdière, Brue-Auriac, Bras, Mazaugues, Signes and Le Revest-les-Eaux, before terminating on the coast at the naval port of Toulon.

GR 97 - The Tour of the Lubéron
This circular walk takes in much of the best scenery in the Lubéron Regional Park. Its 100 miles (161km) take about a week to walk. The tour is coincident with the walk in this book from Montjustin (Day 13), east of Céreste, to Saint-Saturnin-d'Apt (Day 15), a distance of about 26 miles (41.8km).

GR 6 - Ocean to the Alps
An ultra-long distance path crossing southern France from west to east. The path starts at Langon, near Saint Macaire, south-east of Bordeaux. On its journey east it passes through Sainte-Foy-la-Grande, Les Eyzies, Rocamadour, Figeac, Conques and Meyrueis to reach Beaucaire and Tarascon in the Rhône valley. From here it enters the Vaucluse, where it is followed for a time as part of the route described in this book (Days 14 and 15). It leaves the region by turning north to Sisteron, from where it heads north-east across the Alps to join the GR 56 and later the GR 5 south of the Queyras.

GR 92
A relatively short variant of the GR 9 in the Lubéron Regional Park, visiting Cabrières d'Aigues.

GR 9 - Jura to the Côte d'Azur
A north to south route starting from Saint Armour west of Lake Geneva (Lac Léman). The path skirts to the west of Chambéry and Grenoble and traverses the Vercors Regional Park. After Le Pöet-Laval, Nyons and Montbrun-les-Bains, the route contours the lower slopes of Mont Ventoux and heads south from Sault to Saint-Saturnin-d'Apt, the section followed in the walk described herein (Days 16 and 17). The GR 9 continues across the Lubéron Regional Park to Vaugines, Grambois and Mirabeau, passes to the east of Aix-en-Provence and reaches Trets. The last section heads east via Nans-les-Pins, Signes, Belgentier, Carnoules and La Garde Freinet to finish at Saint-Pons-les-Mûres, 4 miles (6.4km) from Saint Tropez.

GR 91 - Vercors to Ventoux
This 106 mile (171km) trail traverses the Drôme and Hautes-Alpes, crossing the

wild and beautiful Barronnies. The path starts in the Vercors Regional Park at Saint-Nizier-du-Moucherotte, near Grenoble, and heads south through the Vercors to Chatillon-en-Diois. Direction is maintained from here to Brantes, north of Mont Ventoux where the path ends.

GR de Pays des Dentelles de Montmirail

A short circular tour between Malaucène and Séguret, west of Mont Ventoux (Day 19). It is co-incident with the GR 4 between Les Gippières and the Passage des Loups, a distance of about 2.5 miles (4km). The waymarking on the route, as with all GR de Pays (local footpaths) consists of red and yellow paint stripes.

GR 42

A trail that follows the course of the River Rhône from Tarascon, south of Avignon, to Tournon, north of Valence, where it climbs north-west to join the GR 7 in the Parc du Pilat, south-west of Lyon. The major places en route are as follows: Tarascon - Saint Roman - Villeneuve - Les - Avignon - Bagnols-sur-Cèze - Viviers - Saint Montant - Rochemaure - La Voulte - Tournon - Satillieu - Bourg Argental - GR 7. The GR 4 is co-incident with the GR 42 between Saint-Paulet-de-Caisson and Saint-Martin-d'Ardèche (Day 21), a distance of about 3.5 miles (5.6km). The GR 42A is a variant of the GR 42 that leaves the main route near Saint-Julien-de-Peyrolas.

E 4 - European Long Distance Path No. 4

This trail, when eventually completed, will run from Montserrat in Spain to Delphi in Greece, a distance of about 4200km (2609 miles). It is coincident with the GR 4 between Saint-Martin-d'Ardèche, Salavas and Les Vans (Days 22 and 23).

GR 4B

This is a short alternative route (3.6 miles; 5.8km) to Labastide-de-Virac via the D217 road and the Aven d'Orgnac, omitting the Mas-de-Serret. It leaves the main route of the GR 4 at a point south of the Mas-de-Serret and from there heads west and south-west to meet the D217 at La Forestière. It then leads north via the Aven d'Orgnac on a route roughly parallel with the D217. It emerges on this road about a kilometer before Labastide near to the *gîte d'étape* Mas des Roches, and is therefore recommended to those wishing to spend the night at the *gîte*.

GR 4F

A relatively short variant of the GR 4, from Salavas (Day 22) in the Ardèche to Bourg-Saint-Andéol, via Saint Remèze and Bidon.

GR 44

A 54-mile (87km) spur of the GR 4, running west from Les Vans (Day 23) to Villefort, Mas d'Orcières, Col de la Loubière and Champerboux. The GR 44A is a short variant of the main trail.

GR 72

The GR 72 links the GR 4 near Le Bez (Day 26) to the GR 7 at the Barre-des-Cévennes. It heads west to La Bastide Puylaurent and then south to the Croix de Grabio, Villefort, Col de Rabusat, Pont du Tarn and over the Col de la Planette to reach the Barre-des-Cévennes.

GR 7 - Vosges to the Pyrenees

Another ultra-long distance route stretching from Ballon d'Alsace to Andorra in the Pyrenees. On the way the route passes through the Vosges, Plateau de Langres, Côte d'Or, Mâconnais, Beaujolais, Lyonnais, Vivarais, Cévennes, Haut Languedoc, Corbières and Pyrenees. It is co-incident with the GR 4 for a few miles between Le Bez and Pra Bargès (Day 26).

R.L.S. Trail

A walk of about 140 miles (225km) following closely the route taken by the celebrated nineteenth-century writer Robert Louis Stevenson in 1878, described in his book *Travels with a Donkey in the Cévennes*. Starting at Le Monastier-sur-Gazeille near Le Puy, the trail traverses the Velay and Cévennes to Saint-Jean-du-Gard. The trail passes through Langogne (Day 26) the end point of the route described in this guidebook. There are plans by the mid to late 1990s to upgrade this historic trail to GR status. For a guidebook to the R.L.S. Trail see Bibliography.

APPENDIX 3
USEFUL ADDRESSES

1. French Government Tourist Office. 178, Piccadilly, London W1V 0AL. Tel (071) 493 3371.

2. Edward Stanford Ltd (specialist map shop). 12-14, Long Acre, London WC2E 9LP Tel (071) 836 1321.

3. The Map Shop. 15, High Street, Upton upon Severn, Worcestershire WR8 0HJ.

4. Au Vieux Campeur. 48, rue des Ecoles, 75005 Paris. Nearest Metro station: Maubert-Mutualité. Extensive range of French maps and guidebooks.

5. IGN Shop. 107, rue La Boétie, 75008 Paris. Just off the Champs-Elysées. Nearest metro station: Georges V. Complete range of IGN maps of France at 1:50000 and 1:25000.

6. Falcon Holidays (charter flights to Nice). 33 Notting Hill Gate, London W11 3JQ.

7. National Express Coach Services. Eurolines. Victoria Coach Station, London SW1. Tel (071) 730 0202.

8. Thomas Cook Group Ltd. P.O. Box 36. Thorpe Wood, Peterborough PE3
    6SB. Tel. (0733) 63200. Ask for details of their Independent Travellers
    Insurance Scheme.

9. West Mercia Insurance Services. High Street, Wombourne, near
    Wolverhampton WV5 9DN. Tel (0902) 892661. Ask for details of their
    insurance scheme for "walking, rambling, scrambling and camping".

10. Comité départemental de la randonnée Alpes-de-Haute-Provence, ADRI
    04 (walking in High Provence). 42, boulevard Victor Hugo, 04000 Digne,
    France.

11. Comité départemental de la randonnée pédestre Vaucluse (walking in the
    Vaucluse). 63, avenue César Franck, 84000 Avignon, France

12. Chamina (*gîtes d'étape* and walking in the Massif Central). Maison de la
    Randonnée Massif Central, 5, rue Pierre-le-Vénérable, 63102 Clermont-
    Ferrand, France.

13. Le Parc Naturel Régional du Lubéron. 1, Place Jean Jaurès - B.P. 128, 84400
    Apt, France.

14. Le Parc National des Cévennes. Château de Florac, 48400 Florac, France.

15. Club Cévenol. Pierre and Pat Valette. 6, avenue du Mont Aigoual, 30120
    Le Vigan, France (send an international reply coupon with any enquiries -
    letters may be written in English).

BIBLIOGRAPHY

1. *Walking in France* by Rob Hunter. Hardback, Oxford Illustrated Press
    (1982), or paperback, Hamlyn (1983). Although a little dated now, this
    classic book provides useful information on all aspects of walking in
    France.

2. *Walks in Volcano Country - the Auvergne and Velay* by Alan Castle (1992).
    Cicerone Press. For those wishing to continue an exploration of the GR 4
    this guidebook describes a 10 to 15 day Traverse of the High Auvergne
    from Volvic, near Clermont-Ferrand, across the principal ranges of the
    Massif Central to Langogne, terminus of the trek described in this
    guidebook. The circular, 8-day, Tour of the Velay, GR 40, is also included.

3. *The Robert Louis Stevenson Trail* by Alan Castle (1992). Cicerone Press. A
    guidebook to the famous trail from Le Monastier-sur-Gazeille in the Velay
    to Saint Jean du Gard in the Cévennes. The route, which passes through
    Langogne, terminus of the walk described in this guidebook, is 140 miles
    (225km) in length and has been divided into eleven daily stages, allowing
    ample time in a fortnight's holiday for general sightseeing and a visit to the

impressive Tarn Gorges west of Florac.

4.   *The Elf Book of Long Walks in France* by Adam Nicolson (1983).   Weidenfeld and Nicolson. The book contains a chapter on a walk across Provence from Aix-en-Provence to Saint Tropez on the GR 9, to the south of the region traversed in this guidebook.

5.   *Classic Walks in France* by Rob Hunter and David Wickers (1985). Oxford Illustrated Press. This coffee-table style book includes a chapter on the circular Tour of the Vivarais, GR 420, a walk in the Ardèche to the north of the region covered in this guidebook.

6.   *France. Off the Beaten Track* edited by Martin Collins (1988). Moorland Publishing Company. Includes chapters on Provence, Ardèche and the Cévennes. Written for the adventurous tourist. Good background reading.

7.   *Gîtes d'étape de Randonnée et Refuges, France et Frontières* by Annick and Serge Mouraret (4th edition 1990). La Cadole. Lists some 3300 establishments including all those in Provence, Ardèche and the Cévennes. In French with an English lexicon.

8.   General tourist guides to Provence and the Massif Central. The following selection should be found useful for general planning and background reading:

   a)   *Provence and the Côte d'Azur. The Rough Guide* by Kate Baillie (1990). Harrap-Columbus. 402 pages.

   b)   *Visitor's Guide to France: Provence and the Côte d'Azur* by Norma Brangham and Richard Sale (2nd edition, 1990). Moorland Publishing Company. 256 pages.

   c)   *Provence, Languedoc and the Côte d'Azur* by John Ardagh (1990). A Collins Independent Travellers Guide. 288 pages.

   d)   *Provence and the Côte d'Azur* by Roger Macdonald (1989). Christopher Helm. A Helm French Regional Guide. 186 pages.

   e)   *Baedeker's Provence/Côte d'Azur. The Complete Pocket Guide* (1985). Published by the A.A. (includes a road map).

   f)   Michelin Green Guides:
         i) *French Riviera and Côte d'Azur*. In English. It includes many of the areas, villages and towns passed through on this walk, including Grasse, Entrevaux, Manosque and Castellane.
         ii) *Provence*. In English. This guide focuses on the western side of Provence and is less useful for walkers of this Trail than i) above.
         iii) *Alpes du Sud. Haute Provence*. In French.

   g)   *Provence* by John Fowler. Photographs by Charlie Waite (1987). George Philip. A large coffee-table style book. 216 pages.

h) *The Visitor's Guide to France: Massif Central* by Barbara Mandell (1990). Moorland Publishing Company. 256 pages.

i) *Auvergne and the Massif Central* by Rex Grizell (1989). Christopher Helm. A Helm French Regional Guide. 218 pages.

j) *The Rhône Valley and Savoy* by Rex Grizell (1991). Christopher Helm/A.& C.Black. A Helm French Regional Guide. 178 pages.

9. *A Guide to Provence* by Michael Jacobs (1988). Viking. The first part of the book is a good general account of the history, art and literature, village life and the cuisine of Provence. The second half is a useful gazetteer.

10. *Travels with a Donkey in the Cévennes* by Robert Louis Stevenson. The classic account of an idiosyncratic journey from Le Monastier, via Langogne, to Saint Jean du Gard, made by the author in the autumn of 1878. Several versions have now been published including a facsimile copy of the first edition (Godfrey Cape, 1980), a paperback version (Dent, Everyman's Library, 1984) and an illustrated edition (Chatto & Windus, 1986).

11. *A Year in Provence* by Peter Mayle. Hardback, Hamish Hamilton, (1989) or paperback, Pan Books (1990). An amusing look at rural life in France by an Englishman who has settled in the Lubéron region of Provence. The sequel *Toujours Provence* (hardback Hamish Hamilton, 1991; paperback, Pan Books 1992) is also worth reading.

12. *Jean de Florette* and *Manon des Sources*. These films, directed in the late 1980s by Claude Berri from the book *The Water of the Hills* by Marcel Pagnol, were acclaimed as two of the finest productions of the French Cinema. They were awarded several British and French film oscars. The films star an elderly Yves Montand and tell a story of greed, passion, envy and revenge, set amidst a background of rural Provence in the 1920s. The photography is stunning. Both films are available on video recordings (French with English subtitles).

CICERONE GUIDES

Cicerone publish a wide range of reliable guides to walking and climbing abroad

FRANCE
TOUR OF MONT BLANC
CHAMONIX MONT BLANC - A Walking Guide
TOUR OF THE OISANS: GR54
WALKING THE FRENCH ALPS: GR5
THE CORSICAN HIGH LEVEL ROUTE: GR20
THE WAY OF ST JAMES: GR65
THE PYRENEAN TRAIL: GR10
THE RLS (Stevenson) TRAIL
TOUR OF THE QUEYRAS
ROCK CLIMBS IN THE VERDON
WALKS IN VOLCANO COUNTRY (Auvergne)
WALKING THE FRENCH GORGES (Provence)
FRENCH ROCK

FRANCE / SPAIN
WALKS AND CLIMBS IN THE PYRENEES
ROCK CLIMBS IN THE PYRENEES

SPAIN
WALKS & CLIMBS IN THE PICOS DE EUROPA
WALKING IN MALLORCA
BIRDWATCHING IN MALLORCA
COSTA BLANCA CLIMBS
ANDALUSIAN ROCK CLIMBS

FRANCE / SWITZERLAND
THE JURA - Walking the High Route and
 Winter Ski Traverses
CHAMONIX TO ZERMATT The Walker's Haute
Route

SWITZERLAND
WALKING IN THE BERNESE ALPS
WALKS IN THE ENGADINE
WALKING IN TICINO
THE VALAIS - A Walking Guide
THE ALPINE PASS ROUTE

GERMANY / AUSTRIA
THE KALKALPEN TRAVERSE
KLETTERSTEIG - Scrambles
WALKING IN THE BLACK FOREST
MOUNTAIN WALKING IN AUSTRIA
WALKING IN THE SALZKAMMERGUT
KING LUDWIG WAY
HUT-TO-HUT IN THE STUBAI ALPS

ITALY
ALTA VIA - High Level Walkis in the Dolomites
VIA FERRATA - Scrambles in the Dolomites
ITALIAN ROCK - Rock Climbs in Northern Italy
CLASSIC CLIMBS IN THE DOLOMITES
WALKING IN THE DOLOMITES

MEDITERRANEAN COUNTRIES
THE MOUNTAINS OF GREECE
CRETE: Off the beaten track
Treks & Climbs in the mountains of RHUM &
PETRA, JORDAN
THE ATLAS MOUNTAINS
WALKS & CLIMBS IN THE ALA DAG (Turkey)

OTHER COUNTRIES
ADVENTURE TREKS - W. N. AMERICA
ADVENTURE TREKS - NEPAL
CLASSIC TRAMPS IN NEW ZEALAND

GENERAL OUTDOOR BOOKS
THE HILL WALKERS MANUAL
FIRST AID FOR HILLWALKERS
MOUNTAIN WEATHER
MOUNTAINEERING LITERATURE
THE ADVENTURE ALTERNATIVE
MODERN ALPINE CLIMBING
ROPE TECHNIQIUES IN MOUNTAINEERING
MODERN SNOW & ICE TECHNIQUES
LIMESTONE -100 BEST CLIMBS IN BRITAIN

CANOEING
SNOWDONIA WILD WATER, SEA & SURF
WILDWATER CANOEING
CANOEIST'S GUIDE TO THE NORTH EAST

CARTOON BOOKS
ON FOOT & FINGER
ON MORE FEET & FINGERS
LAUGHS ALONG THE PENNINE WAY
BLACKNOSE THE PIRATE

*Also a full range of guidebooks
to walking, scrambling, ice-climbing,
rock climbing, and other adventurous
pursuits in Britain and abroad*

---

*Other guides are constantly being added to the Cicerone List.
Available from bookshops, outdoor equipment shops or direct (send for price list)
from CICERONE, 2 POLICE SQUARE, MILNTHORPE, CUMBRIA, LA7 7PY*